What Is an American Muslim?

WHAT IS AN AMERICAN MUSLIM?

Embracing Faith and Citizenship

ABDULLAHI AHMED AN-NA'IM

OXFORD
UNIVERSITY PRESS

OXFORD
UNIVERSITY PRESS

Oxford University Press is a department of the University of Oxford.
It furthers the University's objective of excellence in research, scholarship,
and education by publishing worldwide.

Oxford   New York
Auckland   Cape Town   Dar es Salaam   Hong Kong   Karachi
Kuala Lumpur   Madrid   Melbourne   Mexico City   Nairobi
New Delhi   Shanghai   Taipei   Toronto

With offices in
Argentina   Austria   Brazil   Chile   Czech Republic   France   Greece
Guatemala   Hungary   Italy   Japan   Poland   Portugal   Singapore
South Korea   Switzerland   Thailand   Turkey   Ukraine   Vietnam

Oxford is a registered trademark of Oxford University Press
in the UK and certain other countries.

Published in the United States of America by
Oxford University Press
198 Madison Avenue, New York, NY 10016

Library of Congress Cataloging-in-Publication Data
Na'im, 'Abd Allah Ahmad, 1946–
What is an American Muslim? : embracing faith and citizenship / Abdullahi Ahmed An-Na'im.
pages cm
ISBN 978-0-19-989569-4 (hardback)—ISBN 978-0-19-989570-0 (ebook)—
ISBN 978-0-19-935073-5 (ebook)   1. Muslims—United States.
2. Citizenship—United States.   I. Title.
BP67.U6N35 2014
305.6'970973—dc23
2013036652

9 8 7 6 5 4 3 2 1
Printed in the United States of America
on acid-free paper

To our "American Muslim" children and grandchildren.

Contents

Acknowledgments

I STARTED FOCUSING on issues of American Muslims and citizenship for a public lecture I gave at Emory University on February 2, 2009, but was already drawing on discussions, research and writing opportunities around related issues during the preceding several years. It is therefore difficult to name all the friends, colleagues, and research assistants who helped me with the themes of this book along the way. I can only express my general appreciation and gratitude to all of them. However, I am pleased to gratefully acknowledge the research support I have received from Emory University School of Law over the years.

Regarding this book in particular, my special appreciation goes to the Carnegie Corporation for their grant under the Carnegie Scholars Program of 2009, which enabled me to conduct extensive research, take leave from teaching for one semester, and organize a series of conversations and critical reviews of written draft chapters. This grant also enabled me to engage Dr. Mary Virginia Pyron, a professional editor, who worked diligently throughout the summer of 2012 to help me render this manuscript as accessible as possible to a general readership. I am particularly grateful to Virginia for "adopting" the manuscript and helping me clarify my thinking and writing throughout the final drafting process, far beyond her formal obligations as editor.

I am pleased to acknowledge my appreciation for the instructive critical reviews of chapters 1 to 4 by, listed alphabetically, Cemil Aydin, Juliane Hammer, Jamillah Karim, Aminah Beverly McCloud, Hussein Rashid, Ulrike Spohn, Amina Wadud, and Adnan Zulfiqar. I am also grateful for the incisive comments and suggestions of Kambiz GhaneaBassiri on chapter 3. All these colleagues are scholars of Islam and related fields from significantly diverse perspectives. I am glad that I opted for seeking critical feedback from specific scholars, instead of attempting to organize a workshop on my draft manuscript as a whole. By seeking the help of these scholars in this way, I have received thoughtful and detailed feedback on each chapter.

What Is an American Muslim?

1

Identity and Citizenship: Beyond Minority Politics

IT MAY SOUND redundant to say that the *only* identity all citizens of the United States share is their citizenship, but there is some value in stating the obvious. Citizens of the United States identify with such a wide variety of identities—racial, cultural, political, religious, and so forth—that there is no fixed or permanent majority or minority. Every citizen of the United States is part of a minority in some respects and of a majority in others. Yet those citizens who think of themselves as members of a minority are keenly aware of it, while those who feel confident in their "Americanness" do not give it much thought. They do not feel a need to prove their identity as Americans to anyone.

As an American Muslim, I have wholeheartedly embraced my Americanness, which entitles and enables me to contribute to what it means to be American. In this book, I will argue that other American Muslims should as well. Certainly, there are those who may be reluctant or ambivalent about asserting their identity as Americans, perhaps because they are unsympathetic to a certain preconceived notion of Americanness, or they feel that others may not accept them in that identity. I am not suggesting that the question is exclusively a matter of subjective perception. There are complex racial, material, political, and other factors that contribute to the formation and experience of identity. Most important, there is a *relational* dimension to identity, a combination of how we feel and present ourselves, and how others perceive and treat us.

Let me from the outset briefly present an Islamic rationale for overcoming my own ambivalence, while explaining how I came to embrace an Americanness that might be appealing to both native-born and immigrant American Muslims, in all the varieties and complexity highlighted in various parts of this book. An initial aspect of my thinking here is that there is no "universally" agreed-upon or accepted notion of Americanness—beyond citizenship—that one is bound to submit to. All American citizens, whether native-born for many generations or first-generation immigrant like me, are entitled and enabled to contribute to defining Americanness for themselves.

One of the more key features of Americanness to me personally relates to what I see as an Islamic religious rationale of immigration, either in a spiritual and psychological sense of moving to an inner community of believers within the society, or in a physical sense. Both types of migration were experienced by the first Muslims, together with the Prophet himself, while they lived in Mecca, and when they physically migrated to Medina in 622. In both stages, Muslims were sharing a realm of what we now call citizenship, in its most rudimentary ancient formations, especially under what came to be known as the Charter of Medina.[1] I would argue that native-born as well as immigrant American Muslims are experiencing one or more varieties of migration, either internal within their communities, or in the sense of physical relocation.

The religious rationale of both varieties of migration is firmly anchored in the Quran and exemplar of the Prophet (i.e., Sunna as the second scriptural source of Islam). For example, verses 2:218, 3:195, 4:97–100, 8:72–75, 9:20, and 16:41 of the Quran (cited by chapter followed by verse numbers) enjoin and encourage believers to migrate (within their societies or by moving away) in pursuit of the freedom to practice their religious beliefs out of honest and candid conviction. For me, this is one of the key features of Americanness: "to be a Muslim by conviction and choice, which is the only way one can be a Muslim...."[2] This is what I call *religious self-determination*: Since this is the purpose and rationale of our migration, whether internal within American society at large for converts and descendants of converts in their communities of believers or by physical relocation in coming to the United States, it is our religious obligation as Muslims to uphold and embrace this understanding of Americanness.

This sense of religious self-determination is what I am calling for in this book. It is time for American Muslims to start talking to each other about who they are—on *their own terms*, not anyone else's—and about how they can proactively embrace citizenship in the United States. What strategies can American Muslims explore, in public discourse and through the political and legal process, to advance their priorities?

To be clear from the outset also, I am *not* concerned here with defending Islam and Muslims against negative stereotyping or charges of "un-Americanness." I do not accept that there is a uniform, monolithic measure of American identity other than citizenship. Within that framework, multiple and overlapping identities will continue to evolve, interact, and cross-fertilize. As a citizen of the United States, I contribute to defining what it means to be American, as I strive to realize that for myself individually, as well as for my religious, racial, political, and other communities.

A Matter of Choice

Both individually and collectively, people can express their right to self-determination of religious belief and practice. Each Muslim has the right to experience her religious beliefs according to her own convictions and choices, and to collaborate with others in debating, and seeking to understand, the Islamic tradition in the specific context of her own community. Accordingly, this book concerns *American citizens who self-identify as Muslims*, regardless of what any other person, group, organization, or institution thinks of their claim.

I want to advance among American Muslims conversations that boldly address questions of identity and citizenship—not with the goal of increasing acceptance within the wider American public, but because I, as an American Muslim myself, believe that these must become priorities for Muslims.

For a community, which is the better choice? To engage such issues in order to appease others, or to avoid engaging issues, for fear of *being perceived* as seeking to appease others? Both choices are equally disempowering. We should neither do nor refrain from doing what we believe is right out of fear or a desire to please other people, whether within or outside our community. The true maturity and self-confidence of members of a community lie in their ability to engage important issues regardless of perceptions, one way or the other.

The Complexity of Being American Muslims

The term "American Muslim," I realize, comprises complex varieties of people and their experiences. I do not claim to speak for all American Muslims, nor do I expect to raise issues of concern for all of them. There is simply no coherent way of regarding all American Muslims as a single monolithic community, or of speaking about them as such—not even in terms of broad categories such as race, gender, "native-born," and immigrant.

How could one ever disentangle the impact of race and gender relations among American Muslims from such relations in the wider society? It is impossible. Indeed, the meaning of race and gender is shaped by experiences that non-Muslim and Muslim Americans actually share, perhaps in more significant ways than they are shared within the American Muslim community.

Moreover, African American Muslims, shaped partly by their experiences of being descended from slaves and being subjects of racial discrimination, may also influence immigrant Muslims' perceptions of implicit racial hierarchy that is grounded in experiences with race in their countries of origin.

I use the term "American Muslim," rather than "Muslim American," because, to emphasize, I am concerned with *citizens who self-identify as Muslims*. I seek to explore the meaning and implications of these Muslims' citizenship in the United States, *not the nature or quality of their religious beliefs*. In a religious context, it may be appropriate to speak of "Muslims who happen to be American citizens," but for the purposes of this book, I speak of "American citizens who happen to be Muslims."

Not every Muslim, I realize, would care to assert his religious beliefs and practice as a matter of "conviction and choice." The majority of Muslims seem to regard themselves as simply part of a received tradition: deemed to be Muslims by destiny, by divine will, or through the influence of family and community. Nor do all Muslims engage in self-reflection and conscious assessment of their religious beliefs and practices. Today many Islamic social and ethical values are internalized through the socialization of children and daily interaction; they are no longer consciously seen as "religious practice."

Yet conscious reflection and moral choice are integral to Muslim identity. The Quran urges Muslims to think and reflect, and the subject of reason and reasoning is one of the dominant themes of the Quran as a whole (e.g., 2:219, 242, 266; 6:32; and 28:60). In fact, the Quran explicitly states that the object of its revelation is to inspire human deliberation and reflection (12:2; 43:3). For any practice—prayer, fasting, or other action in compliance with Islamic precepts—to count as religious at all, it must be done deliberately and intentionally (i.e., with *niya*). Abstaining from eating, drinking, and engaging in sexual conduct, for instance, is not "fasting" unless it was deliberately intended as such.

In other words, human action acquires Islamic value when it is done with deliberate intention. Muslims must engage in self-reflection and critical evaluation of their beliefs and practices—"religious self-determination" is the right and the duty of all Muslims, regardless of what form it ultimately takes.

Who Are We to Ourselves? To Others?

To seek a clear sense of identity, whether individual or collective, is to follow a complex path. Human beings tend to have multiple, overlapping, and intersecting identities— a wide range of affiliations and interactions. Furthermore, as we go through life, we sometimes acquire new identities, adapting or redefining preexisting ones.

For instance, I am an African from Sudan who is now a naturalized American citizen. I am a Muslim; a husband, father, and grandfather; an academic lawyer and a human rights activist. Since I support certain social and economic policies that are commonly attributed to one of the two major political parties in the United States, my political identity may place me nationally in either the majority or the minority (and that may change), regardless of my other identity affiliations. Yet some of those other identities may influence which priorities I choose to support among the policy options that my party advances. Sometimes I may not even be consciously aware of an identity until it becomes relevant in a specific context.

What's more, my identity is relative. I am constantly re-negotiating my identities in my interactions with others, asserting or de-emphasizing certain facets of myself. Depending on the context and my motivation, I am a member of majorities in some respects and a member of minorities in other respects. In contrast to my mostly permanent attributes like sex or race, my affiliation with an identity group may depend on the context: *At that moment, who do I choose to be?* For instance, African Americans strongly identified with the liberation struggle in South Africa during the Apartheid regime in that country, but did not assert that racial identity to other parts of sub-Saharan Africa at the time, and did not continue to identify with South Africa after two decades of black majority rule. Jewish Americans may strongly identify with the State of Israel when it is under attack, and may equally strongly distance themselves from Israel when it is building settlements in the Occupied Palestinian Territories. Similarly, the significance of being a Muslim is unlikely to be the same for all Muslims in all situations or regarding all issues.

As we consider the role of others in our process of identity formation and negotiation, the layers of identity continue to stack up: *Do other people accept my claim to an identity, or reject it? Do they attribute to my identity a meaning different from the one I believe it possesses?* Thus, identity formation is relational and contextual: the identity we work with in a particular setting emerges from the interaction between *our own* perception and experience of that identity, and *other people's* perception and experience of it.[3] In other words, we don't have exclusive control over our various identities and how they interact among themselves and in our relationships with other people.

To continue from my own example: I believe myself to be a Muslim; other Muslims, however, may not accept my assertion of this identity, because they strongly disagree with my understanding of what Muslim identity means. Some non-Muslims may attribute a particular meaning to Muslim affiliation, regardless of how Muslims understand their religion—as recent controversies in the United States attest. Since I am an immigrant to this country, my idea of what it means to be an African American may differ widely from the meaning held by native-born African Americans.

Mediating the formidable tensions between self-perception and the perceptions of others—both within and outside the identity group in question—is central to the task of promoting and safeguarding positive public discourse about identity and citizenship. The identities we claim for ourselves or ascribe to each other are contingent, ambiguous, and contested. In any particular context, the meaning of an identity results from dynamic negotiation among relevant actors and is guided by specific tactical and strategic choices. In other words, the identities that link us to purported majority or minority populations are both strategically constructed and contextually determined.[4]

Drawing on this widely accepted insight, I argue that *deliberate strategies and proactive action* can change the perceptions of our identities and their meanings. The experiences of other religious communities, discussed in the next chapter, illustrate this theory.

Although being a Muslim is no indicator of what kind of American citizen one might be, being an American citizen is a way to contest and negotiate what a particular identity (religious or otherwise) means for people, both individually and collectively. By embracing citizenship, people can define the meaning and implications of being a citizen—a status that is, itself, an evolving and dynamic concept.

Embracing Citizenship

To realize this vision of citizenship and meaning for themselves, and to uphold it for others, American Muslims must join general political and social life—in solidarity and common cause with other citizens—and begin exercising their rights to democratic self-governance. To earn the rights of citizenship, Muslims must assume the responsibilities of citizens. In engaging a proactive citizenship, American Muslims should seek to integrate on their own terms as persons and communities, rather than abandoning their religious self-determination through passive assimilation. This includes the constant evolution and reformation of American Muslims' identities in relation to national identity.

To some readers, this framing may seem to concede the same logic of minority/majority politics that I am seeking to challenge. In my view, however, American Muslims already confine themselves to minority status—as does the wider American society. We can acknowledge this without accepting it as either inevitable or permanent.

I frame this issue in terms of two hypotheses:

1. To the extent that American Muslims and the wider society are already relating to each other beyond the framework of minority politics, I hope to further advance and facilitate that relationship. By "minority politics" I mean engaging in political strategies and practices that are premised on or motivated by one specific identity, religious in this case, to the exclusion of other identities and the dynamic of multiple, overlapping identities that I am calling for.
2. To the extent that this is *not* the case, then I hope to make the case for transformation and also to advance and facilitate its practice.

On both counts, I remain firm in my objectives: urging American Muslims to take a proactive, affirmative view of citizenship and to seek religious self-determination, including the critical self-understanding of their identity and of conditions under which self-determination can be exercised.

Citizenship and Identity

While the traditions of many countries and civilizations have much to teach us about citizenship, it's worth recalling how the concept of citizenship developed in the European/Western tradition, the primary antecedent of citizenship in the United States as we know it.

That review, though, begins with a caveat: Despite the strengths in European/Western theories of citizenship, the coherence and credibility of this broad tradition, over time, have been contradicted in practice by the exclusion of women and poor classes at home, and also by brutal colonialism abroad, during which the leading powers demonized native populations in order to justify their systematic extermination and displacement by European settlers. Similar contradictions persisted in colonies like the United States, where it took first a civil war and then a constitutional amendment to end the institutionalized practice of chattel slavery, then another century or more of struggle as African Americans and other marginalized groups sought to obtain civil rights. For centuries, the ideal of citizenship in the United States also was seriously diminished by the exclusion of Asians and other peoples.

All these problems are a matter of historical record, which only goes to show that more work must be done to secure the advances made thus far, and to facilitate further development of the concept and practice of citizenship in the United States. The European/Western tradition has shown the capacity to evolve, and within this theory of citizenship we can find the means for overcoming both its past limitations and its current constraints.

Ancient Greece and Rome: Status-Based Citizenship

The institution of citizenship in American public discourse can be traced back to Ancient Greece (750–300 BCE), where citizenship was not merely an identity affording certain rights and responsibilities but the framework for a moral, communitarian life. From birth, people internalized the governmental, military, and religious values of citizenship, along with an understanding of a citizen's duties, such as serving on a jury and attending assembly meetings. A citizen stripped of such functions was described as *atimos*, an ancient Greek term that literally meant being without honor and value. But the honor and value of citizenship at that time was limited and exclusive; the citizen had to be a male of known genealogy, a patriarch, a warrior, and the master of the labor of others, normally a slave owner.[5]

This principle of limited and exclusive citizenship was continued by the Romans, but the meaning of the concept changed over time. Initially, during the Roman Republic (500 BCE–27 CE), the *civis Romanus* corresponded to the Ancient Greek paradigm in which citizenship was rooted in the social and political community, but it eventually came to denote only a person's legal status. Thus, a Roman citizen came to mean someone who was free to act under the law, to ask for and expect the protection of the law, and to enjoy legal standing within the Roman legal community.[6]

With the increasing Christianization of the late Roman Empire, membership in the state church replaced citizenship in satisfying people's social, political, and legal needs; religious bonds began to count more than civic standing.[7] During the medieval period, the status of *citizen* was granted only to the members of a quasi-aristocratic minority. These few held exclusive access to certain privileges, immunities, and resources, and the honorable recognition of one's independence as a *civitates* countered feudal forms of dependency.

The Beginnings of Rights-Based Citizenship

Political leaders during the European Renaissance not only looked to Ancient Greece and Republican Rome for a sense of the active political citizen but also sought to reaffirm the legal implications of citizenship developed by Imperial Rome. The city-states of Italy based their citizenship regulations on Roman law as defined in the *Corpus juris civilis* of Justinian. Citizenship became a more dynamic concept, the subject of constant litigation. The Italian Renaissance influenced other European territories to adopt (and adapt) citizenship to their own sociopolitical situations. Scholars who came to Italy to study Roman law carried the concept of citizenship back to their homelands, where it was subsequently grafted onto feudal practices.

In France and other territories, power increasingly became centralized in the monarch. As a result, the powers and rights of individuals could not be denied by the king as long as the citizen remained obedient. By the early sixteenth century, Italian ideas had fused with French legal and legislative practices to produce principles of national citizenship. Those principles were clarified and organized into coherent theories by jurists and political thinkers such Jean Bodin, who conceived citizenship as signifying a personal relationship between the individual and the king. During the absolutist period of the seventeenth century, the Renaissance tradition of active citizenship was transformed into a more passive practice of service to the monarch.[8]

The evolution of citizenship continued as the Reformation introduced new changes, and the state replaced the king as both the focal point of power and allegiance and as the source of rights. With the establishment of what came to be known as the *nation-state* after the Peace of Westphalia in 1648, the concept of national citizenship emerged. Political philosophers like Thomas Hobbes developed theories surrounding the direct relationship between the individual and the state. John Locke, building upon Hobbes, constructed a rights-based theory of citizenship, which became the characteristic feature of European political philosophy in the eighteenth century. As the state grew more powerful, it increasingly attracted demands for the extension of rights. The growing structure of government—complex and bureaucratic—also increased the possibilities of interaction and communication between citizens and the state, thereby promoting the democratic principle of rule-by-consent.[9]

National Citizenship and the Welfare State

The 1689 British Declaration of the Rights and Liberties of the Subject, along with the French and American revolutions, firmly established the idea of territorial (national) citizenship. In the French Revolution, citizenship was linked not only to the Declaration of the Rights of Man and the Citizen, which promised universal and egalitarian citizenship, but also to the obligation of civic and military service to the nation. The view that emerged from the French Revolution—that of citizenship not only as an individual political, social, and legal status but as a collective national identity—was inspired by Jean-Jacques Rousseau's idea that "a community could be united by a 'general will' that transcended social conflict."[10] Rousseau also promoted the concept of popular sovereignty, whereby sovereign individual citizens enter into a social contract with the state. This view was adopted by the American Revolution in the Declaration of Independence, which explicitly vested sovereignty in the people.

Eighteenth-century European conceptions of citizenship, however, had to struggle with the question of demographic scope. Initially, for instance, foreigners could claim French citizenship; but as France's wars with other countries militarized the idea of the nation and therefore the idea of citizenship itself, the scope of citizenship narrowed. European states gradually extended citizenship within their borders, while at the same time excluding those who were not seen as sharing the same national identity.

The next significant development in the European/Western concept of citizenship led to the welfare-state paradigm. According to this view, citizenship is essentially a matter of ensuring that everyone is treated as a full and equal member of society; thus, the fullest expression of citizenship requires a liberal democratic welfare state that guarantees civil, political, and social rights to all. The welfare state ensures that *all citizens* are full members of society, able to participate in that society and to enjoy its common life. If these rights are violated, people will be marginalized and will be unable to participate.[11]

Citizenship: Multilayered, Multifaceted

Citizenship, from a broad perspective, has both a vertical and a horizontal dimension. The vertical dimension links individuals "upward" to the state by reinforcing in those citizens the idea that this is "their" state, that they are full members of an ongoing association that is expected to survive the passing generations. The horizontal relationship consists of citizens' positive identification with each other as valued members of the same civic community. Here, citizenship works "across" a population to reinforce empathy and to sustain solidarity among the wider political community.

Citizenship *unites* what the activities of parties and interest groups can so easily divide; it helps to overcome the forces of demography. But citizenship is also a malleable and contested institution. The task is to find a basis for cohesion without suppressing the capacity for difference, because a mature democratic polity must positively affirm different ways of being and the different goals to which they lead.[12]

Citizenship remains an institution of the state. It is based on financial contributions (taxes) and services (e.g., military or civic service) that presuppose a reciprocal relationship between rights and obligations and imply a relationship between rights and specific territory. It does not extend beyond the state. At the same time, however, the practices and benefits of citizenship do extend beyond the state, because people, ideas, images, products, values, and concerns tend to cross borders. Multilateral arrangements and international agreements now implicate citizens in a web of rights and responsibilities concerning trade, the environment, refugees, crime, minorities, war, children, and many other issues.

Furthermore, citizenship is never a single, unalloyed concept; rather, its multifaceted meanings have to be worked through and developed in terms of the particulars of sociopolitical location and history. Since the 1970s, intensified flows of capital, goods, and people have produced an increasingly complex network of global relationships, which not only challenges social cohesion within nations but also requires a more inclusive notion of what it means to be a citizen. The nation-state remains the primary site of citizenship, but globalization is highlighting the tensions between nationalism and multiculturalism, individualism and collectivism.

Citizenship in Today's Diverse World

Diversity in this context refers to the demographic fact of religious (possibly racial or ethnic) difference, which may or may not be accepted or at least tolerated among the various groups. I realize that there can be many appropriate ways of approaching these and related issues. In terms of what I am calling for in this book, I see acceptance of difference as indicating a proactive sense of seeing difference as a positive and creative factor. Toleration of difference indicates a lower level of acceptance, which may be sufficient to avoid or to at least minimize the risks of political instability and social strife that can follow from refusal to accommodate the facts of difference. This refusal is what I call *exclusive diversity*—of seeing our identity group as exclusive of other identities—which can easily turn into hostility toward people we deem to be alien or foreign to our preferred identity.

Democratic citizenship seeks to mitigate the negative consequences of exclusive diversity either by assimilating it or by making it the central feature of national identity—what we call multiculturalism. In a multicultural society, citizenship is a multilayered amalgamation of identities and belonging, a system of rights and responsibilities, a legal mechanism and a shorthand descriptor, a narrative of identity and culture that connotes both sameness and difference.[13]

In recent years, multiculturalism has spread both as a political discourse and as a set of international legal norms.[14] These policies seem to be driven by conflicting impulses. On the one hand, there is pessimism about the destabilizing consequences of ethnic politics; on the other, optimism about the prospects for a peaceful and democratic form of multicultural politics.

In a multicultural society, citizenship does not stand apart from or transcend other identities. For instance, the creation of a common British citizenship was quite compatible with being Scottish, English, Irish, or Welsh, thus allowing for the idea that there were different ways of being British. From this perspective, there should be no objection to expanding the number of constituent communities, all of which have a right to belong to the whole as well as to speak up for themselves and for their vision of the whole. Such negotiations are a natural part of citizenship.

Since citizenship is not monolithic, it is not strictly a legal and political identity. Rather, citizenship manifests itself in many settings—in voluntary associations, community organizations, trade unions, newspapers and media, and educational and religious institutions.

Dimensions of Citizenship

Citizenship is a public identity because it involves concerns that are "public," such as social justice or environmental issues, even though these concerns can be advanced in private settings—say, a trade-union meeting or a mosque. Because citizenship is public, it requires some degree of "national" consensus around foundational principles and values. Such consensus is not necessarily inconsistent with multiculturalism. Strong multicultural identities are not intrinsically divisive, reactionary, or subversive; however, they need to be complemented by vibrant national narratives and rituals that give expression to a national identity.[15] While this process does not require a single mono-lithic "national identity," it does require sufficient commonality—an overlap-ping consensus on some shared values—to sustain large-scale social cohesion and political stability across a country's population.

The question is one of degree and balance: How can unity and diversity coexist, whether within or among differing religious, ethnic, socioeconomic, or political communities? A state need not consist of one uniform, domi-nant "national" identity—but a state cannot persist for long when irrecon-cilable differences divide communities, rendering them incapable of working together to articulate and pursue national goals.

Whether from a general historical perspective or during the lifetime of a single person, political identity through citizenship is just one among many identities. What's more, political identity may not be one's primary identity. Other identities—social, ethnic, religious—are more likely to arise earlier in a person's life, or to be of greater importance to that person, than political identity experienced through citizenship.

We must avoid, however, drawing a sharp distinction between political identity and citizenship, because identities continually overlap and inter-act. Ethnic and religious identities, for example, have political dimensions. Within political identity and citizenship, there may be social, emotional, or psychological aspects. Acknowledging this fluidity, this interaction, is central to understanding the politics of identity and citizenship.

Politics and Identity

Identity is at work in all politics. For instance, identity influences how issues are framed and choices are made, how people understand their concerns, and how those concerns are described by politicians to their constituencies. Iden-tity also influences how people react to factual claims or to symbolic refer-ences in political discourse.

We tend to be mostly concerned with whether the connection between politics and identity is positive or negative, which is, of course, a matter of perspective or value judgment. The term "identity politics," for example, is sometimes used in a negative sense—to mean a divisive appeal to an ethnic, religious, or other marker of identity. Yet whether an explicit or implicit reference to identity is negative or positive depends on a host of other factors.

An appeal to national identity, as we often see in references to "American values," can be positive when invoked to generate political support for social justice initiatives or assistance after natural disasters. National identity also may be invoked, however, for chauvinistic, even fascist ends, as we have seen in the appeal to Serbian nationalism during the disintegration of the former Yugoslavia.[16] While identity is integral to all politics, we shouldn't underestimate the ambiguity and contingency of this connection.

A nationalist view of identity politics promotes the notion of stable, essential identity, and as such, it privileges difference over the reconciliation of differences. In contrast, a relational view of politics assumes that identity is always the product of relationship and therefore never an essential aspect of a person's identity. Relational politics aims to overcome the threat of conflict by privileging the flux of relationship and social conversation over the stability and privilege of identity.[17]

If we take a more inclusive and collaborative view of national identity among citizens, the persistence of the nation-state need not lead to divisive identity politics. The more multicultural a national identity becomes, and the more relational and collaborative identity politics is, the less conflict there is likely to be.

The Nature of States

Today, all of us live in a world governed by states. Yet the very nature of states remains deeply contested, with a range of competing theories offering very different views of how states actually operate—or should operate.[18]

Until recently, the bounded, territorial, and sovereign state has been the foundation of modern understandings of political space. As the patterns of world politics undergo major transformations through the competing processes of global integration and local fragmentation, new and complex relationships emerge to challenge the nation-state system.[19] Addressing the challenge to think beyond the nation requires a reassessment of the very categories we use in understanding local, national, and international politics, and a re-imagining of the nature of political space itself.[20] These developments tend to undermine the assumptions of a state-centric approach to the politics of identity and citizenship.

The territorial nation-state organizes modern societal spaces and also influences the organization of groups of people and their relations with each other. The state produces differences between "citizens" and other groups: "foreigners," "refugees," and "immigrants." It distinguishes between those who are "inside" and those who are "outside." The modern state can thus be called a social and political practice of *inclusion and exclusion*, because it arranges relationships between people and communities through what it deems to be significant differences and similarities.

Through this approach, however, the state tends to serve the interests of those elites who control its institutions, although it often does so in the name of neutrality of the state or the public good. Since identity groups based on such classifications as class, ethnicity, religion, or gender seek to promote their interests, they are bound to come into conflict with those elites—who actually control the state in order to advance their own interests. We should therefore expect varying forms and degrees of tension between identity politics and what the ruling elites might assert as a homogeneous national culture.

In this struggle, claims by identity groups and social and political dissidents are likely to be characterized as threats to national security, political stability, or the public good. In the usual course of majority politics, officially sanctioned discourse tends to strengthen certain groups' identification with the nation-state, while at the same time marginalizing other groups and attempting to delegitimize their claims by characterizing them as threatening to the social order.

Identity politics works in a variety of spheres, from cultural discourse and legal claim, to political alliances and social movements. The nature and likely outcome of these processes are affected by various factors, including the role of the state in the formation and transformation of identities, and whether the state is sympathetic to multicultural policies. For instance, the French state adopted a policy of mass expulsion of the Roma people in 2011–2012, which reflected manipulation by the state of widespread prejudice against this minority ethnic group.[21] Moreover, technology and the media help social and political actors to manipulate people's identities through rituals, myths, and symbols in order to consolidate the social authority and/or political power of elites.[22]

The Potential of Human Agency

Since perceptions of majority and minority status are created and managed through the processes just outlined, such perceptions can also be resisted and reformulated through the same processes. Members of the presumed majority would be unlikely to voluntarily give up their relative power and privilege, but members of the presumed minority have the ability to contest and challenge the balance of power.

We must not underestimate the role of human agency—of citizens and their politics—in the negotiation of identities beyond the simplistic dichotomies of "majority" and "minority," which are neither accurate nor productive. This claim may seem to be contradicted by the case of race as a permanent marker of difference that historically has shaped majority/minority relations in the United States. But when we consider, for instance, the shifting balance of persecution among the Hutu and Tutsi in Rwanda from the 1950s to 1990s, we can clearly see that the operative issue is not race or demographics as such, but power relations.

I would argue that majority/minority relations are always political, and therefore can change significantly over a relatively short period of time: consider race relations in the United States over the last fifty years (though much remains to be done).

The politics of identity should aim, first and foremost, to advance recognition and respect for the racial, ethnic, political, socioeconomic, professional, and other identities that unite some citizens in some respects, even while differentiating among them in other respects. On closer examination, we will see that no member of any identity group belongs, in every respect, only to that group, but is also a member of another group indicated by a different marker of identity. No majority or minority anywhere is united or divided in all identities. This is as true of American Christians, for instance, as it is of American Muslims: both groups are not only divided by racial, cultural, economic, and political factors, but also in their religious beliefs and practice as Christians or Muslims.

For American Muslims, Where Can "Beyond Minority Politics" Lead?

My call for Muslims to transcend the perceived limitations of minority status does not mean that they should abandon their personal and communal interests as Muslims and simply disappear into the melting pot of wider society. I do not assume that there is a completely level playing field for American Muslims, nor do I expect them to be welcomed in solidarity by the American public at large. As is evident in recent controversies about the so-called banning of Sharia and the Park 51 mosque in New York, there are some clear indications that both irrational hostility and profound ignorance of Islam and Muslims exist among significant segments of the American public.

This is far from the whole story, however, because there are also clear indications of genuine acceptance from many—I would say most—segments of American society. As a close observer of such concerns on a global scale, I think that acceptance of religious difference and willingness to learn about other religious communities is relatively higher in the United States than in other parts of the world. Seeing both sides of this equation, I am calling on American Muslims to take a proactive, affirmative view of their citizenship in order to advance their personal and communal concerns.

The Politics of Equal Citizenship

Recall that I use the term "minority politics" to indicate engaging in political strategies and practices that are premised on or motivated by one specific identity, religious in this case, instead of the dynamic of multiple, overlapping identities that I am calling for. Generally speaking, what lies beyond minority politics for American Muslims is "the politics of equal citizenship," in which *all citizens* are neither disadvantaged nor privileged by their religious affiliation or by a lack of it. When I call on American Muslims to exercise their full agency and rights to cultural/religious self-determination as citizens of the United States, I am enjoining them to fulfill their obligations and claim their entitlements in the same way other citizens do. There are no particular advantages or disadvantages in this process that are peculiar to Muslims or any other community.

To begin with, the simple fact that someone self-identifies as Muslim is irrelevant to that person's entitlement to equal citizenship and protection of the law—just as irrelevant as it would be for someone who self-identifies as Christian, Jewish, Hindu, or any other religious affiliation, or none. With a firm grounding and self-confidence in their *equal citizenship*, American Muslims can, in fact, contribute to the further development of the meaning and practice of citizenship in the United States. While early conceptions of citizenship derived from elites, in this age of popular self-determination the field is now wide open. Most likely, not all citizens would want to engage in such contestations, and not all of them can effectively do so; but the option is available—and it has nothing to do with religious affiliation.

American Muslims should recognize that it is possible to engage in deliberate integration into the social, political, and cultural life of the United States at large, rather than retreating into helpless and passive assimilation. I use the conditional word "possible" because whether or not that promise of integration is realized will depend both on what Muslims do and on what the wider society does, over time. As I will discuss in chapter 2, other religious communities, including those who are already well-established among the country's population, have had to struggle for acceptance; some are still struggling. The practice of citizenship that I am recommending is not, by any means, perfect. Nor is it secure against failure or regression. But I do believe that the door to citizenship, in this concept and through this practice, is sufficiently open for us to expect as much relative success as one could hope for anywhere in the world today.

Facing the Preexisting Realities

Nevertheless, in developing and pursuing their strategies of deliberate integration, American Muslims must realize that they are dealing with preexisting social, political, cultural, and legal realities. Assumptions or claims as to the neutrality of a legal system hide the fact that every constitutional and legal system actually flows organically from the values and institutions of the underlying cultural/religious tradition.[23] I am not suggesting that there is no value in relative neutrality; striving for neutrality enhances the symbolic authority of the law. Every legal system needs that symbolic authority. How else can it achieve the minimum degree of legitimacy that will win voluntary compliance from most of the population?

No legal system can maintain its authority in the face of massive and persistent violation of its norms by its human subjects. Successful legal systems, therefore, actively cultivate perceptions of neutrality among their subjects through commonplace means: the use of specialized language for legislation; a formal dress style and manner of communication between judges and lawyers; and ritual procedure for the presentation of evidence and the deliberation of judges and juries.

Even if we accept the logic that supports a need for this relative neutrality, however, we should not assume that a legal system is totally independent of the culture and religion of the society it serves. On the contrary, the organic connection that links legal norms to the community's culture and religion is the fundamental rationale of democratic governance and self-determination. People need to see their values and concerns reflected in the norms and processes of their legal system if they are to accept it as legitimate and comply willingly with its commands.

American Muslims, especially African American Muslims, may hold a strong perception that their values and concerns have not been integrated into the state and federal legal systems of the United States. Muslims are not alone in this perception, of course, and their religious values can be more intentionally represented in American legal systems than might now appear to be the case. But the primary issue here is a matter of an individual's or a group's experience of marginalization.[24] I believe that we should neither lose sight of such concerns, nor allow them to overwhelm us.

The fact that Muslims—or the people of any other religious community—are not dealing with a culturally neutral constitutional rule of law does not necessarily mean that they can never come to terms with that system, or that it has no value for them. Nothing human can ever be neutral. The issue is how to redress both the reality and the perception of exclusion or marginalization. What does the particular constitutional rule of law do? How does it work? And when Muslims and others find something to be wrong or problematic with the system, what can they do about it?

Religion and US Law

Instead of succumbing to either paralysis or blind rejection, it is better to seek an accurate understanding of the system and its underlying assumptions in order to develop appropriate strategies to engage it. The constitutional rule of law anywhere will set boundaries for political debate in order to maintain its own survival, though systems may differ on the nature and manner of their limits of toleration, and on whether the constitutional system allows challenges to its norms and assumptions. For religious communities, in particular, the US Constitution determines the scope and manner of legal tolerance of religious beliefs.[25]

As I will discuss in chapter 4, the scope of constitutional toleration of religious activities in the United States is appropriate, and it does permit reasonable opportunities for debate and contestation. Two major issues for American Muslims are the question of whether Sharia family law should be enforced by state courts, and the broader question of whether Muslims accept in principle the separation of religion and the state. For American Muslims—as for all other religious and cultural communities—there is a general framework within which to debate and contest these issues, namely the established constitutional rule of law of the First Amendment.

The First Amendment mandates that the state can neither establish any religion nor restrict the practice of any religion. In light of that framework, one of the main questions for this book is the following: Can American Muslims engage in internal discourse to transform their understanding of Sharia and how it applies in their lives? Or should they keep their traditional understanding of Sharia and its practice intact, and seek whatever accommodation the wider society is willing to grant them? To explore this, let's begin by examining the overarching relationship among Islam, the state, and politics, and then consider the more specific question of whether Sharia can be enforced by secular courts.

Here's my rationale for raising these questions: Among the American public at large, there is a perception that these are challenges facing Muslims everywhere, including American Muslims. I am not assuming that most American Muslims are particularly concerned about these questions, or that they consciously view them as "questions" or "issues" at all. Yet we need to raise such questions, or at least to explore methodologies and strategies for addressing them, in view of the relational nature of identity and also the role of the wider society in transcending minority politics. Proactive citizenship and religious self-determination, the dual objectives of this book, call for taking the apprehensions and concerns of other citizens seriously and trying to address them, even if we don't find those concerns credible or relevant ourselves.

More important, in my view, these issues may in fact influence the attitudes and experiences of American Muslims more than we realize. Concerns about the secular state, for instance, may inhibit the political participation of American Muslims, while heightening their anxieties about the practice of Sharia norms for family relations. The answer for this dilemma may be for American Muslims to participate in the political process in order to try to influence what is enacted into the family law of the state. But they must also accept that all aspects of the law of the state, including family law, will remain secular.

Furthermore, I will argue, the two aspects of the First Amendment (disestablishment of religion and free exercise of religion) are in fact *required by*—not merely tolerated or accepted by—Islam and Sharia. True, this is only my view of Islam and Sharia, but that is always the case: *every* view of Islam and Sharia is simply that of some person or group of persons, regardless of how widely or narrowly it is accepted. I am presenting my view so that it may be debated among American Muslims and the American public at large, and am happy to debate others, or to accept their view if I find it superior.

It may also be helpful to note our tendency to declare a general conclusion out of a vague and unsubstantiated "impression," sometimes in clear contradiction of established facts. I find this to be particularly true in public discourse about Islam, the state, and politics. It is remarkable that opinion leaders, prominent journalists, and sometimes scholars and intellectuals assume an inherent or permanent unity of Islam and the state as the "self-evident" truth of the history and current politics of Muslims. In historical fact, the notion of an "Islamic state" that will enforce Sharia emerged for the first time in the late colonial period (1930s–1940s). In current politics, the claim of unity of Islam and the state is based on an impressionistic view of the current situation in three or four (Iran, Pakistan, Saudi Arabia, and perhaps Sudan) out of more than forty Muslim-majority countries in the world today. I say "impressionistic" view because I am confident that upon close examination we will find this claim to be untrue even of those four countries. My plea is that when we encounter such assertions in public discourse we should ask the question: What is the evidence given or referenced in support of the claim? How does the person making this claim explain the consistent evidence to the contrary, not only on a global scale today, but also through fourteen centuries of Islamic history?

Islam, the State, and Politics

As noted earlier, the general framework within which American Muslims may debate their identity—including what I call religious self-determination—is established by the First Amendment, which forbids the state from establishing or restricting the practice of any religion. This framework applies to all religious and cultural communities in the United States. Further, within the parameters of the First Amendment and its jurisprudence, any group of citizens can practice their religion or address the concerns of their religious community openly and freely.

Throughout this book, I will be asking: How can American Muslims negotiate their religious self-determination within the existing framework? As one more step toward answering that question, I would like to present a model of a "secular state," one that is both consistent with the First Amendment and legitimate from an Islamic point of view.

The Secular State

This secular state, by definition, is neutral toward religion but is neither indifferent nor hostile toward it. I believe that the secular state—more so than even a so-called Islamic state—provides the best environment in which one can be a Muslim by choice and personal conviction, which is the only valid way of being a Muslim.[26]

A few caveats are appropriate here. First, I mean the secular state: not secularism, as a human philosophy that may be hostile to religion; and not secularization, as the privatization of religion or its exclusion from the public sphere. On the contrary, my purpose in calling for the religious neutrality of the state is to enable religion to have an appropriate and legitimate role in public life.

Second, I mean a state that is neutral regarding religion in particular, and not neutral about matters of public policy for such concerns as economic development or social justice.[27]

Third, the secular state is always inherently contextual and historical; every society's experience is unique. I am not seeking to engage continuing controversies about the historical contextual development of the secular state in the United States or elsewhere in the world. My limited purpose here is to introduce and illustrate the application of this model from an Islamic point of view.

The idea of an Islamic state that enforces Sharia as the positive law of the state is, from an Islamic point of view, both conceptually untenable and practically counterproductive. It is untenable because, once Sharia norms are enshrined in law, they cease to be the religious law of Islam and become the political will of that state. Moreover, given the wide diversity of opinion among Muslim scholars and schools of thought, enacting any of those norms as state law will mean having to select among competing views that are equally legitimate. Since that selection will be made by whoever happens to be in control of the state, the outcome will be political, rather than religious. Why will this process be counterproductive? By suppressing competing views, it will necessarily deny some Muslims their religious freedom.

I am therefore advocating the institutional separation of religion and the *state*, while recognizing and regulating the unavoidable connection between religion and *politics*. This distinction is necessary. It is practically impossible to prevent religious believers from acting politically in accordance with their beliefs, and they are entitled to do so through the democratic process, just as nonbelievers may seek to advance their philosophical or ideological views.

Where do we draw the line? The *state* is the more settled and deliberate operational side of self-governance, while *politics* is the dynamic process of making choices among competing policy options. Although the state and politics may be seen as two sides of the same coin, they should not be completely fused. The state is not simply a reflection of daily politics; it must be able to mediate and adjudicate among competing views of public policy, which require it to remain relatively independent of everyday politics. In essence, the state is the structure in which politics operate.

It is true that complete separation of the state and religion is not possible, because those who control the state will be influenced by their religious views. Moreover, in a democratic state, elected officials will usually attempt to implement the policies on which they campaigned—perhaps including some policies that are religiously motivated. This connection between religion and politics is a reality; therefore, in order to protect the separation of religion and the state, it is necessary to strive toward regulation of the connection between the state and politics. Although this paradox—separation of religion and the state despite the connection of religion and politics—cannot be completely resolved, it can be mediated by constitutional and human rights safeguards.

The Role of Civic Reason

How can this tension best be managed? Policies should be advanced on the basis of what I call *civic reason,* which consists of two elements:[28]

1. Citizens should be able to accept or reject such proposals, and counter with other proposals, through public debate, without having to challenge the religious beliefs of others.
2. Proposed policies must be debated publicly and openly, rather than assumed to follow from personal beliefs and religious motivations of either citizens or officials.

It is impossible, of course, to control people's intentions, but our objective should be to promote civic reasoning while diminishing reliance on personal religious beliefs through civic education, public discourse, and cultural activities.

Principles of constitutionalism, human rights, and citizenship must safeguard the role of civic reason in negotiating the relationship between religion and the state. Consistent institutional application of these principles gives all citizens the ability to participate equally and freely in the political process; it also protects them against discrimination on religious grounds. Protected by such safeguards, citizens will be more likely to contribute to the formulation of public policy. They also may be more likely to rely on civic reason when they object to proposals by others. Religious believers, including Muslims, can make proposals that emerge from their religious beliefs, but they must argue for them in a way that is accessible to those of other faiths (or none).

Negotiating the Relationship with the State

Since the relationship between religion and the state and its implications for public policy are matters of continuous debate and negotiation, any attempt to predict particular outcomes would be both inappropriate and unwise. We might, however, try to identify relevant factors and actors, determining how to regulate their interaction so as to improve the prospects for genuine and sustainable state neutrality. The basic tension in such negotiations arises from the need to protect the autonomy of religious authority while respecting the legitimate political and legal authority of the state.

On the one hand, the state needs to control religious institutions to the degree necessary for the state to fulfill its obligations: keeping the peace, protecting the rights of others, maintaining political stability, and achieving social and economic development and justice. On the other hand, religious communities need to maintain their autonomy in matters of legitimate religious doctrine and practice, as determined by the religious communities themselves, without interference by state officials.

The modern state is a centralized, bureaucratic, and hierarchical organization composed of institutions and offices that are supposed to perform highly specialized functions through predetermined rules.[29] To fulfill its obligations, the state should be distinct from other kinds of social organizations in *theory*, while remaining deeply connected to them in *practice*, for its own legitimacy and effectiveness. For instance, the state must seek out and work with various constituencies to maintain law and order and to provide education, health, and transportation services. State officials and institutions therefore cannot avoid having working relationships with various groups who hold competing views of public policy—nongovernmental organizations, businesses, political parties, and pressure groups—any of which may be religious. These working relationships not only enable the state to fulfill its obligations, but they are required by the principle of democratic self-governance.

If they develop an appreciation for civic reason, religious believers will have more opportunity to promote their religious beliefs through the regular political process, without threatening citizens who do not share those beliefs. Again, the separation of religion and the state alongside regulation of the relationship between religion and politics can best be achieved when religious beliefs are neither privileged nor suppressed—a condition that facilitates genuine and respectful negotiation of public policy.

In summary, a state that is neutral regarding religious doctrine, without being indifferent or hostile to religion, is *more consistent* with Sharia than is a so-called Islamic state. A secular state neither depoliticizes Islam nor relegates it to the so-called private domain. Rather, the influence of religion in the public domain is both open to negotiation and contingent upon free exercise of human agency by all citizens, believers and nonbelievers alike. Believers are entitled to keep their religious beliefs and practices exclusive when they apply that to themselves. But if they wish their religious beliefs to have general public application, they must be open to debate and contestation by nonbelievers.

These conditions provide a necessary framework for negotiating the relevance of Sharia to public policy and law. In this gradual and tentative process of consensus-building through civic reason, people may agree on one issue but disagree on another, and consensus-building efforts on any particular topic may fail or succeed, but none of these outcomes will be permanent and conclusive. Whatever the *substantive* outcome on any issue at any time, that outcome will be the result of—and also can change through—the process of civic reason, based on the voluntary and free participation of all citizens.

A more specific question remains for an established and stable secular state like the United States. Regardless of one's view on the broader question of Islam, state, and politics discussed here: *What is, should be, or is likely to be the role of Sharia in secular democratic Western states?*

Sharia in Secular Courts

Must American Muslims advocate for the enforcement of Sharia by secular courts? The issue here is not whether American Muslims owe allegiance to Sharia, because being a Muslim at all requires fidelity and voluntary compliance with relevant aspects of Sharia—doctrine, ritual practices, and social ethics. The question is whether there is another—public and legal—aspect of Sharia to which Muslims also owe allegiance and which they should seek to enforce through secular courts.

I have argued against this view, whether Muslims constitute the majority or the minority of the population.[30] Some questions, however, must be asked: *Is this view shared by American Muslims? And, if so, how do they understand their allegiance to Sharia in the context of the United States of the early twenty-first century?* The issue is complex, because of two factors. First, Muslims themselves tend to be ambivalent to or strongly disagree about the role of Sharia in a pluralistic modern state like the United States. Second, the exaggerated fear and irrational hostility of some Westerners toward Islam and Muslims may act as a self-fulfilling prophecy, strengthening extremist Muslims while undermining the moderate ones. This fear is exaggerated because it is totally out of proportion not only to the number of Muslims in Western countries, but also to the power of poor recent immigrant Muslims (as well as African American Muslims, in the case of the United States) measured against that of the dominant Christian or secular population. It is practically impossible for a tiny number of Muslims to impose their will on the vast numbers of established and entrenched non-Muslims.

The hostility is irrational because those who are promoting it fail to mention any evidence whatsoever in support of their claims. Yet such exaggerated fear and hostility can lead to a hardening of attitudes on both sides, thereby increasing the risk of incidents that seem to vindicate the original unfounded claims.

Consider the persistent charges that Muslims are trying to impose Sharia in secular courts. There is absolutely no indication of such an effort in practice. And even if there were, how could Muslims, who constitute about one percent of the population, possibly succeed in enforcing Sharia in the United States? The wave of laws banning Sharia might induce some Muslims to wonder: What is the motivation behind this?

Could Secular State Courts Enforce Sharia?

For now, let me clarify what constitutes the enforcement of Sharia by state courts. We must consider whether there is a clear distinction between these two situations:

1. Enforcement of a norm that happens to be endorsed by Sharia, but the authority of the judge and court enforcing it is *not derived from* Sharia;
2. Enforcement of the same norm as part of a religious, ethical, and social system, where both the authority of the court and the competence of the judges are grounded in Sharia.

In precolonial Muslim-majority lands, Sharia was part of an integrated system of Islamic education, comprising networks of scholars who performed the role of consultants to judges (*muftis*) as well as the judges selected by the parties to a dispute.[31] The caliph or sultan may appoint judges in the capital and perhaps in other major cities, but that does not preclude the parties from seeking judges of their choice. Moreover, the whole system was founded on the premise that Sharia norms are developed by independent jurists outside state institutions, and that the state would never claim any role in enacting Sharia norms. When parties submitted a dispute for adjudication, even the task of identifying the "law" applicable to the facts of that particular dispute was performed by an independent scholar (*mufti*) and was applied by the judge.[32]

Just because a law happens to be consistent with Sharia does not mean that the government is enforcing Sharia, any more than banning the death penalty means that a government is enforcing Catholic doctrine. What designates an enforcement of Sharia (if such a thing is even possible) is that the source of the authority—both of the norm and of the court that is enforcing it—is religious, as is the broader context in which the norm is being enforced. There can be a lot of general overlap between Sharia (and other religious and moral norms), on the one hand, and state law on the other. But that does not mean that the state is "enforcing Sharia."

For instance, theft and fraud are prohibited by both Sharia and state law, but the source of authority and the exact definition of the crime are very different. The Sharia norm is derived from the Quran and/or Sunna (traditions) of the Prophet, through a particular methodology (*usul al-fiqh*) leading to specific formulation of the norm and its consequences. By contrast, state law derives from the state's political authority to legislate—expressed in the particular formulation of a statute or a code, to be interpreted and applied by state-appointed judges.

Because of such differences in sources and methodology, each system has its own definition of stealing. Theft (*sariqa*) under Sharia is strictly limited to secretive taking (*khefiya*) of the private property (not public property) of another person above a specific value (*nissab*) from a locked container (*hirz*). It does not include the taking or misappropriation of public property, and it does not extend to fraud or embezzlement, whether public or private. These features of the prohibited conduct, determined by the scriptural sources and their interpretation, cannot be changed by judges or state legislators. The rationale of such limitations—which may seem odd from a modern public policy or a rationalist point of view—is that the prohibition is imposed by God, and therefore it is not for human beings to modify. In practice, however, applying these limiting features was believed by Muslim scholars to be more merciful than rejecting them because either they restrict the scope of the offense, or they create ambiguity (*shubha*), which can be the basis of avoiding enforcement of the strict punishment.[33] The rationale of their thinking was that it is better to let a guilty person go than to risk punishing a person who is not guilty by Sharia standards.

If a legislator wishes to punish theft under Sharia, he must adopt its exact definition and not change any aspect of it (e.g., by punishing theft of public property). Moreover, imposing the same punishment under a non-Sharia system is not a Sharia punishment at all. In sum, the authority of the norm, of the judge, and of the process of application must all derive from Sharia.

To offer an example, the enforcement of so-called Sharia-compliant contracts by secular American courts does not derive its authority from Sharia itself.

Such a contract can, of course, be enforced by an American court when it is consistent with American law, but the outcome would be an application of American law, not of Sharia. Each of the two normative systems is sovereign and supreme on its own terms. If there is a coincidental overlap, such as a conclusion that one party or another is liable for breach of contract, then that is merely an interesting point of comparative law. It will be a decision authorized by American law, which happens to agree in outcome with Sharia.

Furthermore, enforcement of Sharia norms by the state is not the only or the most appropriate way for Muslims either to comply with Sharia, or to respect their religious/cultural identity. Sometimes the claim that religious or cultural communities are entitled to some degree of legal autonomy or exemption from the general law of the land is stated in terms of the desirability of "legal pluralism." Since the official legal system is in fact that of the dominant culture, some argue, other cultural normative systems should receive equal recognition as legal systems.[34]

How Does "Legal Pluralism" Work?

The problem with calling this approach "legal pluralism" is that if we designate every normative system as a legal system, the term "legal" becomes too broad to be useful. Setting up such autonomous systems can even add to the marginalization of the very groups seeking such protection. Moreover, communal autonomy through legal pluralism does not work for those who lack an institutionalized hierarchical organization that can speak on their behalf.[35] This risk is particularly relevant to American Muslims because of the religious diversity among them and their lack of centralized hierarchical religious leadership. At the most obvious level, a Shia Muslim, for instance, should not be represented by a Sunni Muslim or subjected to a Sunni norm.

The notion of legal pluralism does, however, succeed in highlighting the diversity of multiple uncoordinated, coexisting, or overlapping bodies of binding norms, which may make competing (and sometimes conflicting) claims on a given population. On the one hand, this potential conflict can be confusing for individuals and groups who cannot be sure in advance which legal regime will apply in a particular situation. On the other hand, the reality of these competing authorities creates opportunities for choice from among coexisting regimes, providing that they are not all called "legal."

A major example of this is in the application of Sharia-based family law norms through state courts not only in more than forty Muslim-majority countries around the world, but also in some secular democratic states like

India and Israel. If Sharia norms are not enforced by official state courts as positive law, they can be accessible to the parties in a family dispute at the level of community-based arbitration, if they submit to that by their own free choice. I realize that "free choice" may be socially difficult to assert, especially by women in traditional societies, but the possibility of voluntary arbitration cannot be denied to all potential parties in any context because of the risk of social coercion in some societies. In practical terms, denial of this possibility may have the ironic outcome of encouraging political demands for the enforcement of Sharia family norms through the positive law of the state.

The main problem is that legal pluralism fails to distinguish between the state and other normative systems.[36] Proponents of legal pluralism do not provide a comprehensive definition of what they mean by "law"—some basis by which to determine what is law and what is not.[37] Their approach holds all normative or regulatory orders as types of law, instead of viewing law as just one type of normative or regulatory regime. It does not distinguish between a binding, authoritative system that one cannot opt out of—which is the case with the territorial jurisdiction of the state—and a religious or cultural normative system, which one may or may not choose to comply with.[38]

An Alternative: "Normative Pluralism"

It makes more sense to think in terms of "normative pluralism," drawing a clear distinction between the law and other normative systems,[39] which would coexist alongside each other. This would serve the underlying purpose of legal pluralism, while avoiding the confusion of having multiple so-called legal regimes. Accordingly, I would restrict the use of the term "law" to state legal systems, as distinguished from other normative systems in a broader sense. State law and religious norms are two different and separate types of normative systems; we should not create confusion by labeling all of them "law."[40]

The two types of normative systems do not stand on opposite sides; they tend to interact and to influence each other. State law is often inspired by religious norms, even though these norms cannot be enacted into state law as religious directives. For instance, theft is a crime and a sin, but it is not a crime *because* it is a sin, and it is not a sin merely because it is a crime. State law and policies, however, can prompt re-examination of religious norms and practices. Muslims' family relations—involving children in particular—have come to be influenced by state law.

Moreover, these systems are not ranked by authority or importance. Normally they operate in different spheres, and when there is conflict, only legal norms can be enforced by the state. For instance, in the prior example, Sharia family norms can be religious when they are practiced voluntarily, but once they are enforced by the state, they become simply rules of state law, divorced from their religious sources. This does not mean, however, that legal norms are superior to religious norms because the state enforces them. In fact, religious norms can be more effective than state-enforced legal norms in regulating human behavior. In practice, religious and legal norms are not in "competition, but tend to support and influence each other". For example, the institution of marriage itself derives from religion, but the state can regulate family relations in ways that modify traditional religious understandings, as with laws prohibiting polygamy.

These issues deserve further discussion, which will be forthcoming. For now, I am only making the point that, since the source and authority of state law differ from those of religious normative systems, using the term "law" for both can be confusing. To indicate the sense of binding norms, we can use the term "normative system," which suggests rules that are binding and authoritative in a different manner from that of state law. To emphasize, there is no strict dichotomy or hierarchy between the two types of normative systems; they tend to interact, and either type can be more effective in shaping human behavior than the other, depending on such factors as the nature and subject of the norm, the circumstances of its invocation, and the people who are invoking it.

Applied to American Muslims—as to all other religious believers—this approach would mean that believers should be free to live by their own understanding of Sharia, as long as that understanding is practiced voluntarily, including community-based mediation and arbitration of disputes, without invoking the coercive authority of the state. It is true that some social or psychological coercion may exist within a family and community, but that is a general problem, not one particular to Sharia.

Take, for example, the complex role of the state in promoting the well-being of its population and protecting the rights of children and other vulnerable persons. How can we balance the rights of parents to raise their children with concerns about "the best interest of the child" under state law? When should state authorities intervene to protect children? Any answer to such questions requires a delicate balance between competing interests and is best assessed on a case-by-case basis.

Religion and the Modern State

Modern states do not permit freedom of religion to override the law. This is true of a host of states, religious or secular, from the most authoritarian to the most democratic. Iran and Saudi Arabia claim to enforce Sharia as state law, but only according to the official interpretation of what that means (Twelver Shia in Iran and Wahhabi School in Saudi Arabia). Secular states like Germany, the United States, the United Kingdom, China, and Japan exhibit a similar variety of approaches.

Even states that lack the resources to ensure consistent compliance with the law would not openly concede exemptions for religious or cultural practice. The only difference between various types of states would relate to their authoritarian or democratic quality and whether the law conforms to constitutional and human rights standards. For example, Saudi Arabia would not permit Shia Muslims to lobby for legislation based on their religious beliefs.

By contrast, the United States, for instance, would enable American Muslims to lobby for legislation and state policies that facilitate their individual and collective religious self-determination. Like other religious communities, American Muslims can seek accommodations for their religious practices within the constitutional, legal, political, and administrative framework of the United States. This action is necessary when private religious observance requires the cooperation of some administrative agencies of the state, such as permits for the construction of mosques, religious instruction in private schools, and compliance with religious dietary requirements (*halal* food).

The cooperation of the state also may be helpful in enabling Muslims to organize their personal affairs privately in compliance with Sharia, when that practice is consistent with constitutional and legal requirements. For instance, as a general rule, a Muslim widow is religiously required to maintain a degree of seclusion for a grieving period of four months and ten days following the death of her husband (Quran 2:234). If the wife happens to be working outside the home and does not want to prejudice her professional career in the long term, she may need to obtain a leave of absence from her work in order to comply with her religious obligation. Drawing on experience with maternity leave and related matters, American Muslims can lobby for legislation that requires employers to grant a Muslim widow leave for that purpose and still allow her to return to her job after the grieving period. It may even be possible to require employers to offer leave with full or partial pay, since the widow might be in greater need of income after the death of her husband.

While such accommodations can be achieved through the democratic political process, it is also true that Muslims may be required to submit to state law even when it violates their understanding of Sharia. This problem, however, is not peculiar to Muslims or even to religious believers. Submission to the jurisdiction of the law of the land is a shared obligation of all citizens, regardless of their religious or philosophical beliefs or political opinions. All citizens must comply with state law, even when they are strongly opposed to it. The advantage of democratic states in this regard is that they permit their citizens, for example, to organize so as to change the law through the political process, or to challenge its interpretation and application through the courts.

This possibility is one of the main benefits that American Muslims can draw from integrating more fully into the political and social life of the United States. Another advantage is that in the United States, Muslims can freely engage in debates about the meaning and implications of Sharia and can address points of tension or conflict between state law and traditional interpretations of Sharia. Such internal discourse might also be useful for legitimizing, from an Islamic point of view, the principle of separation of religion from the state.

Sharia and Religious Self-Determination

The personal and collective interests of American Muslims are better served by community-based practice of Sharia under the principle of normative pluralism, than by a policy whereby Sharia norms are enforced by state courts in the name of legal pluralism. Sharia cannot be enforced as state law and still retain its religious quality; that quality differs inherently and permanently from state law, which does not claim divine authority.

Another reason for denying to state law the religious sanctity of Sharia is the unavoidable need to select among equally legitimate views of Sharia. Allowing the state to claim such authority is inconsistent with the religious nature of Sharia, because no human being can decide religious truth for other human beings.

Furthermore, Muslims need not undermine the religious legitimacy of Sharia in this way, because they have other ways to exercise their right to religious self-determination:

1. Private social practice of Sharia within the framework of state law and constitutional safeguards;

2. Consideration of Sharia as a normative source for state law through civic reason in the democratic political process, without claiming that Sharia as a religious normative system can be state law; and

3. Religious discourse and cultural transformation, to mediate tensions between historical interpretations of Sharia and modern constitutional and human rights principles.

On the first count, Muslims can, in fact, behave in ways that conform to the vast majority of Sharia norms without coming into conflict with state law in a democratic society. For example, Muslims can refrain from taking or charging interest on loans (*riba*), an act that is prohibited by Sharia, and instead can establish financial institutions that conform to their understanding of Sharia under the framework of existing state law. Muslims can also observe Sharia requirements about marriage and divorce voluntarily, without having those requirements imposed on everyone. Any conflicts that may exist between Sharia and state law at this level of private social practice can be mediated through the other two processes.

In the second process, the premise is that any legal system should reflect the ethical values, priorities, and interests of the political majority, subject to the constitutional rights of all citizens regardless of their political standing. The concept of "beyond minority politics," we recall, means that American Muslims may be among either the political minority or the political majority of the day, because political affiliation neither determines nor is determined by religious identity. All religious or cultural communities have the right to organize and to act collectively, and to contribute to public policy and legislation through civic reason in the democratic process, provided they submit to the same principles of constitutional governance. For example, Muslims can lobby for recognition and accommodation by the state for some of their religious holidays or practices, such as leave when employed by the state to travel to Mecca for Hajj. State recognition and accommodation may assist Muslims in negotiating similar treatment by private employers, who may be influenced but are not bound by state policies as such.

The third process of religious self-determination for Muslims—and a critically important one—is Islamic discourse on the interpretation of Sharia in the modern context. Since what Muslims uphold as Sharia today results from human interpretation of the Quran and Sunna of the Prophet, that interpretation can be modified by re-interpretation of the same sources. From an Islamic point of view, such modification would be as legitimate as any earlier interpretation of those principles, if Muslims accept them as such. The only manner in which any principle of Sharia came to be established in the past was through what I call intergenerational consensus, and this remains valid today. Sharia norms became norms simply because succeeding generations of Muslims accepted them, never through an "enactment" moment or process. Rather than a human authority or institution establishing Sharia norms for Muslims to comply with, it was always ordinary Muslims' acceptance of the norms that established those norms as authoritative among believers.[41]

Our purpose here is to redress problematic historical interpretations of Sharia regarding, in particular, the rights of women and freedom of religion. In relation to family law, for instance, Sharia does not require men to take more than one wife, but permits them to do so provided they maintain justice among co-wives—which the Quran itself says is not possible to attain (cf. Quran 4:3 and 4:129). Some scholars have already suggested that this combination of verses indicates that monogamy should be the rule, and polygamy the rare exception. For example, if the first wife is unable to have children, she may consent to her husband taking a second wife instead of terminating their marriage. If it is the husband who is unable to have children, then the wife has the right to seek termination of the marriage, if she wishes to do so.

The fact that there is much diversity of opinion among schools of Islamic jurisprudence on these issues supports the approach that I am suggesting. Instead of resorting to state courts, which are bound to enforce legal uniformity of state law, Muslim spouses may prefer to have their differences mediated through community-based arbitration. Sharia norms are premised on personal piety and subjective judgment, which are better observed and accounted for through voluntary community-based mediation, not state enforcement. The existence of serious discrimination against women under traditional interpretations of Sharia is also better addressed through public debate among Muslims than by state courts. The judicial system of the American state has neither sufficient competence in Sharia to pretend to enforce its norms, nor the Islamic religious authority to intervene in controversial religious doctrine and practice. I return to these issues in chapter 4 of this book.

It must be emphasized, however, that none of these elements of religious self-determination would permit Muslims to opt out of the application of state law, or to have Sharia norms enacted as state law, except through the regular democratic process and subject to constitutional safeguards. Nor would these elements permit Muslims to plead Sharia as justification for violations of state law. Rather, our object is to enable Muslims to exercise their right to religious self-determination within the framework of state law and its constitutional safeguards—just like any other religious or cultural community.

2

Negotiating Citizenship in the United States

FOR AMERICAN MUSLIMS who want to embrace their citizenship in the United States—along with their right to religious self-determination—the outlook is promising.

From its early exclusion of certain groups on grounds of race, slavery, and gender to its present far more inclusive and dynamic status today, US citizenship has traveled an ambivalent and meandering path. In that historical process, native-born citizens, at various stages in US history, have tended to be more assertive than immigrants, and the Anglo-Saxon Protestant majority has tended to place itself above all others. Part of the guidance we should now draw from that history is that citizens have been able to resist exclusion and marginalization, and have asserted their right to full and dynamic citizenship. In the past, citizens have been able to contest and negotiate the quality of their own citizenship, becoming its authors and guardians. For example, despite its limitations and frustrations, the civil rights movement achieved significant success on the issues it tackled. The fact that citizenship of the United States has *not* always been humane, enlightened, coherent, or rational offers hope for a more inclusive future.

Although citizenship law and practice, in the past, have fallen far short of ideal, they have evolved—and can evolve further. How can American Muslims contribute to this evolving process?

The Evolution of American Citizenship

Differences in race, language, religion, and ethnicity have always produced waves of hostility toward cultural minorities in the United States, even after Congress repealed the quota system for immigration. Much of this hostility comes from the human tendency to assign labels to ourselves and to others.

A Sense of Belonging

Every human being desires to belong, and every person needs that sense of belonging to survive and thrive. Through self-labeling—which we all do—we seek to understand the ways in which we are similar to some people and different from others. In the end, however, each person is unique, because no person's list of labels is exactly the same as someone else's.

Our individual labels, in combination—whether self-selected or assigned to us by other people—guide us into groups and niches of society, affirming our individual and collective identities. By telling me where I belong, my group identity also tells me that another person, someone who does not wear the same identifying labels, does *not* belong and is an "outsider." Over time, we can become entrenched in our group identity, because it is what we know and understand. Human beings tend to fear the unknown; therefore, we learn to distrust "outsiders" and perceive them as threats to our ways of life. We learn to repress whatever is beyond our realm of understanding and acceptance.[1]

Cultural differences can breed feelings of danger and fear, particularly in times of national trouble. At such times, "[i]t becomes convenient to make scapegoats of 'them'—the people who look different from 'us' or whose language or behavior is foreign to our own."[2] In the wake of World War I, for instance, the practice of what is known as "Americanization" gained momentum, with the goal of getting perceived outsiders to conform to the American way of life—"socializing" the "foreigners," and thereby transforming them into genuine "Americans."[3]

Although Americanization may have seemed well-intentioned, it involved some level of coercion. To force conformity is a way of securing power over others, and also a way of reinforcing the security of those who belong to the dominant culture. There seems to be a presumption that citizens of relatively recent alien origins are not loyal to the United States. During wartime, when patriotic fervor weakens usual restraints, this presumption is amplified.[4]

Our identities, however, are not solely cultural—and neither is the definition of citizenship. I am urging American Muslims not merely to meet the official requirements of citizenship, but to engage its full meaning and significance. Stepping up to full citizenship implies participating in the political as well as the socioeconomic life of the community. To participate in this way, people must be able to see themselves not as "foreigners" or members of a separate group; they must have a sense of belonging. I am not suggesting or implying that this will be easy, as entrenched interests are bound to resist challenge to the status quo. In fact, resistance is usually an indication of the need for change.

As Richard Bellamy argues, democracy cannot function in its full capacity unless trust and solidarity exist among its citizens, enabling them to promote social and political cohesion:

> Citizenship is a condition of civic equality. It consists of membership of a political community where all citizens can determine the terms of social cooperation on an equal basis. This status not only secures equal rights to the enjoyment of the collective goods provided by the political association but also involves equal duties to promote and sustain them—including the good of democratic citizenship itself.[5]

My idea of dynamic, integrated citizenship matches his.

The Problem of Exclusion

Citizenship is now closely associated with democratic politics, with "membership of an exclusive club—those who make the key decisions about the collective life of a governed political community."[6] This view of citizenship is in fact a very recent development; it was not true of the vast majority of countries, including European countries, as recently as the early twentieth century. Moreover, different levels of exclusion can occur inside or outside the political community on such grounds as race, gender, and lack of property. Voting—the pinnacle of citizenship—is just one example of a right that was denied to women much longer than to men. Even today, in most US states, prisoners who are citizens are denied the right to vote.

But exclusion can happen in more subtle, albeit equally problematic, ways. For instance, nationality is often taken to be synonymous with citizenship, though that assumption can be seriously misleading. Nationality supposedly indicates a legal bond, based on a social fact of attachment, a genuine connection of interests and sentiments that comes with reciprocal rights and duties.[7] Nationality also supposedly indicates belonging to the same "nation," an affiliation that fosters a sense of community among individuals, derived from shared culture, history, traditions, and language.

That presumed commonality, however, is often true of only a small or at least limited proportion of the population, who then project this "national identity" onto everyone else. The discourse of nationalism tends to hide the cultural, religious, and other diversity of a citizenry. This has been the case through much of US history, as Anglo-Saxon Protestant communities presumed to define what it means to be "American," to the exclusion of native peoples, African Americans, Hispanics, and Asians, as well as some Europeans who did not fit the mold.

Citizenship has many dimensions. It can mean legal status, in which persons are both empowered and protected by equal rights. It has a political dimension, conferring the right of active participation in the political process. And it has a cultural element as well.[8] The legal dimension, however, is particularly important, because the law, to paraphrase Ulrich Preuss, connects people who are strangers. It creates a minimum of trust, which allows people to engage in mutual commitments. From this trust and engagement, people come to feel confident in the future and in the constancy of the society. That confidence, in turn, encourages them to develop skills and knowledge that they can transmit to subsequent generations.[9] Legal citizenship is the baseline from which more fully realized citizenship can grow.

With that observation in mind, let's look at the legal development of citizenship in the United States.

How the Legal Dimension Developed

The Constitution did not define citizenship until the ratification of the Fourteenth Amendment in 1868. At present, there are three established ways for someone to become a citizen of the United States: being born in the United States, being descended from parents who are citizens, and through the process of "naturalization."[10] These grounds were established through a protracted and contested process, as specific court cases illustrate.

In *Dred Scott v. Sandford* (60 U.S. 393, 1857), the Supreme Court held that African Americans were not citizens. According to Chief Justice Roger Taney, whether an African American was slave or free made no difference; citizenship did not apply. As a slave, Dred Scott was considered property and had no right to bring suit in federal courts. In 1866 Congress sought to overrule this decision by providing for citizenship under the Civil Rights Act, and then included this definition in Section 1 of the Fourteenth Amendment: "All persons born or naturalized in the United States and subject to the jurisdiction thereof, are citizens of the United States and the state wherein they reside." Debate about the passage of this amendment in Congress sought to make it expansive enough to remedy the problem of the Dred Scott decision, but did not include American Indians or every child born in the United States.[11]

Further judicial and congressional regulation of citizenship by birth continued. In *Elk v. Wilkins* (112 U.S. 94, 1884), for example, the Supreme Court held that children born to members of Indian tribes and governed by the legal systems of the tribes were not US citizens. Congress acted to correct that injustice by extending citizenship to all Indians under the Indian Citizenship Act of 1924. In *United States v. Wong Kim Ark* (169 U.S. 649, 1898), the Supreme Court ruled that children born in the United States to noncitizen parents were US citizens.

For those not born here, the Naturalization Act of 1790 explicitly allowed only "white free persons" to become citizens (1 Stat. 103). Nearly a century later, under the Act of 1870, the only aliens who could be naturalized as US citizens were "free white persons," "aliens of African nativity," and "persons of African descent" (16 Stat. 254). In *Ozawa v. United States* (260 U.S. 178, 1922), for instance, the Supreme Court ruled that since Ozawa was not Caucasian, he did not qualify for naturalization. The meaning of being "white" for the purposes of naturalization was not necessarily the same as being a "white" American citizen.[12] Although anthropologically speaking, people of the Indian subcontinent are considered Caucasian, the Supreme Court refused in *United States v. Thind* (261 U.S. 204, 206, 1923) to accept that racial classification as "white" for naturalization purposes. Such racial exclusion continued in one form or another until the mid-twentieth century, when naturalization was finally opened up to men and women of all races and ethnicities, through the Immigration and Nationality Act of 1952 (66 Stat. 163, 239).

Termination of Citizenship

Another legal dimension of US citizenship, relevant to its meaning and significance, is the question of termination. Generally speaking, governments may want to terminate citizenship for such reasons as protection of public order, punishment for certain offenses, and failure or termination of allegiance.[13] In the United States, Congress occasionally passes statutes, such as the 1907 Expatriation Act, requiring expatriation for those who swore allegiance or took an oath to another state. Under the 1940 Act, grounds for self-expatriation included wartime desertion and treason. In 1944, leaving to avoid military service was another way to relinquish citizenship. Still later, in 1954, the list expanded to include certain criminal acts. All of these reasons relate to allegiance in some manner.[14]

Now, however, the Supreme Court has all but eliminated the power of Congress to terminate citizenship. In a series of cases, such as *Trop v. Dulles*

(356 U.S. 86, 1958) and *Kennedy v. Mendoza Martinez* (372 U.S. 144, 1963), the Supreme Court overruled legislation that decreed denationalization for various reasons. In *Afroyim v. Rusk* (387 U.S. 253, 1967), the Court held that the Fourteenth Amendment provided protection against forcible removal of citizenship. Then, in *Vance v. Terrazas* (444 U.S. 252, 1980), the Court held that the act of relinquishing citizenship and an intent to relinquish citizenship must be proved by a preponderance of the evidence.

"American" versus "Foreign"

Citizenship also includes cultural and social dimensions, such as the idea of "Americanness" versus "foreignness," regardless of legal citizenship. Thus, "if a person is racially identified as African American or white, that person is presumed to be legally a US citizen and socially an American... [but] these presumptions are not present for Asian Americans, Latinos, Arab Americans, and other non-black racial minorities. Rather, there is the opposite presumption that these people are foreigners; ... Asian Americans are still identified as foreign, even after several generations."[15] Although people of Asian descent who are born in the United States are citizens under the Fourteenth Amendment, it was not until the 1940s and 1950s that people of Asian descent could be naturalized.[16] This history reinforces an American hierarchy of race.

The juridical categories of "citizen" and "alien" and the parallel social distinction between "American" and "foreign" seem to be taken as clear and accepted. For Asian Americans, and probably for American Muslims of African and Asian origins, the racial considerations render the coincidence of being both a citizen and an American much less certain. "A Japanese-American citizen in 1942 was easily considered 'foreign,' thus making possible the judgment that likelihood of disloyalty was high enough to justify wholesale internment."[17] The tendency to consider Asian Americans outsiders in their own country often leads to their feeling like guests in someone's home, where they are expected to "know their place." This "outsider" feeling has pressed Asian Americans to try to assimilate to the superior white Americans.[18]

A clear example appears in the case of Chae Chan Ping, a Chinese-born laborer living in California. During a visit Ping made to China, Congress passed the Chinese Exclusion Act of 1882 to ban re-entry of Chinese to the United States. Ping found out about this new regulation after he arrived back in San Francisco, and in 1889, before the Supreme Court, he challenged the denial of his re-entry. The Court sustained the act, reasoning that Chinese are "racially different" strangers in the land, who resisted assimilation by bonding together and retaining much of their traditional culture. The Court emphasized the danger to the United States presented by the growing Chinese population, and found the Chinese Exclusion Act valuable for the protection of the country. Further, the Court found the power to exclude inherent to sovereignty, authority to conduct foreign affairs, and self-preservation.[19]

Asserting Equality

The preceding review is not intended as a comprehensive history or critique of American policies and practices. Instead, my aim is to argue that, regardless of how Muslims feel about their place in American society, the only response must be engaged and proactive citizenship. This response is possible today, because citizenship has become egalitarian. Marginalized persons and groups can use their citizenship as legal and political support for claiming their rights.

In a modern democratic society, citizenship must apply to all equally and must be transparent in its application. People can identify themselves as citizens more easily than with any other identity, because citizenship means inclusion in a grand community, and it recognizes the individual while promoting cohesion among the many. Citizenship promotes stability and solidarity by requiring participation by all persons and communities.[20]

In the words of legal scholar Kenneth Karst:

> The most important constitutional development in the 20th century may have been the emergence of equal citizenship. Since everyone is presumed to have equal citizenship, individuals have freedom to choose their identities. Individuals have more liberty in choosing which cultural groups, racial groups, or religious groups to associate with and to what degree they wish to associate. The law has assisted in removing hurdles of self-identification…. These constitutional advances have fostered respect and dignity. Equal citizenship has effectively eliminated stigma and badges of inferiority.[21]

For many decades, people and groups have struggled for—and have realized—their equal citizenship in the United States. The challenge, however, remains: Equal citizenship must be asserted and sustained; it can neither be taken for granted, nor given as a gift.

The Evolving Framework and Practice of Citizenship

Accounts of the relationship between religion and state in the United States often take place in the context of what may be called "the founding myth": the idea that a consensus was reached at the time of the American Revolution. A review of that history may help us balance the need to contest (or even demolish) that myth and the value of building on it to affirm a consensus that is empirically truer and more sustainable. If we can believe in an established consensus, one that is supported by facts, we are likely to be more successful at maintaining that consensus into the future and expanding it to include Muslims and others.

The "Founding Myth" of Religious Freedom

According to the basic myth, the revolutionary leaders had diverse religious beliefs, but they agreed broadly on a set of principles for the new nation, including one of primary concern to us here: the right of each individual to hold and exercise religious beliefs without compulsion from church or state. Further, they held that there should be no established state church, no religious test for public office, and freedom of religious practice for all. As provided by the First Amendment:

> Congress shall make no law respecting an establishment of religion, or prohibiting the free exercise thereof; or abridging the freedom of speech, or of the press; or the right of the people peaceably to assemble, and to petition the Government for a redress of grievances.

As scholars have commonly observed, this provision sought to protect the government from religion, while simultaneously protecting religion from government.[22] But there is much more to the First Amendment than we see from this text alone. Though the separation of church and state is not an explicit constitutional principle, it has found its way into the American doctrine and discourse because of a famous letter that Thomas Jefferson wrote in 1802, in which he spoke of "the whole American people which declared that their legislature should 'make no law respecting an establishment of religion, or prohibiting the free exercise thereof,' thus building a wall of separation between church and State."[23]

From Pluralism to "Public Religion"

Arguments for pluralism took two forms. The first was theological, arguing that God, not the state, should set the righteous path. The second was political, in which a multiplicity of sects was seen as the best possible check on theocratic abuses by any one sect. In that context, the state held a twofold role. First, it was to provide a space in which a multitude of religious sects could thrive. Second, it was to refrain from interference with the religious practice of any group. During debates over ratification of the Constitution, speakers often called not only for a guarantee of religious freedom, but also for restrictions on religious freedom. "Expressions of this nature, on the one hand upholding freedom of religion and on the other restricting it, exemplified the fact that Americans habitually viewed Church-State relations within the framework of a Christian or Protestant society."[24]

Although state neutrality toward religion had strong constitutional basis at the founding, in practice it was based on a pluralism of Protestant Christian denominations and was restricted in application to action by the federal government. At the state level, religious freedom was widely practiced but not constitutionally guaranteed until the middle of the twentieth century; its existence depended on how far a group strayed from dominant forms of religion.

At times the definition of "religion" was expanded to all Christians, including Catholics, or to all theists, but never to African slaves or Native Americans. "Many states, however, still dealt discriminately with religious minorities, particularly those [minorities] of high religious temperature or low cultural conformity."[25] Occasionally one of the founding fathers would voice the opinion that religious freedom in the United States was truly expansive, covering all manner of belief and nonbelief.[26] This opinion may have been a minority position, but more important it was a *hypothetical* view, because the vast majority of the country's recognized citizens practiced some form of Christianity, providing them with an underlying set of shared beliefs and principles.

Religion and Public Education

There was general agreement that religion was quite relevant to public education, because it helped people to develop an understanding of citizenship and its responsibilities. Yet, much of the contestation concerning the relationship of religion to the state took place in the field of education. In this combination of contestation and agreement, we see the complexity and ambiguity that have characterized the separation of church and state.

The public school (or common school) movement in the United States began in the 1820s, motivated by a desire to provide sufficient education so that the rural citizens arriving in the cities and participating in public life would be able to make informed political decisions. Not only were schools expected to dispense basic education in reading, writing, arithmetic, and civ-ics; they were also supposed to provide moral education. In the United States of the early nineteenth century, however, morality was not distinguishable from religion.[27] Secular schools, therefore, were not plausible, let alone man-dated by the First Amendment or concepts of religious liberty, which applied only at the federal level.

Early proponents of public education faced a problem: how to teach religion in a country of diverse Christian sects. "The solution lay in what was coming to be called 'nonsectarianism:' the claim that there were moral principles shared in common by all Christian sects, independent of their particular theological beliefs."[28] At that time, nonsectarianism in education was realized through readings from the Bible, which were not commented upon by teachers but left to the interpretation of the students. Though that approach addressed early concerns about religious education in public schools, it quickly raised opposition from the rapidly expanding Catholic population. "From the perspective of the new immigrants, the idea that the Bible would be read, in the Protestant King James Version, and that children would be encouraged to decide on the meaning of the Bible for themselves, ran headlong into Catholic teaching that conferred authority for bibli-cal interpretation on the church's priests and saw the church-sanctioned Douay-Reims translation...as the only legitimate English version of the Bible."[29]

American Catholics first challenged the Protestant bias of religious edu-cation by establishing their own parochial schools and then appealing for state funding. They argued that public schools violated their freedom of con-science and that Catholics were being taxed for schools they could not use.[30] State prohibitions on funding of sectarian schools, which targeted Catholic schools in particular,[31] caused these efforts to fail.

Catholics then called for eliminating Bible reading from the public school curriculum.[32] That view was resisted on the ground that nonsectarianism was not an exclusionary doctrine, and that Christian education was essential to the function of the public schools. The prevailing view at that time held that the government was to stay out of religion, but that there was also a role to be played by public religion in the affairs of society and the workings of the state.[33] Catholics, for their part, gradually accepted the nonsectarianism of the public schools, and the schools made small accommodations to create a place for Catholic students.[34] Nonsectarian religious education continued until shortly after World War II, when it was challenged by rising scientific rationalism.

Religion and State Relations

Another dimension of the complex, ambiguous religion-state relations in the United States has been the rise of materialism, of science, and of a range of secular doctrines that sought to undermine Christianity—particularly, evangelical Protestant Christianity—as a "de facto national principle."[35] In debates over such issues as the teaching of the theory of evolution in schools, a preexisting tradition of "free thought" asserted itself. While the debates represented a wide range of political views, "the one political concern that did unite all freethinkers was their support for absolute separation of religion and state, which translated into opposition to any tax support of religious communities—especially parochial schools."[36]

Since World War II, religion and state relations have continued to be defined by vigorous disagreement over the role of religion in public and political life. Particularly helpful to American Muslims, I believe, is a famous confrontation in 1925 between American secularism and American fundamentalism, a case known as the Scopes Monkey Trial. This episode is valuable for American Muslims because it shows that the meaning of "separation of religion and the state" is established through negotiation and contestation *over time.* It also helps us to see that the underlying issues of concern are similar for all religious communities. American Christians have continued to be as divided about what it means to integrate faith and citizenship as American Muslims are likely to be.

In the Scopes Monkey Trial, a teacher was prosecuted under a Tennessee statute for teaching Darwin's theory of evolution. The strong secularists in that state lost the case: the law prohibiting the teaching of evolution was ruled constitutional by the trial court, and the defendant, John Scopes, was fined $100 for teaching evolution in a Tennessee public school. When the Tennessee Supreme Court heard the case on appeal, it affirmed the constitutionality of the law, but overturned the conviction on the ground that the jury and not the judge should have assessed the fine. That effectively ended the suit and prevented an appeal to the US Supreme Court.[37]

The struggle between the strong secularists and the fundamentalists, both before and shortly after the Scopes trial, resulted in uneasy tension and subtle accommodation of the new diversity of belief in the United States.[38] Although the states did not actively suppress secular views in the public square, such toleration was not a constitutional mandate until several decades later, when the Supreme Court decided in *Epperson v. Arkansas* (393 U.S. 97, 1968) that it was unconstitutional to prohibit the teaching of evolution in public schools.[39]

The First Amendment was first applied to the states in *Cantwell v. Connecticut* (310 U.S. 296, 1940). Then, in *Everson v. Board of Education* (330 U.S. 1, 1947), a New Jersey school district adopted a plan allowing the reimbursement of schools for the transportation of students to private schools. The constitutional question was whether paying for the busing of parochial school students violated the Establishment Clause. In this case the Supreme Court formally incorporated the First Amendment prohibition of establishment of religion into the Fourteenth Amendment's due process clause and applied it to the states. For the majority of the Court, however, even though the assistance might make parents more likely to send their children to such schools, the authorization did not unduly assist the schools. Justice Black, writing for the majority, set the legal terms as follows:

> The "establishment of religion" clause of the First Amendment means at least this: Neither a state nor the Federal Government can set up a church. Neither can pass laws which aid one religion, aid all religions, or prefer one religion over another. Neither can force nor influence a person to go or to remain away from church against his will or force him to profess a belief or disbelief in any religion. No person can be punished for entertaining or professing religious beliefs or disbeliefs, for church attendance or non-attendance. No tax in any amount, large or small, can be levied to support any religious activities or institutions, whatever they may be called, or whatever form they may adopt to teach or practice religion. Neither a state nor the Federal Government can, openly or secretly, participate in the affairs of any religious organizations or groups, or vice versa. In the words of Jefferson, the clause against establishment of religion by law was intended to erect "a wall of separation...." That wall must be kept high and impregnable. We could not approve the slightest breach. (*Everson v. Board of Education* (330 U.S. 1, 15–16, 18, 1947)

On the factual issue in this case, however, the majority held that New Jersey had not breached the "high and impregnable" wall of separation between church and state. It is worth noting how fine and intricate the line is: although all the Justices were agreed on the constitutional principle, they were divided 5 to 4 on its application.

While the Supreme Court has reaffirmed the constitutional prohibition of giving preference to one religious community over others, specific issues keep coming up before the courts, such as the question of religious language in the pledge of allegiance and the display of religious monuments in public places. Questions arise, too, about the treatment of new or unfamiliar religions, such as the Church of Scientology, the International Society for Krishna Consciousness, and the Unification Church. It remains to be seen how such issues are resolved both legally and politically.

An Evolving Context for Negotiation

Clearly, the legal separation of religion and the state does not permanently settle the status of religion in political and public life.[40] The context for negotiating religious self-determination in the United States is constantly evolving and adapting.

What can American Muslims find instructive as they seek to realize their religious self-determination? I would emphasize this point: The absence of an officially established state religion has had important consequences for the religious and political life of the country. Without state support, churches had to rely on voluntary membership and financial support; consequently, they became less formal in worship, more democratic and local in their organization, and practical in their goals. Various commentators on American religion have remarked on American religions' tendency to "this-worldly" political and economic pragmatism, which has been the case "at least since the early-nineteenth century…predominantly activist, moralistic, and social rather than contemplative, theological, or innerly [*sic*] spiritual."[41] Whatever one may think of that view, it should not be assumed to apply to American Muslims and their communities.

Experiences in Exclusion and Inclusion

American Muslims can look for guidance from other religious communities—Catholics, Jews, and Mormons—that have become integrated into the larger American society. But for these groups, self-removal or exclusion played a role in the perception that they were incompatible with American political culture.

Self-Containment versus Proactive Engagement

The more self-contained a group is perceived to be, the more it is seen as having withdrawn from the larger society; and the more evidently a group attempts to live separately, the more likely it is to be regarded as incompatible with the community at large. By contrast, when a community attempts to engage civic and political culture, even if it is initially rebuffed, it is more likely to gain acceptance. These are not the only factors, of course. Racism, xenophobia, economic exclusion, legal segregation, and many other factors are relevant.[42]

For American Muslims, proactive engagement is critical. To me, the main question is: Granted that such conditions as racial prejudice, fear of the "other," and economic competition exist, what can people in American Muslim communities do to overcome the challenges they face, and to improve their situation? They may not succeed in overcoming all of those challenges—or even most of them—but they will not know what difference they can make until they try. And they will not try if they assume that the situation is hopeless.

Integration, as we shall see, has necessitated accommodation and acculturation; and engagement has usually been on the majority's terms—meaning that it was rooted in Protestantism. This is hardly surprising, because in the universal human experience, both historically and globally, the established order does its utmost to maintain its supremacy and hegemony. Another universal experience is that things always change. Absolutely nothing human stays the same, whether in social relations, political institutions, or economic conditions. Engagement with American civic and political life is a crucial way of gaining recognition in the wider society.

How does such engagement work? In the nineteenth century, the meaning of the First Amendment had a distinctly Protestant flavor. For instance, Robert Baird, whose 1844 book, *Religion in America*, was one of the first texts to note the diversity of religious life in the country, premised his recognition of pluralism on a Protestant view of American civic life. As R. Laurence Moore explained:

> The religious neutrality of the Constitution had not prevented individual states and municipalities from passing laws that favored the interests of Protestant evangelical groups. Sabbath laws were enforced in many parts of the country. The King James version of the Bible was read in most public schools after they were founded. Blasphemy was punished. American jurists praised Protestant Christianity in their written court decisions. These measures did not strike Baird as parts of a religious establishment nor were they so legally defined at the time. He regarded them as reasonable compromises through which the nation sought to preserve both a genuine religious tolerance and a proper Christianity.

Baird's religious view set sharp limits to pluralism....In short, Baird regarded the United States as semi-officially a Protestant nation.[43]

A century later, however, when Will Herberg described the impact of this assumption on American religious life, he also protested the sacrifices that minority religious communities have been forced to make in order to gain acceptance into the public sphere. His book *Protestant, Catholic, Jew* was a protest against the tendency of religious groups to forget their specific traditions and their willingness to merge those traditions into an uncritical nationalism.[44] There was no American national character, Herberg argued, to be found in "a single source of national unity."[45]

Such a paradigm shift, however, also must acknowledge the all-too-human factors that generated and sustained the Protestant standard in the first place—in particular, the fear of the "other." A generational factor, too, has been at work. To begin with, the immigrant community's "foreignness provides fertile ground for all sorts of speculations about their traits and intentions. At the same time, immigrants often lack sufficient knowledge of the new language and culture to realize what is happening and explain themselves effectively."[46]

By contrast, descendants of immigrants and subsequent generations have often mobilized to exercise their political and civic rights as citizens precisely because they feel compelled to respond to the nativist fears and campaigns that had targeted the first generation. The descendants of immigrants, unlike their parents, were fluent in English and more in tune with American culture—and thus acquired a stronger voice, which they used to reaffirm identities that were previously attacked with impunity.

In the late nineteenth century and early twentieth century, migrants were commonly perceived as politically dangerous, because of a broad-brush stereotyping that linked immigrants with political movements in their home countries. The stereotyping occurred, paradoxically, from both ends of the political spectrum. Conservatives, seizing on socialist ties among educated portions of immigrant communities, painted all immigrants as a radical socialist/anarchist menace. Liberals, seizing on a perceived "docility" among uneducated migrants, painted the opposite picture, depicting immigration as a threat to the American labor movement. Thus Finnish and German immigrants could be described simultaneously as a radical threat to the American political system and as a lazy undermining of American labor standards.[47]

Arbitrary factors, such as poverty and urban conditions, fed into fear of the immigrant "other," as the crowded immigrant quarters of any American city were taken as confirmation of the moral and social corruption of urban life.[48] This fear of the immigrant "other" also fed on economic hardship and competition, enabling many American employers to use immigrant workers against domestic labor organizations: "By dividing workers along national lines and assigning them different pay and working conditions, employers reinforced ethnic identities over class solidarity."[49]

Catholics

Anti-Catholic bias in America can be traced back not only to the original colonies, but also to the preexisting attitudes and experiences of the Europeans who settled them. Many of the founders of the original thirteen colonies brought with them vivid memories of conflicts between Protestants and Catholics in Europe. Although the settlers were able to establish colonies in which their own beliefs could be instituted and maintained, this license did not translate into greater freedom of religion in general.[50] Colonial charters and laws contained specific proscriptions against Roman Catholics having any political power. In 1642, Virginia passed a law prohibiting Catholic settlers. Five years later, a similar statute was enacted by the Massachusetts Bay Colony. Even where there had been originally Catholic colonies, the sheer numbers of Protestant settlers eventually overturned them. In 1692, colonists in the formerly Catholic colony of Maryland established the Church of England as the official religion and forced Catholics to pay heavy taxes toward its support.[51] Pennsylvania alone became a safe haven for Catholics, because its founder, William Penn, granted religious toleration and civil rights to all who believed in God, regardless of denomination.[52]

Over the centuries, the reasons for anti-Catholic feeling in the United States may have shifted, but at the heart of every argument is some idea that Catholicism is un-American or anti-American.[53] Phillip Jenkins notes, "[A]s the notion of Americanism has gone through periodic transformations over time, so has the popular concept of the religious tradition that supposedly represents its darkest negation. Modern anti-Catholicism is built upon these multiple layers of ideological precedent."[54] Early American political ideologies linked the Catholic Church with the denial of personal liberty.[55] The Pope was regarded as an alien, foreign threat, and thus anti-Catholicism was bolstered by nationalist feeling.[56]

By the time of the Industrial Revolution, a different type of anti-Catholic feeling had begun to emerge, as poor immigrants arrived, desperate for work, in urban areas. The stereotype of the Catholic changed from the threatening foreign power to the "poor and ignorant" worker.[57] Non-Catholic blue-collar workers resented the Catholics as rivals for jobs. Educated Protestants began to see Catholic immigrants as symbols of "everything that was wrong with emerging urban-industrial America, including its blatantly corrupt political machines."[58] Many anti-Catholic activists asserted that religion should not intermingle with public services in any way, and should compromise with the liberal, scientific, modern worldview. This led to bitter conflict, in which neither side was willing to compromise.

By the 1850s, the Roman Catholic Church was the country's largest religious denomination. In the late nineteenth and early twentieth centuries, Catholics continued to grow in numbers, from 7 million to 20 million, and in power. With this increase came a wider network of schools and charities, such as the National Catholic Welfare Conference, leading to criticism that Catholics were refusing to assimilate. Some critics went so far as to accuse Catholics of attempting to set up a "provisional government" and feared that Catholic schools were indoctrinating children in intolerant views.[59] These critics argued that the traditional view of the United States as a "melting pot" was threatened by the Catholic desire to remain a culture apart.[60]

The Catholic experience, particularly after the great wave of immigration, is one of attempting to negotiate multiple, weighty identities. There was a long debate among American Catholics between liberal "Americanizers," who sought engagement with American society, and conservative Catholics who felt that the role of the Church was to temper America's excesses. At the same time, however, "there has been a general conviction through two hundred years of American Catholic history that the American environment was good for the Catholic Church. Even the conservatives who felt that there was a considerable danger in becoming too Americanized, nevertheless were prepared to admit that if sufficient care was maintained, the religious freedom in American society provided an extremely healthy environment for the prosperous development of faith."[61]

The controversy pitted late-nineteenth-century immigrants—newly arrived, and looking to hold on to the traditions of the homeland—against established Irish American communities and clergy who controlled the American hierarchy and insisted that Catholics should actively become as "American" as possible. The Americanists believed that Catholicism was fully compatible with the national traditions and democratic institutions of the United States, while their opponents feared that as Catholics became more Americanized they would surrender their unique spiritual traditions and imperil their souls.[62] These opponents of Americanism, however, were not anti-American. People on both sides of the Americanist controversy perceived themselves as loyal Americans.[63]

"Americanization," in fact, frequently meant rather different things, ranging from organizing the Church along lines that one thought appropriate to the American political environment and putting aside Old World customs and language, to assuming practically all the values and culture of American society. This approach includes support for the separation of church and state in the United States, as well as an openness and willingness to try new methods and structures.[64]

It was important for Catholics not to be perceived as segregating themselves from American society. Ironically, though, this segregation was often the result of discriminatory practices (many of them springing from economic factors). Yet, regardless of what motivated the separatist tendency, the more a community operated as a self-contained group, the more likely it came to be perceived as incompatible with the American civil religion and political life.

Anti-Catholic sentiment often found expression in organized political movements, such as the American Protective Association at the end of the nineteenth century.[65] A more violent expression of anti-Catholic feeling erupted in the 1920s with the Ku Klux Klan (KKK), which terrorized Catholics as foreign aliens, "the unassimilated hordes of Europe," who would put an end to American racial purity. At its height, the KKK had between 5 and 8 million adherents. Such organized opposition frustrated the efforts of Catholics to play a greater role in American political life. The 1928 Democratic Party candidate for president of the United States, Al Smith, an Irish Catholic from an urban setting, was defeated largely because of widespread anti-Catholic sentiment.

For their part, Catholics resorted to showing their political power. On September 21, 1924, for example, over a hundred thousand Catholic men marched in Washington as representatives of the National Catholic Holy Name Society; they were addressed by President Calvin Coolidge at the end of the march.[66] Such demonstrations of political power were becoming more and more common, although more so among the English-speaking "assimilated" Catholics who controlled the Church's leadership than among immigrants from Mexico and from southern and eastern Europe.[67] Anti-Catholicism itself actually encouraged the development of a stronger network, by forcing the Church to respond to its attackers and to defend Catholics' rights.

Although anti-Catholicism persisted at a low level, national cooperation during World War II and the Catholic Church's strong anti-Communist stance led many Americans to view Catholicism more favorably in the mid-twentieth century.[68] At the same time, liberals' consternation over federal education funding being given to Catholic schools along with public ones, in both elementary education and through the GI Bill, led to "a tremendous revival of anti-Catholic feeling."[69] Such contestations, as well as Catholic negotiation of citizenship, were subsequently reflected in a range of issues. In 1951, for instance, President Harry Truman sought to extend diplomatic recognition to the Vatican, to which the United States had previously merely sent the president's "personal representative." The response from American Protestants was immediate—and so negative that not only was the plan abandoned, but the post of the president's "personal representative" to the Holy See (the Vatican) was eliminated. When the issue was taken up again in 1983, however, President Ronald Reagan successfully established diplomatic relations. At that time, the Protestant backlash paled in comparison to Catholic support.[70]

The greatest victory for Catholics who were hoping to be seen as a fully integrated group rather than an alien minority was probably the 1960 presidential campaign of John F. Kennedy, which is generally believed to have finally overcome the perception of Catholics as untrustworthy and politically disengaged.[71] Even in that context, though, some Catholics were critical of Kennedy's campaign, believing that he went too far in reassuring the hostile electorate of his loyalty to the United States. "But what the Catholic critics did not seem to understand is that only the strongest sort of language would break through the hard shell of nativist prejudice."[72] Kennedy's convincing arguments in the primary essentially asserted that Catholics were not a people apart, and that he, as a presidential candidate (and later as president), was an American as much as—if not more than—he was a Catholic. His actions in office, which neither favored Catholics nor turned on the advice of the Church, finally convinced Americans that Catholicism was compatible with American political culture and civil religion.

Jews

The first Jewish communities to settle on the territory of what is now the United States began to arrive in the 1680s, in New York, and later (in the 1730s) in Savannah, Georgia.[73] Jews enjoyed a relatively high degree of acceptance and toleration from British authorities, particularly compared with the harsh discrimination that was practiced against Jews in Europe. Jews were not full members of the political community, however, because of the long-standing perception that they were a separate nation and were therefore incompatible with "non-Jewish" political communities.

"Jews in the British colonies could neither vote nor serve in public office; they had no civic existence. Their exclusion from public life extended to the possibility of informal influence, as well, for there is no evidence to suggest that they served as advisers to public officials or participated in public debates on political issues."[74] Despite this exclusion, American Jews did make consistent attempts to engage in the political and civic life of the United States. During the American Revolution, "most Jews took sides in the struggle, in a majority of cases declaring themselves for the American side, but in some cases for the British."[75]

After the founding of the United States, Jews were as civically engaged as they were permitted to be. Nevertheless, discrimination against them persisted, though it never reached the level of anti-Semitism that many Jews fled Europe to escape. "Numbering less than 1 percent of the American population, they enjoyed far greater freedom and acceptance in America than they had experienced in Europe, but anti-Semitism lived here, too. Stereotypes of Jews gaining enormous wealth by illegal means had long been part of European folklore, and non-Jewish settlers brought that folklore with them to America."[76] Jews' inability to break into American civil and political life was not for lack of trying; it was the result of Protestant hegemony, which defined Judaism as simply outside the acceptable normative religious framework of the United States. By the end of the nineteenth century, "a self-defined 'white' Anglo-Saxon Protestant social elite had placed its schools, businesses, and clubs beyond the reach of Jews and others it deemed outsiders. Despite those difficulties, Jews felt themselves to be part of America...served in America's civic associations, militias, and armed services. Nineteenth-century Jewish men voted in elections and contributed to political parties."[77]

The Jewish minority organized its civic life along lines that intersected with the larger American civic society. Charitable organizations were formed, particularly to assist new migrants. Jews exercised what they perceived to be their legal protections under the American Constitution to fight discriminatory legislation, often allying themselves with other religious minorities (usually marginalized Christian groups). Jews also engaged the US government in efforts to protect Jews abroad who continued to suffer under more strident forms of anti-Semitism in Europe and elsewhere. There was a persistent effort among the Jewish population to participate in the civil, political, and cultural life of the nation.[78]

Changes in the practices of American Judaism accompanied these efforts. In the nineteenth century, the Jewish American Reform movement—led by Isaac Mayer, editor of the *American Israelite*—advocated such reforms as simplifying Jewish practice and rejecting dietary laws and some traditional customs. These changes were part of a larger movement that started in Germany in the early nineteenth century. Before the immigration wave that began in 1880, German Jews made up most of the American Jewish population, and they were economically successful as merchants and businessmen. Reform Judaism retained the principles of the Jewish faith that were considered rational and in keeping with modern life. For instance, "worship service featured mixed male and female seating, choirs of men and women, a sermon in the vernacular delivered by the rabbi along with vernacular prayers."[79] The American Jewish population at that time generally did not keep traditional dietary laws or maintain strong ethnic and linguistic ties. They were thoroughly integrated, being closer in practice to non-Jewish Americans than to the Eastern European Jews who would arrive later.[80]

The great wave of immigration from 1880 to 1924 changed the dynamics of Jewish integration, bringing 2.5 million Jewish immigrants to the United States and thus overwhelming the existing Jewish population of approximately 300,000.[81] These new arrivals disrupted the established social patterns that Jews had built over many years. By 1880, the American Jewish population had become largely middle-class, acculturated, and politically conservative.[82] In contrast, the new Jewish immigrants were largely working-class, and many had sympathies for socialist or communist parties in Europe.[83] The greatest difficulties, however, arose from the new industrialization of labor in the United States, which meant that Jewish immigrants became increasingly concentrated in ethnic, urban enclaves with poor living conditions.[84] This combination of factors hampered the efforts of the established Jewish population to achieve civic and political engagement. New Jewish immigrants' isolation in urban enclaves separated them from the rest of American society and exacerbated perceptions of their "otherness" and incompatibility.

Tension was particularly acute between the established Jewish population of German origin and new immigrants. On the one hand, the existing Jewish community in America did create Jewish organizations, like the Hebrew Emigrant Aid Society, to aid the immigrants. At the same time, they also felt an obligation to differentiate between immigrants who "will become citizens of whom we may be proud" and immigrants who were incompatible with the American way of life.

As expressed by Augustus Levey, secretary of the Aid Society, "the mode of life of these people in Russia has stamped upon them the ineffaceable marks of permanent pauperism; only disgrace and a lowering of the opinion in which American Israelites are held by this community can result from the continued residence among us of such an addition to the Jewish population. Every crime against property or the person committed by one of these wretches will throw obloquy over our race throughout the land."[85]

The existing American Jewish population therefore feared the effect that the new immigrants would have on their position within American society. To avert such negative consequences, established American Jews concentrated most of their efforts on attempting to assimilate the new immigrants.[86]

It was not easy, however, to create a sense of unity within the expanding community. On the one hand, the persecution of Jews in Russia strongly affected some well-established American Jews and motivated them to help immigrants. On the other hand, agreement among different Jewish communities was very difficult to achieve. As one immigrant Jew explained: "It wasn't only the differences in our daily language and manner of speaking that got in the way. That wouldn't have been so bad. It was the deeper differences in inherited concepts and customs that separated us. With the best intentions in the world and with gentle hearts they unknowingly insulted us."[87]

By the 1890s, conditions in urban tenements had become so poor that something urgently needed to be done, and "immigrant distribution was regarded as the solution to the problem of adjustment and assimilation."[88] The success of immigrant relocation programs varied, but immigrant aid networks were determined "to remove all past false traditions regarding the Jew; to in every way make himself one with his neighbors; to stand off from them only in his religion."[89] Their efforts met with some success, despite the difficulty of persuading recent immigrants to leave the cultural security of the cities. Data gathered in 1955 and in 1976, however, show that American Jewish populations remained primarily on the East Coast, with only a few large communities located on the West Coast.[90] There were scattered communities across the entire country, and statistics indicate that they continued to spread. By the latter half of the twentieth century, American Jews were evenly divided between pluralistic communities and the more culturally homogeneous communities in the Midwest and the South.[91]

Despite these efforts, prejudice remained, though on a much smaller scale than found in Europe, and apparently declining in the United States.[92] Since the early 1900s, however, the way in which Jewish Americans are viewed has changed significantly. While anti-Semitism still exists, it is in sharp decline. Jews are no longer parodied in the media and in songs, as they were in the early 1900s.[93] Whereas in the early 1900s Jews were frequently refused employment, banned from hotels, social clubs, and summer resorts, and subjected to university quotas, discrimination against Jews in employment, housing, and higher education has also been severely curtailed.[94] World War II was a clear turning point, not only in that non-Jews began to see Jews as Americans, but also in that many Jews began to see the United States as a place where Judaism could thrive. Jews began leaving urban neighborhoods and resettling in the postwar suburbs, dispersing among the larger population.[95] They also began to build their religious institutions, and the Conservative movement emerged as a uniquely American style of Judaism and a particular accommodation to American culture.[96] As a result, the postwar Zionist movement took on a different character in the United States, where many American Zionists rejected the idea that Israel should be the *sole* homeland for Jews.[97]

Scripture has always been used by Christians to justify anti-Jewish sentiments, but in the United States this manifested more often in individuals rather than in positions taken officially by churches—although many people felt that anti-Semitism was implied in the way that religious texts were interpreted in official publications. "Jews were portrayed as Christ killers and as having called on themselves a curse from God for their actions."[98] As the public view of Jews changed, churches responded slowly. For some Christian denominations, this change involved a challenge to the way they traditionally interpreted scripture; many congregations tried to reconcile the newfound acceptance of Jews with their faith. The mobilization of other religions in support of Jewish Americans has, in short, been slow and reactive rather than at the leading edge of Jewish efforts.

The Jewish community has sought to combat anti-Semitism and its own feelings of powerlessness through the work of such organization as the Anti-Defamation League, founded in 1913. According to the organization's website, "ADL fights anti-Semitism and all forms of bigotry, defends democratic ideals and protects civil rights for all."[99] It is also relevant to note that Jewish Americans have been able to achieve middle-class economic success, particularly through education. By the latter half of the twentieth century, as Jews overturned the quotas and other restrictions on their enrollment, 80 percent of Jewish high school graduates went to college, in contrast to 40 percent of the general population. Education was a key factor in Jews' acceptance in American life.

A good example of this Jewish approach to affirmative integration can be seen in their celebrations of American national holidays: "Jews used national holidays not only to demonstrate their loyalty to American ideals but also to put forward their vision of American civil religion—one that made room for the inclusion of Jews within a largely Christian culture.... National holidays provided an opportunity for Jewish groups not only to rehearse their own history but also to define their place in America, and often to define America itself."[100]

American Jews are frequently held up as an example of a minority community that has assimilated well, yet still maintains a distinctive subculture. While conforming in lifestyle with prevailing perceptions of Americanness, they have not lost their essential identity as a distinctive ethnic and religious community. Some Jews felt that the focus on maintaining their own culture came at the expense of addressing national problems. Albert Vorspan, director of the Commission on Social Action of Reform Judaism of the Union of American Hebrew Congregations and Central Conference of American Rabbis, stated:

> The American Jewish community is silent on the paramount moral choices facing the nation.... As the inner city has become the new racial frontier in American life, Jewish groups increasingly lag behind Christian involvement in the urban setting. Christian leaders talk about the urban crisis the way Jews talk about the Israeli crisis—as a matter of sheer survival.... Most synagogues stand in suspended isolation from the central problems of the community.[101]

This may be a dated view that is no longer valid, or an exaggerated impression. The point for us here is a warning to all communities—whether nativist or immigrant, whether Protestant or Catholic, Mormon or Muslim—not to defeat the end by the means. Inclusion and integration is never an end in itself, but a means of sharing human solidarity, confronting our social and economic challenges, and ultimately enhancing the quality of life for all citizens.

Mormons

The history of the Church of Latter-day Saints (LDS) in the United States is filled with episodes of persecution, and, to a greater degree than either Catholics or Jews, Mormons continue to be a target of ridicule and scorn in contemporary American society. "A flood of books and pamphlets are produced annually that challenge Mormon beliefs, question the integrity of the Mormon scriptures, and call into question the work of Joseph Smith."[102] Founded in 1830, the LDS Church faced extreme hostility among established Christian denominations because its claims—including Joseph Smith's claim to prophecy, the revelation of a new sacred text, and historical claims about Jesus Christ's appearance on the North American continent—directly challenged Christian orthodoxy.

None of the religious sects that sprang up in the nineteenth century inspired "such fear and loathing."[103] Yet the success of Mormonism was in some ways a result of American society's Protestant roots. "Mormonism exposed the weakness of a system that relied on the self-sustaining vigor of a 'general Christianity' surrounded by structures of mobility, democracy, and competition. These forces created the very potential for inversion in which Mormonism was born."[104] Thus the Protestant narrative itself caused a minor rebellion in the form of a sect claiming that the then-modern Christian witness was "corrupt" and "infected with hypocrisy and decay."

The Mormons were also able to use legal theory, created by American courts, to defend themselves and, in particular, to defend polygamy. According to the democratic principle of voluntarism, a majority of the citizens of a state or territory were allowed to create an alternative legal structure. The Mormons therefore held forth that in Utah, there was nothing illegal about polygamy or any other aspect of Mormon practice. Protestant principles had also become a part of American jurisprudence by this point, however, and through the application of state blasphemy jurisprudence, polygamy was declared prohibited by the common law.

Among the many contentious issues that the LDS Church raised, polygamy proved the most divisive. Many Americans were appalled by the notion and felt that polygamy was at odds with American culture; and it certainly was, if American culture was measured by the Protestant standard, as the Supreme Court seemed to confirm in *Reynolds v. U.S.* (98 U.S. 145, 1879):

> So here, as a law of the organization of society under the exclusive dominion of the United States, it is provided that plural marriages shall not be allowed. Can a man excuse his practices to the contrary because of his religious belief? To permit this would be to make the professed doctrines of religious belief superior to the law of the land, and in effect to permit every citizen to become a law unto himself. Government could exist only in name under such circumstances. (*Reynolds v. U.S.,* 98 U.S. 145, 166–167, 1879)

The Court further noted in *Reynolds* that marriage was the foundation of governance, and polygamy the foundation of despotism (*Reynolds v. U.S.,* 98 U.S. 145, 165–166, 1879). In *Davis v. Beason* (133 U.S. 333, 1890), the Supreme Court held that mere membership in a religious organization that believed in plural marriage was sufficient grounds for denial of voting rights. "In addition to laws aimed at plural marriage, ostensibly neutral legislation was passed that excluded past or present polygamists from juries and from voting.... Women, who had been given the right to vote by Utah's territorial legislature in 1870, were deprived of that right by Congress in 1887."[105]

Such systematic harassment continued, culminating in legislative dissolution of the Church of LDS and confiscation of Church property in excess of $50,000, including the Temple—an action that was confirmed as constitutional by the Supreme Court (*The Late Corporation of the Church of Jesus Christ of Latter-day Saints v. United States*, 136 U.S. 1, 1890). The jurisprudence surrounding Mormon cases thus had begun, more and more, to institute Protestant scriptural and moral prescriptions "from a basic fact of American legal culture before the Civil War, into a constitutional code by 1890."[106]

Faced with such pressures, the president of the LDS Church at the time issued the 1890 Manifesto, which led to the termination of the practice of plural marriage. "However, quite a few Mormons were distressed that the church had abandoned a practice that was, after all, the will of God, a doctrine received by a divinely inspired prophet of God. Once the church got serious about ending polygamy, the stalwarts withdrew into their own splinter organizations and continued the practice of plural marriage. And so things continue today, with tens of thousands [*sic*] of Latter-day Saints living in polygamous households in the intermountain West. And they, like their forebears, suffered plenty of persecution."[107] As polygamy was officially rejected and Utah was incorporated into the United States, with Mormon senators and congressmen accepted into the national legislature, integration and acceptance into America life became the goal.[108] As we have seen, the Jewish response to prejudice was to integrate into American society, while retaining key parts of the traditional Jewish identity. By contrast, the early Mormon response to persecution was to withdraw from American society and to create a parallel society within America, held apart from the wider culture. This caused many more far-reaching problems for the Mormon community than it resolved, and it encouraged misinformation and rumors about Mormons and their practices. The focus of much early scholarship by and about Mormons was the issue of polygamy. In fact, there was an enormous void of scholarly works on the Mormons during the first half of the twentieth century, a situation that naturally resulted in a fundamental lack of understanding between Mormon and non-Mormon communities. In that huge vacuum, the predominant literature about Mormonism was mainly editorializing from a secularized Protestant standpoint about such issues as polygamy.[109]

Not until the 1950s did the Mormon Church open up, becoming less of a remote, separate community and more of an assimilated regional religion.

Mormon scholarship broadened, too, and became more mainstream, partly because Mormon youths began to travel outside their home communities for college education. The increased flow of information has eliminated much of the inaccuracy surrounding the religion, and thereby has caused its members to become better accepted in American society. Not surprisingly, the tone of works written about Mormons has become more respectful and respectable. "The vast majority of social scientists who address this issue, however, think the Mormon subculture has traveled a long way down the road toward modernization, accommodation, and assimilation with American society more generally. They have therefore tended to focus on some of the symptoms and consequences of the process, while recognizing some resistance to it as well."[110] The Mormon Church, actively seeking to improve how it is perceived by outsiders, has now developed a vast public relations system.

A Context for Understanding

It is clear from the preceding review that the experiences of each of these religious communities are unique. We cannot make point-by-point comparisons among them, nor can we assume that Muslims will have similar experiences. Rather, these three histories will offer a context for understanding, from which American Muslims can benefit when challenges and opportunities arise.

As we move on to specific experiences of American Muslims—regarding, for instance, education, family law, and accommodation by public authorities and private employers, as well as implications of the First Amendment—the histories of Catholics, Jews, and Mormons will continue to be relevant.

For now, I would like to note two general points:

1. The experiences of other American religious communities indicate that Muslims are not, in any general way, exceptional. Of course, each religious group is unique, and lives in unique circumstances. But religious minorities in America do share many common experiences. In short, there is nothing exceptionally good or exceptionally bad about American Muslims, and their history echoes that of other groups. Muslims must consider their situation in perspective and context, just as Catholics, Jews, and Mormons have.

2. All religious communities have an obligation to seek to engage in intellectually honest, well-informed, and civil public discourse regarding their rights to religious self-determination. In my view—and as we shall

consider in more depth later—the more we improve the quality of our public discourse, the sooner and more likely all parties to any conversation or controversy will reach an acceptable and sustainable outcome.

Civil Religion and the Task of Nation-Building

Here, I'd like to raise another question: Can American Muslims subscribe to what is known as the civil religion of the United States? I do not expect to offer a satisfactory answer, merely to introduce the question for further exploration in subsequent chapters.

Civil Religion: What Is It?

Within the United States, there is a diversity of religions and religious denominations. There is also an entrenched constitutional principle of nonestablishment. In light of these two conditions, religious pluralism has become a widely held political and cultural value, and has opened new possibilities for the development of independent churches.[111]

The inclusive view of Christianity, however, combined with the patriotism that accompanied the development of independent churches in the post-Revolutionary period, has given rise to what has been called "American civil religion." The term "civil religion" has a range of different meanings, including these: folk religion, transcendent universal religion of the nation, religious nationalism, democratic faith, and Protestant civic piety.

Each of these meanings, however, carries different nuances. *Folk religion* is the common religion of the people—the faith they all have in common. *The transcendent universal religion of a nation* is a common religion with a built-in standard: not simply what folk religion is, but what it should be. In *religious nationalism*, the object of glorification is the nation itself. *Democratic faith,* by contrast, glorifies the democratic system. *Protestant civic piety* fuses Protestant (Puritan) faith and nationalism, emphasizing the denominational origins of civil religion.[112]

What happens to any definition of civil religion when we add the word "American?" Does the word merely describe, indicating a place where civil religion is practiced, or does it prescribe what civil religion *must* be, in order to fulfill particularly "American" requirements? For either answer, who defines what is "American"? Is the term used in this context simply in contrast to, for instance, Canadian or Mexican, or does it signify a distinctive set of values or ethics?

One quality of American civil religion is that it has never been hostile to the clergy or militantly secular. The American form of civil religion "was able to build up, without any bitter struggle with the church, powerful symbols of national solidarity and to mobilize deep levels of personal motivation for the attainment of national goals."[113]

Between the Civil War and World War I, evangelical Protestantism primarily aligned itself with a number of movements that sought the cultural and moral purification of American political and civil life, including prohibition of alcohol.[114] The churches also have become important participants in public decision-making about broader issues, such as currency reform, redress for corporate abuses, arbitration of international conflicts, and "direct democracy" through the processes of initiative, referendum, and recall election.

These trends are evident, too, in political parties and their campaigns around various issues. For instance, the campaigns against "obscene" schoolbooks, the Equal Rights Amendment, and gay rights appealed most strongly to evangelical Protestants, who saw their involvement as a crusade in defense of traditional Christian values and institutions.[115] Organized political activism, however, is not limited to conservative Christians. Churches on the left of the political spectrum have a similar history of political lobbying, whether on behalf of race relations, the war on poverty, or ending the Vietnam War. They also seek to influence the foreign policy of the United States in favor of their views. Social activism on the left has been driven primarily by mainline Protestants, African Americans, and Jews. The Catholic Church also has been active on foreign policy and economic issues, as well as on questions such as abortion and homosexuality.[116]

A Republic or a Liberal Constitutional State?

Robert Bellah did not invent the term "civil religion," but adopted it to describe a phenomenon he was observing in the United States in the 1960s. While Bellah's ideas about civil religion have generated much debate and disagreement, his concepts are useful here as a way to describe how various groups negotiating the task of American citizenship—and, particularly, of "Americanness"—are perceived. In drawing on Bellah's thinking for purposes of this book, it may be helpful to ask: Is the United States a republic that is dependent on republican citizenship, or is it a liberal constitutional state that is primarily concerned with balancing conflicting interests?

These two systems differ. A republic must actively nurture its citizens, root out corruption, and encourage virtue. According to Bellah, a republican state has an ethical, educational, even spiritual role, because its survival depends on its ability to reproduce republican customs and citizens.

Liberal constitutionalism, by contrast, assumes that a good society can result from the actions of citizens motivated by self-interest alone, when those actions are organized through the proper mechanisms. In this model, the state is supposed to maintain public order so that the economic market can produce wealth, and so that the free market in ideas can generate the wisdom that society needs to function properly.

Bellah sees republicanism and liberalism as not only different from each other but "profoundly antithetical. Exclusive concern for self-interest is the very definition of corruption of republican virtue.... And yet the American regime from the beginning has been a mixture of the republican and the liberal regimes and has never been a pure type of either."[117]

Religion as the Mediating Force

To Bellah, religion is the mediating force that negotiates the tension between republicanism and liberalism. Two elements are at work in this negotiation. The first is the civil religion, with its elevation of the political virtues enunciated in the Declaration of Independence and its quasi-ritual practices of national devotion. The second is the religious communities themselves, which supplement a necessarily thin civil religion. Civil religion needs to be minimalist to avoid strong conflict with liberal constitutionalism. "Yet the religious needs of a genuine republic would hardly be met by the formal and marginal civil religion that has been institutionalized in the American republic. The religious superstructure of the American republic has been provided only partially by the civil religion. It has been provided mainly by the religious community entirely outside any formal political structures."[118]

Bellah refers to Alexis de Tocqueville on the importance of religion in inculcating the values and mores that make the American republic function: "Tocqueville saw that naked self-interest is the surest solvent of a republican regime, and he saw the commercial tendencies of the American people as unleashing the possibility of the unrestrained pursuit of self-interest. But he saw religion as the great restraining element that could turn naked self-interest into...a self-interest that was public spirited and capable of self-sacrifice."[119]

Bellah's argument, however, does not address the serious risk of excluding some citizens when religion becomes the nexus of the nation—even in a society that purportedly embraces pluralism. If religion and civil religion combine to define civic virtue, the dominant discourse—Protestantism, in the American case—becomes the arbiter of what is allowed or excluded from public life.

For all their usefulness in tempering the dangers of liberal self-interest, the values that were seen as both religious and compatible with the civil religion were those of the Protestant churches, the mainline Protestant churches in particular. R. Laurence Moore notes that the history of religion in the United States is commonly narrated as the history of united, mainline Protestantism, and that this Protestantism sets the stage for an ideal of religious unity (around Protestant beliefs and practices), despite the untold history of diversity and conflict.[120]

Phillip Hammond, Bellah's co-author, acknowledges that conflict is inevitable in a society with diverse religious views. He sees civil religion, however, as the locus of mediation for this conflict: "In the religiously plural society, churches cannot resolve conflicts, at least between parties from different churches. But legal institutions *are* called upon to do so. Without claiming that legal institutions—and they alone—are responsible for American civil religion, I argue only that law has played a critical role in that civil religion's development."[121] Hammond then raises the following questions, essentially asking whether civil religion can rise to the task of negotiating conflict in a religiously diverse society:

> Religious pluralism need not imply *entirely* different sets of "common-ultimate ends," of "impersonal and independent criteria," or of "moral architectures." But it may be argued that some level of sharedness must exist for institutions to exist, and religious pluralism would appear to reduce that sharedness. But does it? Once a society permits multiple meaning systems to exist side by side, does it cease to *be* a society? Doubtless that can happen, but it is more normal for a society to work toward a new, more generalized, common meaning system. It is easier to form a social contract than for all to go to war against all. Still, as is now recognized, "mere" social agreement, a rationally derived document, is insufficient. Commitment to its rightness is also required. Every contract has its noncontractual element, Durkheim said; every legal order possesses its charismatic quality, Weber noted. And that noncontractual element, that charismatic quality, that commitment is articulated finally in terms that are (by definition) "religious." In a single society, then, can more than one set of religious terms exist? And if they coexist, can they continue to function as they are thought to function in a society with a religious monopoly?[122]

Hammond goes on to narrate a history of American civil religion that begins with the Protestant Reformation's notions of tolerance and the early American Protestant concepts of disestablishmentarianism and free exercise. He concludes that legal institutions in the early United States began by working from religious notions of morality but eventually progressed from religious rhetoric to civil religious rhetoric, where the stamp of morality remains veiled in religious language but is abstracted beyond any one religion.

Civil religion is thus a site where persons can come together for republican devotion and also where the deeper moral formation of persons that occurs in their different religions can be mediated to maintain the coherence of the "nation." But in Hammond's account of civil religion, the problem of exclusion again comes to the forefront. Arbitrating between diverse religious traditions by appealing to a "common" civil religion sets the stage for determining which religions are compatible—and which ones are incompatible—with the civil religion.

"Incompatibility" Is Not the Last Word

Civil religion helps to clarify what is happening when Jews, Catholics, and Mormons are believed to be incompatible with American culture, particularly when they are seen as incapable of participating in the public sphere. On the positive side of this story, each of these groups were able—through determination and perseverance—to challenge such notions and, by being active in the public sphere, to dispel notions of incompatibility. On the negative side, this situation generally required that the groups alter their traditions and practices to become more like those of American Protestantism.

While it is important and useful to reflect on the experiences of other religious communities in our effort to understand and advance the experiences of American Muslims, we should pause here and remember that comparative reflection has its limitations. In particular, we must remember that over-generalization is always a risk. In the larger picture, every religious community has its own demographic, cultural, and socioeconomic context, one that makes them different from other communities in both obvious and subtle ways. This awareness—this caution—is necessary among all religious communities; it's also essential among the various communities of Muslims themselves.

3

Religious Self-Determination for American Muslims

AS STATED AT the outset, the central argument of this book is that American Muslims must take a proactive, affirmative view of their citizenship of the United States. They should explore strategies to pursue, both in public discourse and through the political and legal processes, their priorities on their own terms—that is, through intentional *self-determination*—rather than through assimilation into the dominant culture.

This approach includes what I call *religious self-determination* as well. For American Muslims, proactive citizenship is about defining and participating in what it means to be American as much as it is about what it means to be a Muslim.

Religious Self-Determination: Individually, Together

Individuals will—indeed, must—exercise their self-determination, both religious and political, in community with others. Membership in such communities can be either ascribed, as in racial or ethnic identity, or elected, as in civic associations and political parties. Yet a large part of the responsibility for generating this proactive, affirmative view of citizenship rests on individual American Muslims.

This is not to suggest that choice is always accessible for individuals, or that individuals can always exercise it effectively. Self-determination, however—the experience and enjoyment of it, the responsibility for it—belongs to the individual. I am emphasizing the role of the individual Muslim here, to highlight the role of human agency in responding to challenges and effecting change.

By *religious* self-determination, I mean both the individual experience and the collective expression of a foundational freedom: the freedom of religious belief and practice, subject to the equal rights of other citizens. It includes the right of each Muslim to experience her religious beliefs according to her own convictions and choice. There is obvious and useful overlap between this concept and religious freedom under the First Amendment (to be discussed in chapter 4). However, I see religious self-determination as a broader and more dynamic concept that should not be inhibited by the constantly shifting jurisprudence of the First Amendment.

Individual Rights versus Community Discourse

How does individual freedom influence collective discourse—particularly whether that discourse is inclusive? A tension exists between two poles: *inclusivity*, to enhance political mobilization and alliance-building; and *relative exclusivity*, to protect the integrity of Muslim identity and community. This tension raises questions that are difficult to answer.

Can every person who self-identifies as a Muslim participate in the discourse, or should there be some sort of criteria for a seat at the table, thus requiring certain people to function as gatekeepers? If a community—say, the Ahmadiyya (originally from the Indian subcontinent) or the Nation of Islam—is excluded, why should members of that community accept exclusion? What about *their* right to religious self-determination? Additional questions stack up quickly: When can some participants impose their criteria on others? Who determines the criteria? And who enforces them?

To exercise and protect religious self-determination, it is important to collaborate with others, both within and outside Muslim communities. That statement, however, raises even more questions: How can people debate what it means to be a Muslim today? Which priorities should a Muslim seek for her particular community of Muslims to pursue, in the context of the social and political diversity of the wider community?

Take, for instance, a controversial issue such as gay marriage. Where should Muslims stand on this volatile issue? Can Muslims distinguish between their religious view as believers and their public position as citizens who share the same state with others? In light of the disparate communities of American Muslims, what does "religious self-determination" mean in practice? How does it—and how *can* it—operate?

Exercising self-determination is always the work of individual persons, not the work of communities or nations in the abstract. Only individual persons can feel, think, believe, and act; collectivities, as such, cannot perform these human functions. We tend to speak of a community as having this or that feeling, or as believing in this or that view, but such language is merely a generalization, seeking to represent the feelings and beliefs held by the aggregate of persons who constitute the group as a whole.

Does this emphasis on the individual person overlook the collective aspect of people's right to self-determination? That aspect emerges through democratic politics in which deliberation about policy options is a joint activity, which cannot be done by any individual alone. Outcomes that result from the deliberative process and voting, the argument goes, represent the collective will of the community, an expression of self-determination.

I do appreciate the fact that the individual is socialized since early childhood by her family and community, and that she continues to rely upon and interact with those collective entities. My point is that a collective entity as such does not have agency independent from the agency of its individual members. In the process of democratic deliberation and voting mentioned earlier, it is only individual persons who engage in reflection, reasoning, and persuasion, not the family or community as such. I believe that my focus on individuals is necessary, for two reasons:

1. To draw attention to the fact that the supposed "will" or "voice" of the collective entity is often appropriated by individuals who speak and act in the name of the collectivity, though they are really presenting their own views. At best, such appropriation tends to subordinate some individual members of the collectivity to what the elite believe to be the group's collective will. In practice, however, this assumed "representation" tends to serve the interests of the elite who are appropriating the collective voice and will of the group.
2. To emphasize that any change in attitudes and practice *begins with the individual*; that it can begin *immediately*, here and now; and that it does not need to wait for some mysterious process of formation of the collective will to be acted upon by "the community."

My purpose in taking this strong view of the individual nature of human agency is to encourage each individual person to advance his or her own interests, whatever he or she believes them to be. If we really want to find out the views of a group, we need to ask its individual members. Asking American Muslims about their Muslim identity and views, though, is not as simple and clear as it sounds.

Who's Asking? And Why?

Consider the main question in the title of this book. The question "What is an American Muslim?" may include another inquiry: "*Who* is a Muslim?" Should the answer be the one I have proposed—"A Muslim is whoever self-identifies as a Muslim"—or should it reflect the application of some criteria? If those criteria are external, who determines and applies them?

Additional layers of complexity appear when we move to the identity of organizations: Should a civil society organization of Muslims be able to limit its membership to Muslims or, even more specifically, to Sunni Muslims? If it is not able to do so, can it still serve its original purpose? Can the difficulty be resolved by enabling some limits to membership, while encouraging the group's leadership to be inclusive and tolerant of diverse views? Lines will always have to be drawn somewhere, but the more inclusive they are, the better.

Whether questions about Muslim identity are appropriate depends on who is asking whom, and for what purpose. While such questions may be fine within a personal or private relationship, an inquirer *outside* such an association—say, a business acquaintance—should not care whether he is dealing with a Muslim or not.

In all *interpersonal* situations, the criteria for answering the question "Who is a Muslim?" should be determined by the person who feels the need to know, as there would be little point in requiring that person to apply criteria decided by others. At the *organizational* level, how can we require members of a Sunni organization to admit people who self-identify as Ismaili Shia, the Nation of Islam, or Ahmadiyya? Open membership in such an organization will likely lead to deadlock or paralysis in the group's decision making. Organizationally, the challenge is to balance the right of existing members to determine the criteria of membership against the right of others to join an organization for whatever benefits they hope to achieve.

A question about Muslim identity normally should not arise in the context of state business, because the state should be neutral regarding religion. For an official to ask such a question may raise the risk or perception of discrimination. In certain cases, however, questions of a personal nature may be unavoidable. A judge or administrator, for example, may need to ask about Muslim identity in order to decide a religious discrimination case. For instance, can a member of Ahmadiyya compete for elections to the board of a mosque identified by some worshipers to be a Sunni site? In such inquiries, I believe that simple self-identification as a Muslim should be sufficient for the purposes of being able to compete for election to the board. State officials and institutions should not claim to assess the quality of religious belief or practice. Sunni worshipers should not be allowed to exclude any person from the opportunity to run for election to the board, but every qualified voter is entitled to campaign for or against any candidate they choose.

The Value of Dissent

I do accept—and take very seriously—the fact that Islam clearly endorses strong communal affiliation and practice, like daily congregational prayers in addition to Friday *Jumah* prayer with its spiritual rituals. Such practices are useful for solidarity and mutual caring among members of a local community. Unfortunately, this humane rationale is lost when Muslims focus on judging who is a Muslim in terms of conformity with *their own view* of orthodox Islam.

When someone judges a Muslim, is the judging person taking a Sunni view or a Shia view? And which particular doctrine or set of practices within the tradition is the person referencing? If the reference is to the Sunni Muslim tradition, is it a Sufi Sunni or Wahhabi? Among the Shia, is it Twelvers (Ithna 'ashari), Ismaili, or Zaydi?

Implicit within this strong diversity of views among Muslims is another important point as well. In the historical reality of Islam, there were many minority views—even some regarded as heretical by the dominant orthodoxy of the day—that, over time, came to prevail. Ahmed ibn Hanbal, for instance, was persecuted and imprisoned for his views, yet he became a founder of one of the four surviving Sunni schools of jurisprudence.[1]

The point for us to remember is this: Dissent should not be repressed, because it can be the source of rejuvenation and dynamism in a religious tradition. None of us holds the key to religious truth; no person can decide for everyone which views are valid. The issue can be complicated when it relates to some benefits of membership in a group, such as burial rights or control over the property of a religious organization. In any case, it is unlikely that all such disputes can be settled by the courts applying legal criteria. I urge all Muslims to avoid such subjective determinations and to support the acceptance of dissent in their communities. Anyone who legitimizes intolerance in the name of "defending Islam" may be laying the foundation for his own stigma and exclusion as a heretic.

For the purposes of this study, my working answer to "Who is a Muslim?" stands as "any person who self-identifies as a Muslim"—regardless of whether that person's beliefs and practices are perceived as conforming to or differing from what might be seen as orthodox or mainstream Islam. In my view, it is neither desirable *nor possible* to judge the validity of a person's religious self-identification.

Race and Ethnicity in Muslim Communities

Islam first came to the United States several centuries ago, with the arrival of African slaves. It is difficult to comment on the demographic composition or religious practices of those early American Muslims, because they were forced either to convert or to hide their religion.[2] By appreciating Islam's early presence in the United States, however, we can gain a better understanding of American Muslims' current experience.

African American Muslims in particular are unlikely to separate their current experiences as American Muslims from the broader struggle of African Americans against slavery and its legacies: racial discrimination, economic deprivation, and political marginalization. This civil rights dimension should enable African American Muslims to act as facilitators for American Muslims in general who are struggling for religious self-determination. That assistance, however, may depend on a key question: Are immigrant Muslims *willing* to accept it?

Scholars have observed, though, that issues of race and ethnicity are likely to arise not only between these two groups but among immigrant Muslims themselves.[3] While the Quran (e.g., 49:13) and Sunna command acceptance of racial or ethnic difference and condemn prejudice on such grounds, Muslims have always had social and political hierarchies based on such distinctions.

Racial and ethnic affiliations are readily apparent among Muslim communities in large American cities such as Atlanta and Chicago, where Muslims tend to socialize with other Muslims who share their specific racial or ethnic affiliation. Immigrant Muslims from the Arab world, India, Pakistan, and Somalia, for instance, usually attend their "sub-communal" mosque where Arabic, Urdu, or Somali languages are used in sermons and social activities.[4]

I should also note here that being a victim of racism does not immunize any of us against holding racist views or engaging in racist behavior. Racism exists within African American communities and among immigrant communities, as well as between these various groups. I would suggest, further, that an obsession with racism can inhibit the human flourishing of the racist himself more than it does the human flourishing of the victim of racism.

There seems to be a correlation between the rising tensions about African American understandings of Sunni Islam and the growth in Muslim immigration after 1965, when the United States repealed immigration quotas. These tensions take several forms:

1. African American Muslims, including those who are orthodox Sunnis, are strongly influenced by the wider African American experience in the United States, which promulgates important aspects of black identity that immigrant Muslims may not value.
2. African American Muslims may see their religion as tied to social activism in a way that immigrant Muslims may not. Immigrant Muslims, on the other hand, may not be as concerned with the social, economic, and political problems (such as inner-city crime and black-white inequity) that African American Muslims view as urgent. Muslim activists of immigrant background who are building organizations such as the Council on American-Islamic Relations (CAIR) seem to be more appreciative of the achievements of the civil rights movement.
3. African American Muslims may see immigrant Muslims as condescending and unwilling to take seriously African American interpretations and understandings of Islam.[5]

A Problem That Must Be Acknowledged

I raise these comparisons in order to challenge the denial and defensiveness around racial and ethnic issues that I have observed among some American Muslims. Failure to confront such concerns is common in all human societies. I believe that Islam condemns racism as well as ethnic or gender chauvinism, but I also see that Muslims have been—and continue to be—engaged in racist and chauvinistic behavior. Believers often fail to comply with religious injunctions, especially the ones that require them to confront deep-rooted sources of prejudice, such as racism and sexism. To overcome such failures, we must first acknowledge that we have them.

Confronting these volatile issues should be a matter of moral principle— for reasons that should be obvious to believers—as well as of pragmatism. On this second count, it seems to me that African American Muslims are distinguished not only by their deeply indigenous roots, but also by the powerful solidarities they share with broader racial, cultural, and political constituencies in the civil rights struggle.

If American Muslims in general are to benefit from each other's strengths, they must *all* find ways of sharing in current struggles for individual freedom and social justice. American Muslims' array of social, gender, and class identities are representative of the American public in general; Muslims should participate in the political struggles and social activities of other American communities, if they expect those groups to reciprocate. To do that, however, Muslims need to engage in internal study and debate in order to arrive at clear positions on current ethical or social issues. The Muslims of a community may, in fact, find themselves in irreconcilable disagreement on such issues, but it is better to have that clarified than to assume agreement where there is none. Then there would be the question of what to do or not to do as a community on ethical/policy issues. For instance, Catholics tend to take a religious position in opposing both the death penalty and abortion. Muslim communities need to first develop their own clear position on such ethical/ policy issues, and then act accordingly: either in solidarity with or opposition to the position of Catholic communities.

In this context, we might raise another question: Which conceptions of Islam are likely to support solidarity and participation across religious boundaries? Since there is no single, monolithic "Islam view" on issues like the death penalty and abortion, local communities of Muslims are likely to be divided. Some may support the death penalty and oppose abortion, while others in the same community may oppose the death penalty and support the right of women to choose having an abortion. It may seem convenient to declare "neutrality" over such controversial ethical/policy issues, but it may be morally wrong to fail to speak for what one believes to be a valid position. Declaring neutrality may also be unwise because we may need other believers to support our religiously motivated positions.

As emphasized earlier, there should be constant debate and contestation about such issues, but never in terms of who is or is not entitled to participate because of their religious affiliation or lack of it. Beyond accepting as a Muslim whoever self-identifies as a Muslim, I also accept the significance of contributions that so-called "heterodox Islamic" groups—such as the Nation of Islam, the Moorish Science Temple, and the Ahmadiyya Movement—have made to the African American understanding of orthodox Sunni Islam.

The Race Myth

For Sunni and Shia Muslims in general, the problem with a group like the Nation of Islam is that Elijah Muhammad accepted and promoted the race myth initiated by Fard Muhammad. In that myth, Yakub, of the original Black Nation, launched a program that bred increasingly white and evil non-Muslim humans. Prophets such as Jesus and Muhammad worked to convert these whites, to no avail. Elijah Muhammad taught that as part of Yakub's plan, the "white devils" enslaved blacks for 300 years and stripped away their religion. Not only does this myth make only superficial references to Islam, but sometimes it directly opposes Islamic teachings, as when Elijah Muhammad identifies Fard Muhammad as "Allah incarnate."[6]

To modern sensibilities, this myth sounds odd and obviously false, but it is not unusual in comparison with the medieval Muslim myth about the Chinese, or the historical Christian myth of Ham, which demonizes blacks. My point here is that Muslims who focus on their disagreement with these views may miss a valuable opportunity to accept African American Muslims on their own terms.

From a broader historical perspective, the Nation of Islam myth has many elements in common with the nationalist or pan-nationalist myths of other Muslim nations and communities. Turkish, Iranian, and Arab Muslims all have highly mythological historical notions that merge ideas about the achievements of Islam with their own national or ethnic contributions. European and white Americans still teach their children myths of Eurocentric supremacy, highlighting a glorious history. The Nation of Islam, a people who had no scholarly resources to draw upon, has constructed a mythic narrative that probably falls within the norm of creation myths found in other human communities.

To find this particular myth deeply objectionable from an Islamic religious point of view does not diminish the appreciation of this narrative among African American Muslims who later shifted to a more orthodox Sunni view of movements such as the Nation of Islam. Those heterodox groups have succeeded in fostering a sense of religious community and identity, one in which African Americans can take ownership. Islam, to these Muslims, is not just a foreign import; it is a religion in which their own communities are rooted.[7] All American Muslims, I believe, should share in that appreciation, or at least should respect African American Muslims' appreciation of those who claimed Islam as their own indigenous religion.

As we proceed in our study of how American Muslims in general can embrace the rights and responsibilities of American citizenship, we must continue to ask: How can we develop and sustain inter-communal cooperation between Muslim groups who do not accept each other as Muslim?

Muslims in the United States Today: The Big Picture

At this point, let's step back and take a broad look at American Muslims in general. When did immigrant Muslims arrive in this country, and from where? Demographically, who are American Muslims? How do they experience living Islam in the United States? Subsequently we will consider the variety of African American Muslims, as background for the discussion of two key issues: leadership and discourse.

Waves of Immigration

Muslim immigration to the United States tended to occur in waves.[8] The first wave, between 1875 and 1912, consisted primarily of immigrants (both Christian and Muslim) from the rural areas of Greater Syria—now Lebanon, Syria, Jordan, and Palestine. Most of these immigrants were economically motivated single men, who intended to stay only temporarily but gradually settled down.

The second wave came from the Middle East after the end of World War I. With the imposition of immigration restrictions by legislation in 1921 and 1924, Muslim immigration declined drastically through the 1930s, limited mainly to the relatives of those who were already in America. The Immigration Act of 1924 limited the annual number of immigrants from any country to 2 percent of the number of people from that country who were already living in the United States in 1890. That limit was down from 3 percent, a restriction that had been set by the Immigration Restriction Act of 1921. The 1924 law aimed to further restrict the influx of southern and eastern Europeans, who in the 1890s had begun immigrating in large numbers, and also to prohibit the immigration of Middle Easterners, East Asians, and Asian Indians.

The third wave, between 1947 and 1960, brought Muslims from Eastern Europe (primarily Yugoslavia and Albania), from the Soviet Union, and some from India and Pakistan, although the National Origins Act and the Asian Exclusion Act were still in effect. The fourth wave followed the passage of the 1965 Immigration Act, which allowed for a diversification among immigrants moving to the United States—Muslim or otherwise—because it repealed the previously held country-of-origin quotas that had favored Western European and mostly Judeo-Christian immigrants.[9]

In the most recent wave of immigrants are Iranians, Kurds, Somalis, Sudanese, other Africans, Afghans, and refugees from the former Yugoslavia. Over the last several decades, Muslims from South Asia arrived in much larger numbers than was the case earlier in the twentieth century. Muslim immigrants from countries such as Indonesia and Malaysia are increasing in number, as are Caucasian and Latino converts to Islam.

Before the 1965 act opened up immigration, indigenous African American Muslims dominated the Muslim population of the United States. Now, however, the country contains a broad range of Muslim ethnicities, cultures, and nationalities.[10] This diversity is constantly growing and changing because of the considerably high rates of conversion, birth, and immigration; Muslims are coming from all across the world, representing almost all races and ethnicities.[11]

Demographic Overview

The present demographic profile of American Muslim communities is difficult to summarize, because there is no reliable way of determining precise numbers.[12] For instance, the US Census does not ask for religious affiliation.[13] I should also note that I am reporting here the findings of some surveys or studies, without necessarily endorsing their conceptualization or methodology. Whichever studies one uses can be criticized in one way or another, as in the apparently conflicting data in different reports of the Pew Research Center.

In 2007 the Pew Research Center estimated the total American Muslim population to be at 2.35 million.[14] Another Pew Reseach Center study published in 2011 found that approximately 2.6 million Muslims lived in the United States in 2010. To put these estimates in global perspective, the world's Muslim population is expected to rise from 1.6 billion in 2010 to 2.2 billion by 2030.[15]

Additionally, the 2011 Pew Research Center study reveals that about two-thirds of the Muslims in the United States today (63 percent) are foreign-born, while slightly more than a third (37 percent) were born in the United States. By 2030, however, more than four of every ten Muslims in the United States (44.9 percent) are expected to be native-born.

According to a 2004 Zogby International Survey, about one-third of Muslim Americans are of South Asian descent; 26 percent are Arabs; and another 20 percent are African Americans. The 2011 Pew Poll, however, found that 30 percent of American Muslims describe themselves as white (including most Arabs, who in large part classify themselves as white Caucasian), 23 percent as black, and 21 percent as Asian. The top countries of origin for Muslim immigrants to the United States in 2009 were Pakistan and Bangladesh. They are expected to remain the top countries of origin for Muslim immigrants to the United States in 2030.

In terms of socioeconomic class, American Muslims tend to be well-educated, affluent, and young. According to one study, for instance, 59 percent are college graduates, 52 percent have an income of $50,000 or greater, 63 percent are under fifty years of age, and 82 percent of those eligible are registered to vote.[16] These percentages may have changed in the past few years with the influx of refugees from Afghanistan, Bosnia, Iraq, and Somalia, who will need some time to achieve levels of education and income that are comparable to those of earlier, by now settled, immigrant Muslim communities.[17]

Socially, the American Muslim population mirrors the general American public in many aspects, a theme that both the 2007 and 2011 Pew polls emphasize. For example, Muslim Americans are equivalent to the rest of society in terms of attaining college degrees and attending graduate school. They are also financially comparable to most Americans, being predominantly middle class. Another study found that the average mosque attendee is thirty-four years old, married with children, has at least a bachelor's degree, and earns about $74,000 a year.[18] Immigrant Muslims tend to be upwardly mobile, because of their high levels of education. Yet it is reported that the earnings of Arab and Muslim men have dropped by 10 percent since the events of 9/11.[19] I should also note that communal aggregate figures like those in the preceding paragraph mask huge economic disparities within Muslim communities.

Religious Affiliation and Practice

The geographical distribution of Muslims across the United States has shifted over the years. The first Muslim communities were in the Midwest, but Muslims also have lived in Boston, New York, and Chicago since the early 1900s. Significant numbers of Muslim communities are now located in many major urban centers, including Atlanta, Detroit, Houston, and other large cities.

Of all Muslims in America, 65 percent identify as Sunni, 11 percent as Shia, and 15 percent have no clear affiliation.[20] More than three-quarters of American Muslims are born Muslims, and 20 percent are converts. Among native-born American Muslims whose parents were also native-born, over two-thirds (69 percent) are converts.[21] In keeping with trends for other religions, the majority of Muslim converts report having converted before the age of 21, while many others report converting between ages 21 and 35.

More than 90 percent of American Muslims report that they adhere to the basic precepts of the religion, such as belief in God, the Prophet Muhammad, the Day of Judgment, and angels. According to the 2007 Pew poll, 86 percent consider the Quran the word of God, and 50 percent believe it should be read literally. Over half (57 percent), however, say that there is more than one way to interpret the religion.[22]

As measured by how many times they pray per day or how often they attend the mosque, almost half of American Muslims (49 percent) claim a medium level of religious commitment, while the remaining percentage are almost equally as likely to claim having a high or low level of commitment; 29 percent pray five times a day and regularly attend mosque; 22 percent rarely engage in these same practices.[23]

Interestingly, a rising trend relates age to religious commitment: the older generation of Muslims (pre-1990 immigrants) tends to be less religious than native-born and younger Muslims,[24] an observation supported by the data collected in the 2007 poll. Muslims under the age of thirty attend mosque at particularly high rates (51 percent attend weekly, compared to 36 percent of those between ages 30 and 54, and just 26 percent of those 54 or older). Additionally, a large majority of American Muslim women report that Islam treats them equally to men (69 percent), while 23 percent believe that the religion favors men. Women also tend to adopt traditional views on mosque etiquette involving prayer. Forty-six percent of all American Muslims (men and women) believe that women should pray completely separately from men.[25]

American Muslim Organizations

As documented by such studies as the Pluralism Project of Harvard University,[26] there is an impressive proliferation of vibrant Muslim organizations throughout the United States that address local, national, international, or other kinds of issues. Some of these organizations can be seen as ethnicity-based, while others are faith-based. Ethnicity-based organizations strive to maintain kinship ties, to provide mutual aid, and to educate others about their shared experiences and concerns. Some clusters within the ethnic groups are made up of professionals who have established guilds to improve their career chances. Faith-based organizations include mosques and Islamic schools.

Islamic centers, while offering educational and devotional services, also have become hubs of local community activism. Through these centers and other networks, Muslim community organizations have demonstrated interdependence across religious, intellectual, and geographical boundaries. They not only have received charitable gifts from their communities, but also have given increasingly to American and international charitable organizations.

This point raises the complex dynamics of charitable versus political funding for Islamist movements abroad, and the ideological influence of those movements on American Muslim organizations and communities. Many

Muslims entered the United States with prior exposure to Islamist movements and little appreciation of a distinction between political causes and
what US authorities may accept as "charitable giving."

In any case, the institutional development of these organizations seems to
suggest that American Muslims are undergoing a significant change in their
understanding and practice of Islamic activism. As they continue to interact
with institutions in the United States, American Muslims may become critical of the ability of traditional Islamic movements to add much value or leverage to the economic, political, and intellectual domains of their daily lives.
It should therefore be possible to develop this trend into wider solidarities,
alliances, and collaborations across religious and secular divides.

Living Islam in America: The Experiences of American Muslims

Between September and December 2010, Shehnaz Haqqani, who assisted
me in doing research for this book, contacted almost 500 different centers,
organizations, and individuals to ask about Islamic life in America. I should
emphasize, however, that I am not claiming that this brief survey was an aca-
demically rigorous study. I have neither the training and expertise, nor the
time and resources, to conduct a study of that quality. Still, I am hoping to
draw some sense of how American Muslims feel about various issues and concerns.

This study endeavored to identify the problems and concerns of Muslims residing in the United States. Equal attention was given to all Muslims,
regardless of their ethnicity, gender, sect, place of origin, educational background, and other factors. Responses from all participants were anonymous,
but fictitious names were assigned to any quoted statements, and a modicum
of true information was added about the speaker to provide context.

On Being Muslim in the United States

Participants in the study were asked to identify the negative aspects of living and practicing Islam in the United States. Many cited the increasing
amount of stereotyping and prejudice against Muslims since the September
11, 2001 attacks, and the negative representation of Islam and Muslims by the
mainstream media. One participant opines that racism and bigotry seem to
increase by the day, and that "freedom of speech means only hating Muslims
and speaking badly about Islam."

Respondents' major complaint, however, focused on the media: "People in general are controlled by mass media and have pre-existent thoughts about Islam and Muslims," says Abdurrahim, a Pakistani Muslim in his early fifties from the Bay Area. Hafsa thinks that "[t]he media is, for the most part, very close-minded about our faith. Given that a lot of Americans don't travel outside of the country, the amount of information they get is huge but limited. So when they see something bad about our faith, they assume it [about] the majority."

According to Abdurrahim, the media also "likes to highlight only controversial subject matters—for example, I haven't experienced any problems [of discrimination relating to my faith] in America, yet the media never talks about the good feelings that Muslims hold about America, [only] how Muslims hate it here."

Some Muslims recognized that the struggle against negative portrayals by the media could be strengthened if Muslims "had stronger representation in professions that give [them] a stronger voice, such as politics, law, media, and journalism." Sameera, a schoolteacher, says, "Muslims must learn to live in this country; it is not just the duty of Americans to accept Muslims or change their system to accommodate Muslims. [Muslims] must change the system, if they believe it is to be changed to suit them, by entering a variety of professions."

"Yet," Sameera notes, "when I have had Muslim boys and girls in my classes, they are forced to become doctors or engineers, not journalists, teachers, social workers, sociologists, psychologists.... It would be great to have some Muslim women in social work and psychology, not just to accommodate Muslims but to show Americans that we are not some fearful 'terrorist' or some stupid female who was married off as a kid and just managed to escape an 'honor killing.'"

On Reaching Out

Zaynab has observed that people in America are curious about Islam—although they do not always know whom, how, or even whether to ask about it—and she considers it Muslims' responsibility to represent Islam well. She shares that she was born and raised in America and maintains "American values," but "some people are nervous around me because they don't understand why I do things like wear *hijab* or pray five times a day, and I would like to encourage those people to ask questions without fear of offending me.... The more we reach out to non-Muslims, the easier life for American Muslims will become. [Thus,] putting energy into our outreach efforts is very important."

What could this outreach look like? Zaynab offers several suggestions: "We could host community *iftaars* [dinner following a day of fasting] and invite local religious organizations, organize more community volunteering activities, help clean up our towns, offer tutoring sessions, open up free clinics or domestic violence shelters." Sameera proffers: "Just like it was before the civil rights movement forced blacks and whites to associate with one another—we fear what we don't know. It is hard to hate somebody who is your neighbor."

Not everyone holds such an optimistic outlook, however. Yusra notes that Muslims across the county have made efforts to increase awareness of Islam, but she laments, "Many fellow Americans have not changed their opinions or attitudes." She notes, however, that this may be due to the current "conservative trend" among American Muslims, "[since] there seems to have been a rise in anti-Islamic sentiment specifically from the political and religious right."

On Discrimination

When asked to state the negative points about American Muslim life, Adam expressed his distrust of law enforcement, saying that there is "an increasing loss of civil rights and liberties, discrimination by public and private institutions, attacks on Islam, feelings of being unwelcomed by many policymakers and the general public, and unwarranted surveillance of innocent people, mosques, and Islamic schools." Adam's perception of a growing prejudice against Muslims in America is shared by many other Muslims. For example, Ahmad, a Shia Iranian American in his fifties from Tempe, Arizona, who has a generally positive view of life in America, laments that "[r]acism [and] bigotry have increased many folds, personal rights are taken away…and freedom of speech is only to hurt Islam and Muslims."

Several respondents, including Adam and Ahmad, expressed the belief that the increasing number of security checks they experience at airports is due to their Islamic faith. Sameera reveals, "I cannot check my baggage at the front of the airport. I must go through the long lines at the airport check-in because of my name. Once, an airline clerk took one look at me and my driver's license and immediately began to process my boarding pass, saying, 'Your last name is on the watch list, so we would have to check even a baby with your name.' I asked her why it took her one second to decide that I was 'OK'—'Is it that you are looking at an older white female and not a Moroccan or other dark-haired Arab?' She refused to respond."

Some informants suggested that Muslim females who wear the *hijab* are more likely to face discrimination or other problems than non-*hijabi* females or Muslim males. Ameera, a forty-one-year-old lab technician living in Salt Lake City, reports regularly receiving "dirty looks" and "a general aura of suspicion" from her non-Muslim counterparts because of her *hijab*. She also believes that wearing the *hijab* can cause economic difficulties: "For women who wear *hijab*, getting a job is so hard. I have my master's and am still looking for a job!" She further suggests that *hijabi* females tend to experience more "random" checks at the airport than non-*hijabi* females.

This impression is corroborated by Jameela, an African American convert in her late forties residing in Atlanta: "Every time my daughter and I are at the airport together, I have to be stopped at security, but my daughter never does. I wear the *hijab*, and she does not. When I asked them why, they said that it was just a random check."

On Ways of Moving toward Change

Faisal, a Pakistani man in his fifties, disagrees that these "random checks" specifically target Muslims: "Being stopped at security at the airport does not happen just to Muslims, and it certainly doesn't happen *because* we're Muslims. It's just that we're not Caucasian." He believes that increased airport security is America's attempt to guarantee the safety of its people, only because of "extremist Muslims who think they have a right to kill innocent people." He suggests that, instead of viewing themselves as victims of the new security system, Muslims "should be condemning those so-called Muslims who think they represent Islam with violent and hypocritical actions."

At least one of the respondents was frustrated with American Muslims' complaints about America and its people. Sameera, a Caucasian American, states, "The bias against America is palpable with many Arabs, more so than with Pakistanis and Indians. I got into an argument with an Egyptian man who was berating America—he had gained his wealth here, yet my country was evil, decadent, terrible. I told him it seemed that everything about my country is bad except for its money. If you are going to live here, then you are obligated to work to change what you think is wrong—don't just sit and complain."

As a lawyer, Hafsa encourages American Muslims to take more civics courses, "because it builds tolerance and appreciation," and to become well-versed in their rights as Americans. Adam also asserts that American Muslims "need to let the media and elected officials know that we are their audience and can be a powerful voting bloc with high income." He believes that Muslims can fight for justice for themselves and can promote positive change in American society by participating in political processes and supporting Muslims who are studying law and running for elected office.

On the Positive Side

Participants in the study were also asked to identify the positive aspects of living in America. For numerous respondents, the answer was some variation of "America is the best place for Muslims to practice Islam." Yusra believes that the positive aspects of an American life include "the freedom to practice our faith as individuals and as a community, access to education, and having space where genuine critique of ourselves can take place without fear of government coercion or retaliation."

Abdurrahim, a Californian Pakistani, summarizes the attitudes of many: "Anyone who complains about their life in America needs to live in a Muslim country for a while to appreciate America for everything it offers us. You have the right not only to study Islam in whatever form you want but [also] to practice how you believe! You cannot do this in Muslim countries because you have to conform." Huda, a Shia Muslim in her early twenties from California, states, "America offers people the freedom to learn about their faith without complications and influence of a particular culture."

The respondents also generally recognized that the freedom of religious practice offered here is not available in all Western countries. As Fatima from Virginia notes, "France has banned the veil on women [in governmental spaces]. In America, you can still practice it without too much criticism."

According to Ahmad, another positive aspect of American life for Muslims is having the opportunity to study Islam more openly and to communicate with other Muslims more freely. He does not believe, however, that Muslims are generally taking advantage of these opportunities. He regrets that "[t]he majority of older generations of Muslims have brought their baggage to America. Many still are not able to adapt and do not care even to learn the language and the culture in order to raise their children properly." The only connection these Muslims seem to have with Islam outside their house, he believes, is through Sunday Islamic schools. Because they do not make any efforts to create an Islamic atmosphere to raise their children, "We see many conflicts with younger generations."

We also asked participants about their ability to perform the obligatory daily Islamic prayers at school and/or work. Most of the informants stated that they have the freedom to pray in private areas at work, or that their schools offer them space to perform their prayers. Most of those who said they do not pray also said that they likely would have no problem if they wished to pray.

Only one participant thinks that she would "have some difficulty getting permission from my supervisor." Ameera, a Shia Muslim from Utah, notes that she prays wherever she wishes—the beach, the park, the street, at school—and has "never faced any problems. People look, but they pass by without saying a word." Generally, the respondents believe that as long as Muslims behave well, carry themselves properly, and maintain good relationships at work or school, they should not experience difficulties performing their prayers at work.

Sameera is of two minds about Muslim life in the United States. On the one hand, she believes that the negative aspects of life for Muslims here "actually outweigh most positives." She states bitterly, "If there are good points about being a Muslim in America, it is only in comparison to being Muslim in Arab countries today with all the governmental unrest, zealots running around loose, and very little tolerance on the part of governmental agents and police. Like Winston Churchill once said, 'Democracy is the worst form of government, except when you look at all the others.' "

On the other hand, Sameera acknowledges, "I rarely have to worry about being killed, arrested, beaten." She also adamantly believes that "the future of Islam lies here in the United States, not in Europe or the Middle East. The changes will come, with the younger generation who has grown up here with immigrant parents. They are of both worlds and they understand this world in ways their parents never will. By the time the third generation reaches adulthood, the world of Islam will be changed forever."

On Concerns within Muslim Communities

The participants in the study were further asked to identify some of the major concerns currently facing the Muslim American population and to provide any suggestions or advice to the Muslim community for improving its current condition. Many respondents focused on immigrant Muslims, whose supposed "frozen values" may hinder them from participating in American society, and advised them to open up to the possibilities for communication with those who do not share their cultural values. The respondents had many suggestions for dealing with this issue, including becoming more involved in their respective communities. Afra', an Indian American Muslim from California who runs her own business, suggests that this can be accomplished by learning English; she encourages Muslim communities to discover commonalities with the non-Muslim community through interfaith dialogues.

A related concern voiced by many respondents was that a significant amount of the discrimination they experience comes from Muslims in their own communities, rather than from non-Muslims. Afra' states, "[In addition to interfaith dialogues,] we also need to be involved in *intra*-faith dialogue, since there are many differences within the Muslim community. We need to learn to accept and appreciate differences among ourselves instead of imposing our own [ideas] on others."

Others also share this perspective, particularly those who reveal that they avoid attending their local mosques. As Aisha, a Pakistani American Sunni Muslim from Alabama, says, "If you express a different belief, or ask a question that you are expected to suppress, everyone looks at you with their heads shaking, as if you've committed a crime."

Hiba, a Pakistani Muslim American graduate student, from Michigan, feels similarly: "Before I put on *hijab*, I felt discriminated by Muslims for not wearing it. I felt as though people automatically categorized me as a 'worse Muslim' than the women who wore the headscarf, on the mere basis of that one element of faith."

Many respondents mentioned discrimination by whole groups, most commonly Arab Muslims. Sameera states, "While it is hard to be an American who has converted, it is also hard to be an American Muslim in the eyes of Arabs." Sameera specifically perceives being judged by the Arab community for her choice to work in order to provide for herself: "I no longer cover to go to work, a choice I made because I have to work. If there has been a problem for me with non-American Muslim women, my working as a single woman has been the source of it."

Sameera continues, "For instance, a Palestinian "Wahhabi" once accosted me about my riding the bus to work. She was upset that I lost my *wudu* [ablution] if a man sat beside me on the bus. [I said that if] she was worried about my *wudu*, she could come pick me up in the morning and drive me to school. That conversation then ended—and I did not get a ride to work."

Hafsa, a native-born African American Muslim from Phoenix, Arizona, complains that there is too much "racism and sexism" within the Muslim community. For example, "There are certain assumptions about me being African American. People don't consider me as a marriage option. I feel less equal to the other Muslims." The biggest conflict among American Muslims, Hafsa believes, results from "imposing an immigrant perspective of Islam in America. I prefer diversity. [The] challenge is not that most immigrants don't understand the American culture, but that they don't embrace the positive assets of the culture. We tend to bash it or equate it with non-Muslimness, or we equate non-Muslims with America—or vice versa."

Many victims of discrimination are Shia, such as Ameera, a lab technician who is currently unemployed, and who says, "Our own Sunni brothers and sisters discriminate against us by hiring Sunnis more than Shias."

Hodan, a female acolyte of the Nation of Islam, residing in Atlanta, also believes that she is most discriminated against by other Muslims: "As Moorish American Muslims, we have different customs and traditions that are not geared to the those of 'al-Islam,' so we're deemed innovators because we have a prophet and don't ascribe to [some of the] dictates of mainstream Islam, such as praying five times a day." Hodan describes other Muslims' treatment of her as "offstandish" because she is the imam, the spiritual leader of her Muslim community, but is not Sunni. She therefore advises Muslims to "come together and share our common goals to strengthen our communities and show unification within Islam, not the divisions. Confusion comes with a lack of communication, which is the key to bringing a better understanding."

Some Muslims have a different perspective on American Muslims' tendency to divide themselves into smaller communities based on ethnicity, not necessarily viewing it as a cause for concern. Salma observes, "The division has more to do with culture, not faith—the Lebanese people will associate with Lebanese people, the Pakistani with Pakistanis, and so on, regardless of their faith," but she also recognizes non-Muslims as a source of much of the discrimination that she experiences.

Unlike participants who reveal stereotypes and discrimination within the Muslim community, however, Adam says that he has never experienced discrimination by Muslims, nor does he expect to experience it: "Muslims in the US don't have the institutional infrastructure to discriminate against others—that is, to develop policies that deny people their civil rights and civil liberties and other opportunities."

Regarding Muslim-on-Muslim discrimination, Huda has a positive outlook on the future. She observes, "[T]he younger generation does not as strongly hold on to cultural norms that keep them strictly within ethnic communities and relationships. Much of the older generation avoids non-Muslims, while the younger generation doesn't." Huda is excited about this and advises Muslims to "learn non-cultural Islam from Muslim scholars who live and know the West rather than those who feel animosity towards it."

While many share Huda's positive outlook, others view intermixing as cause for concern. They predict that the increased intermixing of Muslims with non-Muslims will lead to a declining sense of identity among Muslim youth. Yusra, an Egyptian educator from Orange County, California, in her early forties, says, "[M]y concern is related to American Muslim youth identity amidst the negative media. Are they likely to drop their Islamic identity to fit in, or will they maintain their identity by isolating through a circle of 'Muslim-only' friends?"

On Muslim Identity, Post–9/11

The consequences of the September 11, 2001, attacks have varied for the Muslims who participated in this study. For the most part, however, the tragedy reinforced their identity as Muslims. Zaynab, a Pakistani graduate student in Ann Arbor, Michigan, notes that the September 11 attacks "made me more aware of my Muslim identity." Unlike some of the other respondents—such as Huda, who recalls becoming more defensive and outspoken about her faith in response to the September 11 tragedy—Zaynab did not feel as though she had to defend Islam in the aftermath of the attacks.

Nonetheless, the study suggests that feeling defensive or protective of their faith is not uncommon among American Muslims. Salma, a Shia from Arizona in her early twenties who is a registered nurse, finds herself "*constantly* explaining" her faith to non-Muslims, although she understands that this "may be a blessing in disguise." She feels a need to defend her religion and beliefs at all times. Salma hopes that through her explanations she can give non-Muslims an impression of Islam that is more positive than the one often presented by the media. Others, like Azima, also feel a continual need to represent Islam well through simple acts, such as "not yelling in public, or always picking up trash from the ground."

As a native-born American who has lived all her life in the United States, Sameera describes how "life has grown dramatically worse since" the September 11 attacks, although she does not think conditions were much better before. She recalls, "I was working here during the first Gulf War and wore full *jilbab* to work. I have been spit on, had beer bottles thrown at me, been verbally threatened, called names—and that was before 9/11." For Sameera, the situation has gotten worse since.

In this time of increased xenophobia, Muslims have advice and requests for non-Muslims. When asked what she wants America to know about Islam and about being Muslim, Azima responds, "I hold fast to my identity as a Muslim. It supersedes my identity as a female and as an Arab, both of which are target identities in the US." Adam "request[s] the assistance of Americans from all religious backgrounds to help eliminate the draconian and discriminatory policies toward law-abiding Muslims: learn more about the values of Islam, visit the [mosques] in the communities, and join interfaith groups to make informed decisions about Muslims and Islam." Like many other participants, Adam is grateful to the "many Americans who reject those who make every effort to slander Muslims and stand for equal rights for all under the law."

On "a Secular State"

The final portion of the study asked participants how they would define "a secular state" and whether they identify the United States as such. Most informants agreed that a secular state is "separate of any religious ideology and should be based on fairness." Azima says, "A secularist state means a state removed from rule of law tied to a religious belief. I don't believe that America is an entirely secularist state and think that many of its values are rooted in religious doctrine."

Azima adds, "However, America is one of the most successful countries in allowing freedom of religion, which, in a sense, must stem from a type of secularism. Unlike other religiously ruled regions, the US truly gives people the freedom to practice as they wish, and although it goes through periods of intense discrimination, usually freedom prevails."

Basimah, an African American convert to Sunni Islam and a teacher at a public school in Atlanta, notes, "A secular state must respect all religions, while seeing value in these religions. This is not true in America. This is a Christian state in so many ways. It might respect all religions, but it does not promote the value of all religions—for example, Sunday is a holiday, but Friday is not; Christmas decorations are provided by state funds, but [are not provided for] other religious holidays."

Adam criticizes the United States for stating "on paper that it does not discriminate based on religion, and [that] its rules and affairs are not influenced by any religions, but in practice, the secular state is full of hypocrisy—its policies are discriminatory based on country of origin, religion, language, gender, and income."

***

The preceding review offers only a limited sketch of the kinds of issues raised by the general theme of citizenship and religious identity in this book. Furthermore, each of those issues—as well as related ones—can be examined from a variety of sociological, political, and other perspectives.

Through this brief review, I am suggesting one basic point: the experiences of American Muslim immigrants do, in fact, fit the usual pattern of adaptation and integration faced by earlier immigrants. It seems clear to me, too, that American Muslims *already have* the human resources, organizational capacity, and initiative to pursue their objectives in solidarity and collaboration with others.

Varieties of African American Islam

A look at the varieties of African American Islam may illustrate how complex the issues of religious self-determination can be.

To recap: My emphasis on *religious* self-determination raises some dilemmas and paradoxes. A basic tension exists between two conflicting freedoms: the right of believers to define and live by their own beliefs, and the right of other believers to choose with whom they wish to associate in social and political work.

Islam would mean nothing if its doctrine and practices are whatever people want them to mean, without reference to the sacred sources and history of the traditions. At the same time, however, believers can be bound only by what they accept as a valid view of those doctrines and practices. Who, then, shall decide the appropriate limits of diversity? It is offensive and alienating to tell people who identify as Muslims that their Islam does not measure up to what Islam is supposed to be, yet such judgments will be made, whether explicitly or not.

Since the large group we call "American Muslims" comprises many diverse groups, speaking of all of them as one category will be misleading. As I sometimes use broad categories such as "immigrant Muslims" and "African American Muslims" for convenience, I also want to emphasize that these are broad classifications, comprising a great deal of internal diversity.

To focus here on the *religious* dimension of diversity within African American Islam, for example, is not to deny that there are also socioeconomic and class differences within the group that I am calling "African American Muslims." I think this classification is plausible, because it has a specific purpose here: to highlight the tensions between African American and immigrant Muslims over their respective understanding and practice of Islam. Again, this is not to assume that all Muslims within one group or the other understand and practice Islam in exactly the same way. Rather, we must understand two points: Perceptions exist that some immigrant Muslims think of themselves as the guardians of orthodox Sunni Islam; conversely, perceptions also exist that some forms of African American Islam are beyond the realm of being Islam at all.

Who Is a Muslim? Five Basic Answers

As noted before, the appropriateness and usefulness of the question "WHO is a Muslim?" depends on who is asking and for what purpose. To avoid any risk of misunderstanding or confusion, here are the basic elements of my position on this issue:

1. Subject to diversity of interpretations and practice, *Islam as a religion has an identifiable core.* To Sunni Muslims, this core includes the five pillars of Islam, namely, confession of the faith, prayer, *zakat* (religious tax), fasting, and pilgrimage (if possible). Ismaili Shia add two more pillars, guardianship and jihad, according to their own definitions of those terms.[27] Twelvers stipulate five principles (*Usul ad-Din*) and ten subsidiary pillars (*Furu' ad-Din*). Their five principles are monotheism, justice, last judgment, prophethood, and imamate. Their subsidiary pillars include prayers, fasting, *zakat*, and pilgrimage, as well as jihad, directing others toward doing what is good, and avoiding what is evil (*al-amr bil ma'ruf wa al-nahi aan al-munkar*).[28]

2. To be a Muslim is to acknowledge that core, as one interprets it, as true and binding as a matter of religious obligation. In view of such differences in the most basic elements of an identifiable core of Islam, none of the members of each of these groups would qualify as a Muslim when judged by the standard of another.

3. It therefore follows that no human being or institution is authorized to declare who is or is not a Muslim, but every person is entitled to decide for herself or himself, and for his or her own private purpose, whom to accept as a Muslim or not.

4. Such private evaluation should not have any official consequences, particularly regarding the person's right to practice according to her or his beliefs.

5. In limited circumstances, a court or other state institution may have to decide who qualifies for treatment as a religious believer, for example, in relation to granting or denying tax exemptions to religious organizations.

A list as brief as this one cannot be exhaustive, and much more can be said to clarify and qualify each element; but I hope that these five points are sufficient to establish a framework for reviewing the varieties of African American Muslims and their relations with immigrant Muslims.

Major Themes Related to African American Identity

My survey of the scholarship on African American Muslim identity indicates four dominant themes of discourse:

1. Scholarly disagreement on whether the Nation of Islam and other African American sects are fundamentally secular or religious;
2. Black historical narratives or alternative histories that seek to tie African Americans to other nations through Islam;
3. Rejections of "mainstream" American culture; and
4. Identification with struggles elsewhere in the world.

Is This Identity Fundamentally Secular or Religious?

Regarding this first theme, Kathleen O'Connor argues that African American Muslims have developed meaningful religious connections to Islam despite their association with Black Nationalism: "It is not secular nationalism that unlocks the meaning of 'Nation conscious,' used in recent years to describe their discourse, but *religious nationalism*" [emphasis added].[29] Although influenced by Black Power politics, the Black Muslim movement was not really a nationalist movement at heart.[30]

Black Historical Narratives and Alternative Histories

On the second theme, Edward Curtis credits "black history narratives" since the 1920s with playing a central role in African American conversions to Islam. These narratives illustrated the belief that the "historical destiny of black people as a whole" was linked to Islam.[31] They offered a version of history in which African Americans were originally linked to other non-white people in Africa and Asia through Islam, but their faith was taken away or corrupted (and superseded by Christianity) through enslavement.[32]

Curtis explains how African American conversions to groups like the Nation of Islam were based on a perceived religious link to a past identity, and not just on secular concepts of "black nationalism:" "The black history narrative," he states, "was an imaginative space where African Americans could explore, debate, and dispute what it means to be a Muslim."[33]

This aspect of African American experience created a native-born branch of American Islam that does not exist in France or Germany, and shows how Islam has already become part of the mainstream American story. Immigrant Muslims could have adopted this legacy to further strenthen the experience of American Islam. This seems to be a historically lost opportunity because immigrant Muslims tend to brand the Nation of Islam as non-orthodox.

Under the "classic" view of early African American Muslim organizations, especially the Nation of Islam, religion is seen as incidental to these organizations' identities. Over the last century, African American Muslims have constructed a dynamic "imagined communal identity" through the history narratives that link themselves to Islam.[34] To show how these narratives were created, Curtis draws upon several examples that pre-date the Nation of Islam:

1. As slaves, former slaves, and descendants of slaves, African Americans have long been able to relate to biblical narratives, such as the story of Exodus. Blacks who converted from Christianity to Islam could easily take this story and others with them.

2. Edward Wilmot Blyden, a Liberian Presbyterian missionary, linked a return to Islam with black liberation. This theme was picked up in the 1920s by the Ahmadiyya missionaries in the United States, who targeted African Americans for conversion by guaranteeing racial equality within Islam.

3. Noble Drew Ali, the founder of the Moorish Science Temple, used a black history narrative as a sacred text in the *Holy Koran of the Moorish Science Temple*. According to the Temple, blacks were actually Moors descended from an Asian people whose original religion was Islam.[35] A lack of faith and honor led to their enslavement, so they need to be saved from Christianity and to return to their Muslim roots.

4. Elijah Muhammed of the Nation of Islam also took up the theme that African Americans are descended from Muslims, and that redemption means returning to their faith.

5. Black history narratives continually incorporate stories surrounding Bilal ibn Rabah, a slave who converted to Islam in Mecca before the Prophet's migration to Medina in 622. This narrative takes Bilal's rejection of slavery and devotion to Islam as model ethical behavior.[36]

Rejections of Mainstream American Culture

Internal perceptions of African American Muslim identity also are evident in the top two reasons why African American and Latino inner-city youth turn to Islam: (1) disillusionment with Christianity and mainstream American culture; and (2) gravitation to Muslim groups, such as the Nation of Islam, that provide services both in the prison and the inner city. Muslim organizations deliver material benefits at a time when state and federal cutbacks have slashed services in these places. The Nation of Islam's "Bringing Allah to Urban Renewal" campaign, for instance, works on issues of jobs, housing, and black economic empowerment without federal money. In prisons, these and other organizations provide education on topics such as HIV and disease awareness, family values, and life-skills training.[37] But this does not mean that the people did not join the Nation of Islam for *religious reasons*.

Chande explains that the Nation of Islam was appealing to so many African Americans because it offered a path to "discipline, self-respect, and the positive reinforcement of self-affirming values."[38]

It is true that many youth conversions occur in ghettos and prisons, where youth are disillusioned with mainstream culture and religion, but conversions also happen on college campuses and among all socioeconomic groups. The commercialization of hip-hop culture, which projects its messages far beyond the inner city through television, the Internet, and movies, also extends the spread of Islam among the young. Richard Brent Turner reports, "Young black Americans currently receive more critical information about Islam through popular culture than any previous generation."[39]

Aminah McCloud argues that no matter which subgroup they may belong to, African American Muslims are conscious of the fact that they are stepping outside mainstream American society to assert Muslim identity, and also that they are preserving their own contributions to Islam, apart from foreign influence.[40] She suggests that African American Muslims feel the need for "a distinction between 'things Islamic' and 'things cultural,' so that African American Muslims are not forced to inherit cultural influences from the rest of the Islamic world as they strive to incorporate Islamic law into their lives and communities."[41]

"For African Americans," McCloud states, "the viability of Islam as a worldview hinged largely on its primary emphasis on social justice, and its ability to provide African-Americans with an historical identity independent of slavery."[42]

Despite the diverse expressions of African American Islam, McCloud predicts that this group is "growing and maturing into a distinct Muslim culture."[43]

Identification with Struggles Elsewhere

The liberation and empowerment of women is a crucial dimension of African American Islam, though it is not necessarily defined in "feminist" terms.

McCloud argues, for instance, that African American women are so beset by racism that this problem is the "commanding force" in their struggles with discrimination, even though they are aware that sexism also exists. Moreover, many black women spurned the feminist movement, which they viewed as driven by racist white women, and so were largely outside the discourse on sexism. As a result, they ended up "torn between fighting racism and [fighting] sexism."[44]

These women, however, have had to deal directly with the stereotyping of Muslim women that accompanied the waves of Muslim immigrants in the last few decades.[45] African American Muslim women have pushed against patriarchy within their own communities by spending time in the *masjid*, participating in education programs, and organizing activities.

Jamillah Karim asserts that American women are drawn to Islam because they believe it actually helps women receive fair treatment, by pushing men to honor their responsibilities toward women. Interviewing women who had been members of the Nation of Islam (NOI) but later moved into more orthodox groups, Karim came to see these women as feminists in their decisions to convert in the first place. Karim found that many ex-NOI Sunni women did *not* remember their NOI experience as a time of being valued only for their biological capacity.[46] She examines several NOI practices that women found empowering even as they struggled against male patriarchy—experiences which the women transferred into their understandings of Sunni Islam. For instance, NOI women's decision to cover their hair and their bodies was a feminist move in that these women took it upon themselves "to protect their bodies from the male gaze."[47]

Furthermore, even while the NOI advocated that men should work and women should stay home, the women whom Karim profiled found that this separation of gender roles could be "empowering for women who wanted better families."[48] Meanwhile, those who wanted to work could challenge the NOI ideology that only men can be providers by finding ways to supplement their husbands' income. In the eyes of many NOI women, "commitment to the race required that black women challenge the limits placed on them by black men."[49]

Similar analysis was undertaken by Carolyn Rouse, an anthropologist whose work focuses on Sunni and NOI women in Los Angeles. Most of her study, titled *Engaged Surrender*, involves detailed ethnography of women's and families' experiences. She draws these conclusions:

1. African American women's belief in Islam and their decision to convert are often responses to their social needs.

2. Islam provided a language with which to direct anger at racism and sexism; therefore, "African American women have surrendered to Islam because of the way Islam has been used in the community as a legitimate framework for challenging racism, sexism, and economic exploitation."[50]

3. African American women's "surrender" to Islam is a "surrender to a faith in Allah," not a revocation of their own agency. Rather, these women have empowered themselves "by situating a discourse of liberation within the authorized discourse of Islam.... [S]urrender does not happen in the absence of engagement with the sources of faith, the texts, and the community."[51]

Inter-Communal Relations

Relatively few scholarly publications discuss the tensions between African American Muslims and immigrant Muslims, perhaps because the division is a sensitive topic.

The prevailing view on this issue, as noted earlier, is that African American Muslims are attracted to Islam as an alternative to "the white man's Christianity." That motivation, however, has sometimes resulted in outcomes that cannot be reconciled with global "mainstream" Sunni or Shia positions. Strong disagreements—to the point of denying that the other is Muslim at all—also exist between Sunni and Shia Muslims. Yet mainstream Muslims generally accept that such differences should not preclude inter-communal acceptance and cooperation. The same could have happened with groups like the Nation of Islam.

As African American Muslims have begun to adopt a "mainstream" view of Islam, though, acceptance and cooperation have been growing among African American and immigrant Muslims. Over time, a number of Muslim organizations have developed that include people from both groups. African American Muslims as well as immigrant Muslims now sit on the board of directors for organizations such as the American Muslim Council (which recently merged with the American Muslim Association), the Islamic-American Zakat Foundation, and the Minaret of Freedom Institute.[52]

The Conflicting Dynamics

Three sets of conflicting dynamics are apparent in inter-communal relations:

Political: African American Muslims are more vocal regarding their views on social and political activism. When immigrant Muslims do engage in political activism, their efforts are concerned principally with foreign affairs, in contrast to African American Muslims' emphasis on domestic issues.

Cultural: Cultural differences are evident in superficial matters, of course, such as the food served at feasts and the language spoken in the community. Much of the scholarship discusses ways in which such cultural differences lead to distinct mosque organizations.

Economic: Muslim immigrants tend to be more highly educated and wealthier than African American Muslims—as indicated seemingly by the fact that many immigrants settle in the suburbs, while African American Muslims typically live in inner cities. Racial tensions are not explicitly discussed in most of the scholarly publications I have examined; nevertheless, in some of scholarship, there seems to be an underlying tension about this issue.

Differences Surveyed

The Pew 2007 survey reports eight primary differences between immigrant Muslims and African American Muslims:

1. Immigrant Muslims are more likely to view themselves as well-off financially.[53]
2. African American Muslims are twice as likely as immigrant Muslims to live with a non-Muslim.[54]
3. African American Muslims are more likely to attend mosque weekly (54 percent vs. 37 percent).[55]
4. African American Muslims are less convinced than immigrant Muslims that hard work brings success (56 percent vs. 74 percent).[56]
5. African American Muslims are less likely than Muslim immigrants to argue that new arrivals should assimilate into American life (47 percent vs. 21 percent).
6. Half of all African American Muslims say they have been the target of bigotry based on their religion in the past year, versus 28 percent of white Muslims and 23 percent of Asian Muslims.[57]
7. African American Muslims express overwhelming support for the notion that mosques should communicate their views on social and political matters, whereas the majority of immigrant Muslims say that mosques should keep out of politics.[58]
8. Immigrant Muslims are twice as likely as native-born Muslims to say they voted for George W. Bush (21 percent vs. 8 percent).[59]

What the Scholars Are Saying

In an extensive *New York Times* article, Andrea Elliot discusses political tensions between African American and immigrant Muslims as she observed them at a joint meeting of two Muslim congregations. One congregation was that of Imam Talib's mosque, serving African Americans in Harlem; the other was the Islamic Center of Long Island, representing immigrants of South Asian and Arab descent.

Elliot reports that many immigrant Muslims seem to see themselves as the rightful leaders of Islam in America, by virtue of their Islamic schooling and fluency in Arabic. Naturally, African American Muslims resent this condescending view, which devalues their religious experiences. This tension is reflected, for example, in the fact that every year, the two largest Muslim conventions take place in Chicago—on the same weekend.[60]

Furthermore, many Muslim immigrants come to the United States with advanced degrees and subsequently prosper. They tend to send charitable donations overseas instead of addressing the problems of poor Muslims in the United States. By comparison, many African American converts have not achieved as great a level of economic success.

Imam Talib, Elliot reports, has found that "when domestic issues jump up, like police brutality, all [of] a sudden we're by ourselves." Elliot postulates that immigrant Muslims may be put off by the racial politics of African American converts. In relation to the post-9/11 context, Muslim immigrants struggle to understand why African American Muslims have been reluctant to meet with law enforcement officials. African American Muslim leaders, for their part, complain that immigrants have failed to learn from African Americans' history of struggle.[61]

Liyakat Takim believes that Muslim immigrants experience Islam "through a cultural prism that is highly resistant to change," because immigrants are nostalgic for their homelands and hold on to the belief that they will return someday. As a result, Takim argues, immigrant Muslims are concerned with foreign affairs—particularly in the Middle East—and are averse to involvement in American social and political discourse. In his view, Muslim immigrants view everything alien to themselves as alien to Islam. From this view arises some of the tension between Muslim immigrants and African American Muslims.[62] A study by the Institute for Social Policy and Understanding likewise found that "African-American Muslims have a much less favorable view of immigrants."[63]

In Jamillah Karim's view, as a result of the cultural-religious authority that Muslim immigrants are claiming over African American converts to Islam,

African American Muslims frequently feel that immigrant Muslims call their group's authenticity into question, asserting their own superiority. At the same time, African American Muslims assert their group's American identity and their slave history over immigrant culture. Tameka, a twenty-three-year-old African American convert to Islam, says, "When I converted, the community was receptive but they wanted to mold me into an ideal based on their culture and experience.... To feel accepted in the community, I need to bring with me a language. I have to reach out more to them." Although Muslim immigrants can speak English, Tameka accepts that "everything is on their terms, definitely, especially since I am such a minority. I attempt to be more like them."[64]

Karim sees the difference in the two cultures reflected in each group's treatment of gender relations. Most mosques in the African American community accommodate Islamic guidelines for gender interaction but maintain the general ethos of gender mixing in American society: men and women sit separately, but share the same prayer space. African American communities are likely to experience casual gender interaction also. For example, there may be song performances at African American lectures and coed fashion shows at the national W. Deen Mohammed convention. Karim finds that immigrant Muslims, on the other hand, are more likely to place a curtain or partition between men and women, reflecting the gender segregation in old-world Muslim cultures.

Amina Wadud echoes the tensions of gender, race, and class that other scholars have observed. Further, she notes that administrative styles differ between immigrant and African American Muslims in mosques, Islamic centers, and other community-based organizations. In immigrant communities, consultative bodies are formed by major financial contributors to the mosque. In African American mosques, however, the imam himself is the head of the community, and any consultative body is organized on an ad hoc basis to address particular issues.[65]

Wadud points out that the imams of most African American mosques must maintain employment elsewhere, whereas in immigrant Muslim communities, the position of imam is a full-time job. Typically, the immigrant imam is himself a foreigner and thus is not well equipped to make decisions over the community; he is an employee of those who hired him. Differences in organizational styles, Wadud believes, contribute to the limited financial resources of many African American mosques, because disagreements within the community are less likely to be resolved by a consultative body, and as a result, groups may leave to establish another Islamic center.

Abdin Chande views the immigrant experience with Islam as an inherited identity, in contrast to the African American experience of Islam as a means of expressing empowerment. He sees immigrant Muslims as moving toward assimilation and success, whereas many African American converts "seek, among other things, closer encounters with Islamic authenticity."[66] Today, Islam in the United States is dominated by immigrant Muslims, with an emphasis on their authority of texts and religious developments within Islam. Chande believes that the tension between African American Muslims and immigrant Muslims is exacerbated by the lack of African American scholars of Islam.

Probably the most concerted response to the issue of "Islamic knowledge" in relations between African American and immigrant Muslims is that of Sherman Jackson, who has examined African American Muslim groups' adjustment to the shift in the basis for religious authority—a change brought about when immigrant Muslims poured into the United States, following the 1965 repeal of the National Origins Act and the Asiatic Barred Zone.

Using the neologism "Blackamerican," Jackson argues that before the post-1965 influx of Middle Eastern and Asian immigrant Muslims, Islam in the United States was dominated by "Blackamericans" as a holy protest against racism, and was oriented toward black people—a phenomenon called "Black Religion," which encompasses Black Christian churches as well.[67] As Muslim immigrants pushed aside this orientation of Islam, religious authority shifted to the "sources and methodologies" of "historical Islam."[68] Consequently, "Blackamerican Muslims found themselves increasingly unable to address their cultural, political, and social reality in ways that were either effective in an American context or likely to be recognized as 'Islamic' in a Muslim one."[69]

Jackson maintains that before 1965, heterodox Blackamerican Islamic groups made their connection to Islam through their own sources, with a sense of ownership that was not easily conceded to immigrants. From this perspective, devotion to Sunni Islam cannot wipe out the influence of Black Religion on the African American Muslim communities. He further argues, however, that the inability to completely master Sunni Islam has created serious identity problems for these communities: "[B]y this single default, that is, nonmastery of Sunni tradition, the critical posture of Black Religion and Immigrant Islam toward America and 'the West,' respectively, would combine to create a Blackamerican Muslim self-definition that was practically dysfunctional, enabling Blackamerican Muslims neither as blacks nor as Americans nor, ultimately, as Muslims in America."[70]

Therefore, according to Jackson, the key for Blackamericans to maintain Islamic identity without losing Black Religion is to master and appropriate Sunni traditions—a process he calls the "Third Resurrection." Jackson is careful to explain that he doesn't advocate merely recognizing Sunni authority without understanding how to use and apply it, because to do so would be to assist in its domination over blacks. Even if most African American Muslims today identify as orthodox Sunni, it is still vital, according to Jackson, to preserve the integrity of Black Religion, because "Islam owes the legitimacy and esteem it enjoys in the black community as a whole primarily to [its] proto-Islamic beginnings."[71]

Jackson believes it is important to emphasize the Black Religion components of Islam, because they represent a distinctly American contribution to black Muslim religious identity, one concerned with challenging white supremacy and overcoming anti-black racism. Furthermore, he contends that it is through blacks that Islam became an American religion. Preserving Black Religion serves as a counter to those in the black community who would fault blacks for joining Islam, a religion they see as dominated by racist Arabs (a perception problem that Jackson calls "Black Orientalism"). This question of religious authority invites discussion of another important issue: leadership.

Leadership: Secular, *Not* Religious

By saying that leadership is critical for religious self-determination, I do not mean to suggest that we should accept the pursuit of "unity" of the community of Muslims (*umma*)—whether local or global, religious or political—as a high priority.

On the contrary, my view of leadership is decentralized and pluralistic, because an emphasis on unity can easily be seen as—in fact, can easily *become*—a way to justify the repression of dissent and difference. Such justification has occurred over and over, in the name of secular philosophies as well as religious beliefs. Because people need unity of their communities to help secure their material well-being and personal security, they are strongly socialized into accepting the demands of unity.

Consensus has played a profoundly important role in the normative development of Sharia and in consolidating the authority of a few schools of Islamic jurisprudence. At the same time, however, consensus also has confirmed that difference of opinion is legitimate—within the range permitted by the methodology of Islamic jurisprudence (*usul al-fiqh*).[72] Thanks to these advances, not only have individual Muslims gained the freedom to choose among a range of opinions on any given issue, but a door has opened to the future development of Islamic thought.[73]

It may be helpful to begin with an overview of differences among Muslims in general over religious authority and organization. These differences are reflected in the Muslim population of the United States, as well as in the distinctive tradition of African American Islam, as seen in the previous section.

Traditional Muslim Religious Organization

First, to establish a general framework: For Muslims, religious authority is vested in the Quran and Sunna (traditions of the Prophet), as interpreted by Muslim scholars between the seventh and tenth centuries and developed through various schools of Islamic jurisprudence (*maddhabi*). Whatever subsequent development of Sharia took place was grounded in the structure and methodology established during that formative period.

In practice, Muslims have tended to seek the advice of local religious leaders and scholars in their communities rather than consult the sources of the schools as such. The main difference between the Sunni and Shia traditions in this regard is the extraordinary authority among the Shia of the Imam, who is a descendant of the Prophet according to a particular chain of spiritual succession for each of the Shia schools (mainly Twelvers and Ismailis).

Shia Muslims, who comprise about 10 percent of the global Muslim population, have a more structured hierarchy of religious leadership than Sunni Muslims do. Most of Ithna Ashari (Twelvers) Shia, now living primarily in Iran, Iraq, Syria, and Lebanon, believe that the twelfth and final Imam disappeared in the ninth century and will reappear at the end of time as the Mahdi (Messiah). In his absence, a group of religious leaders (Ayatollahs) guide their respective communities of followers. For the minority of Shia, known as Nizari Ismaili, authority is vested in their own Imam, currently Aga Khan IV, whom they believe to be a divinely inspired, direct descendant of the Prophet. Always a male designated by his predecessor, the Ismaili Imam interprets the Quran and offers spiritual and material guidance to the global Ismaili community, including those living in the United States. The Shia Muslims of the United States are therefore served by their local religious leaders.

A second framing point: Traditional practices of religious leadership depended on trust in the leaders' spiritual guidance and technical knowledge of Sharia. True religious leaders, these men had an intimate knowledge of local communities and their cultures; indeed, they were vital parts of their communities. Such relationships and authority were possible in closely knit communities, but they arose out of frequent and intimate interaction, which enabled followers to observe the genuine piety, generosity, and humane qualities of the leader. This type and extent of interpersonal relationship is normally very difficult to replicate under urban conditions of life in the United States.

A third framing point is that the Imam—the supreme religious leader of the entire Shia community, or the true religious leader in both Sunni and Shia communities—must be distinguished from the *local imam*, who is the leader of daily prayers in a mosque. The routine function of leading prayer can be performed by any competent Muslim man. In theory, any Muslim may move forward out of Muslims lining up for prayer, though in large cities of Muslim-majority countries, the position of imam has become a regular, often paid, position for a specific man. It's true that a particular imam may come to acquire great authority among a local community, but such a rise would come about by virtue of his charisma, religious knowledge, and piety—not from his role in leading prayer. In my view, it is very problematic for an ordinary imam, one who simply leads daily prayer, to assume a much more visible role of religious leadership, a position similar to that of a Christian pastor/priest or a Jewish rabbi. An ordinary imam has no religious authority to speak in the name of the community or its members.

The evolving role of the imam in local Muslim communities raises questions about the nature of imams' religious education and their social and political orientation. In Muslim-majority countries, imams traditionally receive "religious" education, but no particular training in how to serve as imams in those countries' local communities. Being an imam as a career option emerged only recently, in response to the needs of immigrant Muslim communities in Western Europe and North America. When expatriate imams are brought over to serve in Western countries, they typically bring the social and political experiences of their home societies into their practice at the new location—in our case, the United States.

The growing number of Islamic colleges in the United States, however, reflects the realization that locally trained imams can learn to serve their communities better. Islamic schools teach both Islamic and US history, using textbooks published by mainstream publishers. Community development groups, such as the Islamic Society of North America (ISNA), train Muslim activists in public institutions of higher education. Also, imams no longer monopolize the teaching of Islam. In the United States, an entire Islamic knowledge industry has emerged to produce and distribute books and other resources that help with Quranic exegesis.

The Question of "Unity"

Again, my emphasis on leadership does *not* accept as a high priority the pursuit of "unity" of the community of Muslims (*umma*), whether local or global, religious or political. Unity is an illusion, one that has been a source of horrendous suffering and bloodshed throughout Muslim history. On the day the Prophet died and before he was buried, Muslims split—on both religious and political grounds—in what came to be known as the Shia/Sunni divide, a separation that still resonates today in the politics of the Middle East.

For unity to be useful, it must comprise some religious beliefs or political interests; these points of view, however, tend to reflect some members of the supposedly united population more than others. Unity will have to be achieved, then, through some sort of imposition, such as the assertion by a dominant elite of its beliefs or interests, or by some degree of compromise in which—because power relations are rarely equal—some parties will have to give more than others.

In any group, an insistence on unity carries a high price: The stronger the claim of unity, the more firmly that claim will be established and must continue to be practiced at the expense of some community members' religious self-determination. Realistically, the notion of "a founding agreement" would be a myth, at least for the subsequent generations of members who could not have been participants in that founding moment. Yet a community that must maintain its unity and integrity must also impose some restrictions on entry and exit. Unity necessarily requires the suppression of dissent, and in order that the alleged founding and continuing agreement can stand inviolate, dissent must be suppressed in direct proportion to the strength of the claim.

Reconciliation—Through Individualism

Reconciling these opposing perspectives often takes the form of a trade-off, whereby we forfeit some of our autonomy in exchange for religious or social unity. Since this compromise seems to be the dominant view for the time being, I recommend that each of us should seek multiple means of unity among a variety of communities, so that some of them may serve as a check against the risks or costs that unity inevitably entails. This "safeguard" measure takes us back to the first chapter of this book, with the discussion of an individual's overlapping identities as ways in which that person can live and act "beyond minority politics."

Each of us, I suggested, is simultaneously a member of various communities, any of which could be in the majority on some issues and in the minority on others. For instance, I could be a member of a *religious minority*, such as American Muslims, and at the same time a member of a *political majority*, by belonging to one of the two major parties currently in the politics of the United States. I could also be a member of a *numerical minority* as a professional—a minority that could in fact exercise greater political influence than its numbers indicate. To avoid being too oppressed by one community or another, I would prefer to participate in multiple communities and strive to make each of them as tolerant of diversity as possible.

Granting that absolute individual autonomy is not possible in the context of social life, a relative degree of autonomy may be achieved by raising awareness of the value of individualism among members of communities. The whole concept of religious obligation and accountability is applicable to individuals, never to a collective as such. Individuals normally need to surrender some of their personal autonomy in exchange for the benefits of membership in communities. To avoid, or at least to minimize, the risks of destroying individualism, members of communities should strive to respect each other's individuality. The argument would be that such communal toleration of diversity is for the benefit of all members, as any of them may one day be socially ostracized or persecuted for his or her views.

Religious versus Secular Leadership

Another way to safeguard one's autonomy is to participate in the selection and continuing accountability of leaders. In this light, I see leadership as a *secular* function, exercised both by leaders and by followers—even when it appears to focus on religious matters.

Such secular leaders may indeed exercise significant religious influence among a given population. Take, for example, the *mufti* who is appointed by the government in power—a purely political institution—and yet who is widely accepted by the Muslim population of the country as exercising powerful influence in religious affairs.

Another interesting case is that of Sheikh al-Azhar, the rector of the ancient "Islamic" university in Cairo. Since Sheikh al-Azhar is appointed by the Egyptian state, the office he holds is political, and the selection is influenced by political factors. The Sheikh would probably follow one of the four Sunni schools of Islamic jurisprudence or a specific view within the school, but his influence may extend to many parts of the Sunni Muslim world.

Some forms of charismatic religious authority are inherently interpersonal—as we find in Sufi communities or in any other setting where authority is conceded internally by each individual person, rather than externally asserted or imposed. I would accept this as religious leadership, but would see it as defying any form of institutionalization, even at an informal level. Such charismatic religious leadership, unlike the leadership of most groups or entities, is entirely subjective and is exercised at the discretion of individual followers.

In religious leadership, only the follower can concede the authority of the leader; religious authority cannot be asserted by the leader himself. Once a leader asserts religious authority—whether that authority is coercively enforced or not—the person's leadership becomes secular, even if the leader and others claim that it is religious. Such claims are intended to insulate the leader from accountability; they should not be taken at face value.

The categories of *religious* and *secular* are not always sharply demarcated, and I know that they tend to overlap in practice. But I do believe that the differences between these two types of authority are both real and significant. I think there are religious and political differences between a form of authority that is externally imposed and one that is internally and voluntarily accepted.

The distinction can be observed throughout Muslim history, where "religious scholars of the state" (*ulama al-dawla*) exercised their religious influence to advance the state's political ends. Serving their own interests, the state's controlling elite would confer material benefits and power on the religious scholars of the state. Such situations undermine the moral authority of religion and encourage hypocrisy among the general Muslim population. The problem of secular leadership in the name of religion has always been extremely serious—in fact, deadly—in much of Muslim history and even up to the present, as recently seen in the case of Khomeini's Iran and Turabi's Sudan.[74]

Leadership among American Muslims

In any Muslim community, including communities of American Muslims, the question of centralized leadership tends to be a complex one, because of two primary factors:

1. Sunni Islam does not have a set hierarchy of religious leaders. Shia does have hierarchies, but with a very high degree of regional and communal variation.

2. American Muslims are extremely diverse ethnically, racially, and in their experiences as immigrant or indigenous Muslims.

In spite of these challenges, mosques and other American Muslim civic organizations have adopted leadership structures, and, whether consciously or not, they also have adopted different criteria or standards for who qualifies as a "leader."[75]

In the evolving American Muslim communities, how does the voice of authority actually arise? And how will new voices of authority emerge in the future?

First, let's look at Islam itself. Islam has always had an identifiable core of beliefs and practices, but even in those presumably universal elements, variations exist. For instance, take the confession of the faith: for Sunni Muslims, this means affirmation that there is no god but God, and Muhammad is God's messenger. Twelver Shia add to this formula an affirmation of the divine authority of Ali, the first Imam of all Shia. Both the Sunni and the Shia orthodoxy require prayers, but the manner in which prayer is performed varies. There are also emerging varieties of Islam in the United States—not only among historically different traditions, but also between African American and immigrant communities of Muslims. "These emerging constructions of self and community are being partially shaped by the debates over who should represent and interpret Islam in America."[76]

The Diverging Generations

In immigrant communities of American Muslims, generational differences have emerged both in private and in public, and language is the key marker of change in this regard. Elders and mosque leaders do not want to adopt English in the mosque, while members of the younger generation tend to prefer it. Young American Muslims, while being well grounded in American culture, are also open to global flows of Islamic information, interpretation, and activity. Further, they have become a stronger voice on college campuses. For instance, Muslim Student Associations (MSA) used to consist mostly of international Muslim students, and the organization lacked a sense of continuity and vision because of the transient nature of its members. Now, however, MSAs are dominated by second-generation American Muslims who have a strong sense of American identity. It remains to be seen whether MSA leaders will later take over leadership of the faith-based and ethnicity-based organizations, or will form alternative organizations according to their own visions.

Many young people tend to be more orthodox than their parents, who tried to become more liberal in their beliefs in an effort to assimilate into mainstream American society. Some young women, for example, wear the veil (*hijab*) to assert their Muslim identity—which may not necessarily mean that they are conservative or traditional in their life-orientation. Some youth want to choose their own marriage partners and exercise their individual freedoms; moreover, many young American Muslim women see Islam as empowering, helping them to argue for higher education or for a marriage of choice. While some American Muslim youth may lose interest in Islam, others may opt for what seems to them a more "orthodox" view of Islam. Although outsiders tend to ascribe to young Muslims a dominant, monolithic "Muslim identity," the young people themselves subscribe, in fact, to various "American identities."

Efforts toward Cohesion

Despite the factors complicating the question of authority within the Muslim community, American Muslims have strived to create a sense of unity in their leadership. The Islamic Society of North America (ISNA), for instance, helped form a "national Islamic *shura* or representative council on religious issues" whose presidency rotates each year between leaders of ISNA, ICNA (the Islamic Council of North America), and two African American leaders, W. D. Muhammad of Chicago and Imam Jamil Al-Amin of Atlanta.[77]

The irony is that African American Muslims actually concede the supremacy of immigrant Muslim leaders, even as they resist it. On the one hand, immigrant leaders who are qualified in so-called traditional Islamic sciences are criticized for a lack of understanding and appreciation of American culture and social institutions. On the other hand, those traditional sciences are re-affirmed as the true measure of what is still Islamic today. Thus, immigrant knowledge of Islam, with all its cultural baggage, prevails, whether applied by immigrant or African American leaders or by the emerging leadership of South Asian and Arab background.

Some African American scholars, like Sherman Jackson, have attempted to tackle this issue.[78] My point, however, is not simply about immigrant versus native-born, but about the cultural attitudes and assumptions on which traditional knowledge of Islam has been founded. An American-born Muslim scholar who is exclusively trained in the Wahhabi view of Islam but communicates that view merely by "translating" it into current American vernacular would be guilty of the same cultural attitudes and assumptions for which immigrant leaders are criticized.

One response to the challenge of leadership is provided by "new" spokesmen of American Muslims who tend to be professionals (medical doctors, engineers, etc.) and businessmen, rather than traditional imams. These spokesmen advocate citizenship and participation. "Without classical training in Islamic history and law, it is they who have stepped forward, speaking authoritatively and publicly on legal issues ranging from citizenship and voting to marriage and family law."[79]

The MILA Example

A good example of an alternative modern American Muslim leadership—and perhaps a better and more sustainable response to the paradox—may be the organization called Muslims Intent on Learning and Activism (MILA). Established in Denver, Colorado,[80] MILA was founded in 1992 by a few long-standing members of the Colorado Muslim community. Members of MILA tend to be educated "lay" religious leaders, consistent with Sunni general Islamic tradition. An underlying goal of MILA is to provide space for participation in the community's religious life for Muslims who have become disenchanted with traditional mosque activities and attitudes. The organization also seeks to bring together disparate groups of Muslims in order to foster community cohesion.

MILA strives to achieve its goals by organizing itself as a nonsectarian and nonhierarchical set of individuals and groups who work together on various projects under the auspices of a steering committee, which functions more like a loose network than an administrative body. The organization hosts large monthly community events that include outside speakers, panel discussions, and seminars for educators and professionals. MILA also offers sessions for the study of the Quran, community service projects, and new Muslim support groups aimed at providing Islamic converts a welcoming environment in which to learn the new way of life.

The organization, however, carefully avoids interfering in the activities of surrounding mosques, or replacing routine religious services such as prayers. The group prides itself on being tolerant, open to a variety of ideas and religious orientations. A measure of the success of MILA is that its event announcements and flyers are present in nearly every mosque in Denver.

MILA has received criticism for being "excessively liberal" and has been accused of irresponsibility in its approach to Islamic teaching. Specifically, Sunni Islamic centers have formally protested the organization's hosting of Shia speakers and its failure to uphold gender segregation in its activities.

Muslim Educational Institutions

Another attempt to foster leadership is the establishment of American Muslim educational institutions aimed at training students to embrace "the best of both worlds." For example, in 2010, the Zaytuna Institute launched an attempt to formalize Muslim leadership training by initiating the Zaytuna College in Berkeley, which opened its doors for an inaugural freshman class of fifteen students, with five faculty members. The college offers training in the Arabic language, theology, and Islamic scholarship, as well as courses in the humanities and social sciences, such as sociology, philosophy, linguistics, and astronomy. Zaytuna's founders are working toward earning accreditation from the Western Association of Schools and Colleges. The Zaytuna College seems to be setting a new standard for American Muslim leadership training: offering the traditional Islamic sciences that historically have been offered abroad, along with a typical liberal arts education common in America.[81]

The Racial Challenge

A delicate problem in the discourse of intra-community authority runs along racial lines. In 2001, African American leaders split off from the immigrant-led Sunni Muslim groups to establish MANA, the Muslim Alliance of North America.[82] African American Muslim leaders made this decision because they felt that the national immigrant-led organizations—with their focus largely on overseas agendas and assimilation into the predominant white American culture—had failed to reflect the concerns of indigenous Muslims.

Sherman Jackson, the African American Muslim scholar and a MANA board member, charged Khaled Abou El Fadl, an immigrant professor of law, with accepting "white America's claims to 'false universalisms' and overlooking or marginalizing African American interpretations of Islam and historical struggle for social justice."[83] Jackson argues that, instead of presenting a "progressive Islam" in glittering generalities, immigrant Muslims should embrace Islam's rich tradition as a pluralistic faith, allowing for diversity in interpretation as well as adaptation of Islamic principles to specific political or social contexts.

A New Paradigm?

A possible new paradigm for American Muslim leadership would call for competencies both in "traditional Islamic knowledge" and in contemporary

American culture. This is the challenge facing American Muslim communities as they try to train and mold the leaders of the coming generation. Whatever the response may be, it must combine Islamic legitimacy with modern social and cultural skills. We also may need to reconsider what *Islamic legitimacy* should mean for modern American Muslims.

In my view, religious self-determination requires the ability and willingness to challenge and reformulate some aspects of so-called traditional Islamic sciences. The drastic inadequacy of traditional Islamic methodology for meeting the challenges of religious self-determination today is painfully clear when it comes to the rights and status of American Muslim women in particular. While I would advocate the methodology of Islamic reform proposed by Ustadh Mahmoud Mohamed Taha,[84] I am only proposing here that this issue should be open to debate among American Muslims. Questions to consider include: Which aspects of traditional Islamic sciences should be reformed today, and according to which methodology? How can we achieve sufficient reform through a coherent and systematic methodology, rather than by arbitrarily selecting from among the diverse views within traditional schools of Islamic jurisprudence?[85]

We must remember that in attempting to respond to the challenge of leadership, *every* strategy is complicated by the general environment of public discourse, which, in the post–9/11 context, seems to be particularly hostile to Islam and to Muslims.

Looking Ahead

Three factors shape the options now available to Muslims in public and political life:

1. The largest Muslim group is still under the voting age. When they gain the ability to vote, they may contribute to changing the future of American politics.
2. Most immigrant Muslims had little active political participation, even in their countries of origin, and the political experience of most immigrant American Muslims in political activism, alliance building, and so forth tends to be limited.
3. The current social profile of Muslims is dominated by wage earners who can provide a comfortable living for their families but cannot wield much impact on national politics because of their limited financial resources. To

the extent that they have resources, Muslims are still learning to "play the political game."

Thus, Muslims have tended to focus on voter registration and attending political party precinct meetings. They have not generally been involved in school boards, local councils, and local civic organizations. Even so, the limited Muslim activism in the public space has engendered mixed responses.

Some groups have welcomed Muslims into their multicultural experience. Some evangelical preachers have expressed intolerance, while other conservatives have embraced Muslims as a potential Republican Party constituency.[86]

American Muslims are increasingly seeking to situate themselves within the civic and political structures of the country. The 2007 and 2011 Pew surveys illustrate highly complex feelings about assimilation. The 2007 poll reported that 32 percent of American Muslims find a conflict between being a devout Muslim and living in a modern society, while 63 percent have no such ambivalent feelings. Within this context, the 2011 poll suggests that 49 percent of American Muslims consider themselves Muslims first, whereas 26 percent consider themselves Americans first.

According to Pew, these numbers illustrate a struggle with identity, despite the majority belief that no conflict exists between modernity and Islam. In the 2007 poll, a plurality of American Muslims (43 percent) advise new immigrant Muslims to "mostly adopt American customs and ways of life," while 26 percent encourage maintaining a distinct identity. In the middle is a group (16 percent) suggesting that Muslims should integrate into American society without losing their religious and cultural identities. Native-born Muslims, especially African American Muslims, are more likely to oppose full assimilation.

The Pew polls also questioned respondents on their personal connections. The inquiry drew closely balanced results, with 49 percent reporting that most or all of their close friends are Muslim, and 50 percent indicating that they have relatively few Muslims in their inner circle.[87]

The 2011 poll, however, also reveals something new and interesting: Muslim Americans largely (57 percent) believe that most Muslims entering the United States today *want* to adopt American customs and ways of life.

As noted at the beginning of this chapter, I am calling on American Muslims to take a proactive, affirmative view of their citizenship of the United States by exploring strategies for pursing their own priorities, especially what

I call *religious self-determination*. Without any pretense of being comprehensive, I have tried in this chapter to highlight various aspects of the social and political dimensions of such strategies of religious self-determination. In the next chapter, I will highlight aspects of the legal process in relation to the overarching themes of this book, namely, how to proactively participate in defining and engaging in what it means to be American, as well as what it means to be a Muslim.

4

Legal Dimensions of Religious Self-Determination

RELIGIOUS SELF-DETERMINATION IS not merely a social or political phenomenon; it has legal aspects as well. Determining what is "religious," who is
the "self," and regulating the circumstances under which self-determination
happens—all are, in part, legal matters. My aim here is to explain these legal
dimensions to lay citizens so that they can decide the most effective legal
means by which to pursue their religious self-determination.

The Key Relationship: Religion and the State

The legal dimensions of religious self-determination are necessarily informed
by the relationship between religion and the state, including its constitutional
framework. My working assumption is that the terms of the relationship
between Christianity and the state in the United States will apply to Islam
(as well as to other religions). I am not suggesting here that the practical outcomes for Muslims are always the same as for Christians, because human judgment also affects the ways in which constitutional and legal provisions are
interpreted and applied.

Such differences, however, are neither inevitable nor permanent. It is possible—indeed, imperative—for people to challenge discrimination and injustice wherever they encounter it, and whatever or whoever may be its source.
The relationship between religion and the state has not always been identical
for Catholics, Jews, and Mormons. But within each of those groups, the citizens themselves, through their own human agency, corrected those problems
by struggling to apply the firmly established set of constitutional and legal
principles on which the system of this country was founded.

The process of effecting change from within the system works differently
at different times, but it continues to be available for all groups, religious or

otherwise, including Muslims. Due regard must be taken, however, of changes and differences in the context in which such processes work.

Efforts to clarify the relationship between religion and the state in the United States began within the framework constructed when Protestant Christian denominations achieved consensus on this subject in the late eighteenth century. That consensus asserted three important principles: that there should be no established state religion, that there should be no religious test for public office, and that freedom of religious practice must be protected.

These principles were expressed in the Constitution and the Bill of Rights, especially in the First Amendment, which states, "Congress shall make no law respecting an establishment of religion, or prohibiting the free exercise thereof...." That ingenious formulation sought to balance the two critical elements of what might be called the American model: separating religion from the state, on the one hand, and protecting the free exercise of religion, on the other. This twofold purpose—protecting religion from government, and government from religion—is simple and compelling, yet profound, as well as difficult to realize in practice. I will not try to tell its whole story here,[1] but will explore only what it might mean for American Muslims.

It is worth noting that the determination to separate religion from the state was accompanied by an equal appreciation of religion as an important source of ethical life that supports a republican form of government.[2] Clearly, religion played a pivotal role in the Revolution itself, when patriots employed religious imagery to build fervor for the cause of independence. By supplying a strong moral consensus amid continuous political change, religion helped to maintain a democratic republic.[3]

The absence of any established state religion, the other side of that founding equation, has had important consequences for the religious and political life of the country. Without monetary assistance from the federal government, the churches had to rely on voluntary membership and voluntary financial backing, which led to their becoming less formal in worship, more democratic and local in their organization, and practical in their goals.[4]

Thanks both to the diversity of Christian denominations in the United States and to the constitutional separation of religion and the state, religious pluralism has become a widely held political and cultural value and has opened new possibilities for the development of independent churches.[5] This inclusive view of Christianity, combined with the patriotism that accompanied the development of independent churches in the post-Revolutionary period, has given rise to what has been called "American civil religion."

American Civil Religion

Bellah's definition of American civil religion is that it is "an institutionalized collection of sacred beliefs about the American nation," which
he sees symbolically expressed in America's founding documents and
presidential inaugural addresses. It includes a belief in the existence of
a transcendent being called "God," an idea that the American nation is
subject to God's laws, and an assurance that God will guide and protect
the United States. Bellah sees these beliefs in the values of liberty, justice, charity, and personal virtue and concretized in, for example, the
words *In God We Trust* on both national emblems and on the currency
used in daily economic transactions.[6]

I am introducing the concept of civil religion at this stage as part of the American religious landscape at large, and also as a prelude to raising the question
later about the mutual relationship with American Muslims. Is this concept
and discourse useful for the process of religious self-determination for American Muslims?

Competing visions of American civil religion are broadly described as conservative and liberal. A partial comparison of these two branches indicates a
number of differences between them:

1. The conservative version is founded on the claim that the United States
    rests on a distinct relation to God, while the liberal version draws on a
    variety of religious values.
2. People subscribing to the conservative view may see the Ten Command-
    ments as "the bedrock of America"; in contrast, religious liberals typically
    value civil rights, international justice, and ecology.
3. In the conservative view, the United States has a special place in the Divine
    Order, while the liberal view taps into a reservoir of sentiment in the coun-
    try about the idea of peace and justice.
4. In contrast to the drive of religious conservatives to evangelize the world,
    people who hold a liberal view are likely to value cultural difference.

In sum, American civil religion is subject to disagreement and polarization,
rather than to consensus or mutual understanding. The two versions of American civil religion appear to have divided along a fracture line, namely, the
inherent tension between symbols that express the unique identity of a nation
and those that associate the nation with a broader vision of humanity.[7]

Whatever view one takes of American civil religion, it does not mean that the First Amendment was a mere sham or cover for a fusion between religion and the state. The combination of separation and free exercise was (and continues to be) real, as reflected in two centuries of jurisprudence and practice at both federal and state levels. Simply put, the American constitutional model was not hostile to religion. Unlike revolutionary France, which sought to establish a republican civil religion to *replace* religion (primarily Catholicism), American civil religion has never been either anticlerical or militantly secular. On the contrary, it borrowed selectively from the religious tradition in such a way that the average American saw no conflict between the two.[8] Both historically and currently, religious terminology pervades US political culture: the founding documents of the American republic, the national anthem, presidential inaugural addresses and declarations, and state endorsements of holidays all contain religious references.

This union of religion and nationalism, which remains such a potent force in political and civic life in the United States today, has established, in effect, a Protestant religious hegemony. The courts were able to continue opposing any formal establishment of religion (i.e., adoption or promotion of a state religion) partly because an informal religious establishment existed. Mainstream churches, thanks to their informal power and leverage, needed little formal support.[9] Evangelical Protestantism has remained an animating force in American political life. During the period leading up to the Civil War, it significantly contributed to the growth of antislavery feelings in the Northern states while, paradoxically, it reinforced the commitment of Southerners to the maintenance of the slave economy.[10]

It should be noted here that liberal does not necessarily mean secular. Quakers, for instance, are as Christian as Evangelicals. Sometimes a person may be liberal because of her Christian values. The implications of this point for our purposes here is that American Muslims should imagine Christian allies instead of conceding that right-wing Christians represent Christianity in general.

Religion: Public and Political

Since World War II, religion-state relations have continued to be defined by vigorous disagreement over the role and extent of religion in public and political life. For the most part, Supreme Court decisions throughout the second half of the twentieth century have served to deepen the separation of religion and the state by excluding religious activity from public space, on public time, and at public expense, especially in the areas of education and public schools, as emphasized in decisions regarding school prayer.[11]

This series of Supreme Court decisions started with *Engel, et al., v. Vitale, et al.* (370 U.S. 421, 1962), in which the Court ruled that state officials may not compose an official state prayer and require that it be recited in the public schools at the beginning of each school day. This ruling applies even if the prayer is denominationally neutral and pupils may, if they wish, remain silent or be excused from the room while the prayer is being recited. In *Wallace v. Jaffree* (72 U.S. 38, 1985) the Supreme Court declared unconstitutional a law that permitted one minute for prayer or meditation. *Lee v. Weisman* (505 U.S. 577, 1992), in which the Supreme Court prohibited clergy-led prayer at high school graduation, was followed by *Santa Fe ISD v. Doe* (530 U.S. 290, 2000), in which the Court extended the prohibition to prayer led by students at high school football games.

Conservative Christians have responded to this with legal challenges as well as political action. Campaigns have been mounted in support of prayer in the schools, voucher programs that allow parents more freedom to choose schools for their children, and freedom for Christian schools to operate with minimal government interference. Conservative Christians also claim to defend the traditional family, orthodox religion, and a strict approach to morality. The campaigns, for instance, against "obscene" schoolbooks and the Equal Rights Amendment (for women) appealed most strongly to evangelical Protestants, who see themselves as defenders of traditional Christian values and institutions.[12]

Organized political activism, however, is not limited to conservative Christians. Churches on the liberal side of the political spectrum have a similar history of political lobbying—for instance, on behalf of civil rights, the war on poverty, and ending the Vietnam War. They also seek to influence the foreign policy of the United States in favor of their views. Social activism on the liberal side has drawn primarily from mainline Protestant denominations, African American religions, and Judaism. Catholicism, too, has been engaged in foreign policy and economic issues as well as questions concerning abortion and homosexuality.[13] This possibility and the tradition of the engagement of foreign policy by religious communities is important, in my experience, for various American Muslim communities. Examples include concerns about the role of the United States in the Israeli/Palestinian conflict, the conflict between India and Pakistan over Kashmir, as well as tension between Iran and Saudi Arabia and its implications for Sunni/Shia relations in the region.

In recent decades, the constitutional commitment of the United States to non-preference among different denominations has been tested in cases involving such groups as the Church of Scientology, the International Society for Krishna Consciousness, and the Unification Church, all of whom are demanding equality under the law. The constitutional prohibition of a state's giving preference to one religious community over others was reaffirmed by the Supreme Court as a matter deeply connected to the continuing vitality of freedom of religion.[14] In these cases, and for the purpose of this prohibition, the question is: *What qualifies as a religion?*

Specific questions in this area continue to come before the courts—for instance, the question of religious language in the Pledge of Allegiance and the display of religious monuments in public places. The legal separation of religion and the state does not permanently settle the status of religion in the political and public life of the country through a simple or strict formula.[15]

This brief review, of course, cannot settle or exhaust discussion of any of these issues. It simply illustrates the kinds of issues and questions that tend to arise from America's constitutional and legal framework. As noted earlier, I'm assuming here that this framework, as it has evolved in practice over time, applies to American Muslims. The process also indicates the potential of human agency to negotiate the scope and meaning of this framework. I hope that this book will contribute to these processes, from an Islamic point of view.

Religion, State, Politics, and Civic Reason

I believe that Muslims everywhere, whether a religious majority or minority of the population, should acknowledge the constitutional principle of separation of religion from the state, while demanding the right to free exercise of religion. This does not mean that I think Islam and politics should be separated. As I have discussed in detail elsewhere,[16] the apparent paradox in striving for the separation of religion and the state, on the one hand, and the reality of the connectedness of Islam and politics, on the other, should be mediated. This paradox exists in all societies that include significant numbers of religious believers, because the believers are bound to express their beliefs and moral convictions in their political choices, whether that connection is formally acknowledged or not.

The Essential Separation of Church and State

My view is premised on the distinction between the state and politics, despite their obvious and permanent connection. The *state* should be the more settled, deliberate, and operational side of self-governance; *politics* is the dynamic process of making choices among competing policy options. Although the state and politics may be seen as two sides of the same coin, they cannot and should not be completely fused. It is necessary to ensure that the state is not simply an exact reflection of daily politics, because it must be able to mediate and adjudicate among competing views of policy, which requires it to remain relatively independent from different political factions.

Why is this separation essential? The institutions of the state (for example, the Department of Justice in the United States), while not changing in their structure, organization, functions, or staff, are required to serve succeeding administrations with very different political mandates and agendas. Here's an example: President George W. Bush was elected to implement certain policies through various national institutions, including the Department of Justice; President Barack Obama also was elected to implement different policies, again through the same Department of Justice. If the civil administration and professional legal services of the Department of Justice are to serve the Obama administration, they must remain distinct from the Bush administration.

The distinction between the state and politics is necessary not only because it supports a democratic change of governments, but also because it assists the survival of the democratic system itself. All political sides must have the incentive to contest elections in a peaceful and orderly manner, so as to have their turn in implementing their policies. Allowing the institutions of the state to be co-opted by partisan politics diminishes citizens' motivation to engage in vigorous democratic politics. What is the point of contesting elections if those who win elections will not be able to pursue their policies through state institutions that are neutral?

Despite its obvious desirability, the complete independence of state and politics is not possible, because those who control the state come to power and keep it through politics, whether in a democratic process or not. Officials of the state will always act politically in implementing their own agenda and maintaining the allegiance of those who support them. This is inevitable; therefore, the state must be separated from politics, so that those excluded by the political outcomes of the day can still resort to state organs and institutions for protection against any state officials' excesses and abuse of power. The fact that *absolute* neutrality is not possible, however, does not mean that we should not aim for the greatest degree of neutrality that is humanly possible. It is because human beings are incapable of complete neutrality that we should strive to safeguard neutrality as much as possible through transparency and accountability. The vigilance of citizens is the ultimate safeguard of their rights.

Today's modern state is a centralized, bureaucratic, and hierarchical organization, composed of institutions, organs, and offices that are supposed to perform highly specialized and differentiated functions through predetermined rules.[17] To ensure its own legitimacy and effective operation, the state should be distinct from other kinds of social associations and organizations in theory, while remaining deeply connected to them in practice.

For instance, the state must seek out and work with various constituencies and organizations in performing its functions, such as maintaining law and order and providing services for education, health, and transportation. Therefore, state officials and institutions cannot avoid having working relationships with various constituencies and groups who hold competing views of public policy. These constituencies include nongovernmental organizations, businesses, political parties, and pressure groups, and any of them can be religious or secular in different ways. Such working relationships are not only necessary for the ability of the state to fulfill its obligations, but they also are required by the principle of democratic self-government. The autonomy of the state is not an end in itself; rather, it is a means toward the end of enabling all citizens to participate in their own government.

Nonstate actors participate in government through formal mechanisms of negotiation and representation, as well as through informal means of communication and mutual influence.[18] Dynamic interactions between state and nonstate actors raise the risks of conflict and competition among all sides, and also can compromise the autonomy of state actors as each nonstate actor seeks to maximize its influence on state policy. These realistic risks should be moderated and checked through the development of stronger state institutions that can keep their relative autonomy in dealing with diverse groups and their competing demands.

Interconnection Through Civic Reason

We must ask, then: How can state actors remain responsive to the wishes of civil society organizations, business interest groups, and others without falling completely under the control of any of them? The state must strive to maintain its autonomy while being embedded in particular constituencies and in the society at large.[19]

The critical need to separate state and religion, while regulating the permanent interconnectedness of religion and politics, requires that a proposed policy cannot be mandated by the dictates of one religion or another—because that would make it both unacceptable to nonbelievers and non-negotiable to believers. My objection is to religious doctrine mandating a policy, not simply contributing to the process of reasoning when presented in terms that are accessible to all citizens. This possibility is consistent with my call that policy and legislation must be founded on what I call *civic reason,* which consists of three elements:

1. The rationale and purpose of public policy or legislation must be based on the sort of reasoning that the generality of citizens can accept or reject, and to which citizens can make counter-proposals through public debate without being open to charges of disbelief, apostasy, or blasphemy.
2. Such reasons must be publicly and openly debated, rather than being assumed to follow from the personal beliefs and motivation of either citizens or officials.
3. Since it is difficult and problematic to entrust any entity with adjudicating what qualifies as civic reason, I consider civic reasoning to be an *ongoing process* of cultivating civic responsibility and empathy with opposing points of view.

It is neither possible, of course, nor desirable to control the inner motivation and intentions of people's political behavior; the objective should be to promote and encourage civic reasoning over time. The requirements of civic reason encourage the development of broader consensus among the population at large, beyond the narrow religious or other beliefs of various individuals and groups.

Further, the operation of civic reason in negotiating the role of religion in public policy should be safeguarded by principles of constitutionalism, human rights, and citizenship. The consistent institutional application of these principles ensures that all citizens can participate equally and freely in the political process; it also protects citizens against discrimination on religious grounds. With the protection provided by such safeguards, citizens will be more likely to contribute to the formulation of public policy and legislation, including objecting to proposals made by others, in accordance with the requirements of civic reason. Muslims and other believers can make proposals for legislation that emerge from their religious beliefs, provided they are able to present and support such proposals to others on the basis of reasons that those citizens can freely accept or reject.

Religion is an important force that competes to influence policy. The practice of civic reason will increasingly diminish the dichotomy between the public and private realms of social existence, thereby making the separation of religion and politics more difficult. But the role of religion in the contested space of civic reason should not be viewed as predetermined, because such an outcome is contingent on various factors. The ability of religious actors to influence public policy is shaped both by historical relations of religion and the state, and by current conditions such as urbanization, demographics, the level of religiosity in society, and relations among religious communities. As such factors themselves shift and change over time, so does their impact on the influence of religion on public policy.

In countries like the United States, where there is no officially established religion, religious actors may have more room to maneuver in politics, a situation that may enhance their ability to influence public policy.[20] Recent events in the United States also indicate the role that the ideological orientation of the government of the day plays in shifting or even transforming the terms underlying the role of religion in civic reason. For example, the policies of the administration of President George W. Bush regarding faith-based initiatives may be viewed as a reconfiguration of the space of civic reason, allowing religion—or, more precisely, specific religious groups—greater influence in public life through increased funding opportunities from the state.

Those policies raised serious concerns among Native Americans who wondered whether they would qualify for the new policies, or be able to benefit significantly from them—because, in these faith-based initiatives, the category of "religion" itself was defined in limited terms that reflected the president's own understanding of religion and his personal beliefs. The list of religions drawn up by the administration was restricted to monotheistic religions that are most familiar to the dominant secular culture and to Christians. Certain groups, such as the Nation of Islam, were also excluded.[21] While such factors tend to distort the processes of civic reason as well as some groups' participation in it, the process would correct itself if applied within the appropriate safeguards of constitutionalism, human rights, and citizenship.

While religion has the potential to operate as a hegemonic discourse in civic reason, nonreligious forces or ideologies can play a similar role. The separation between religion and state is compromised when the dictates of a particular religion, as interpreted by religious authorities or the ruling elite, are made a prerequisite for participation in civic reason. But this can happen, too, from a nationalist or so-called secular perspective. For instance, consider the controversy over recent French legislation that prohibits Muslim girls from wearing a headscarf in schools. In that policy, republican secularism served to enforce cultural uniformity among French citizens, especially among immigrant populations.

The debate over the headscarf and French secularism must be located as well in a wider context of post-colonial relations, including the ambivalent relationship of France to its former colonies, and stereotypical perceptions and anxieties about Islam and Muslims. Muslims are uniformly perceived and treated as outsiders to French society, even though significant numbers of them have French legal citizenship.[22]

The separation of religion and state is a necessary but insufficient condition. If this separation is to serve its purpose of safeguarding political pluralism and ensuring a space of civic reason, it must be confined to a necessary minimum of normative content. A necessary minimum of normative content would include support for the principle of the separation of religion and the state, and pluralism as an ideological commitment beyond mere toleration of difference. That is, religious, cultural, and other differences are demographic facts, but acceptance of such difference as a positive force in social and political life is what I mean by pluralism in this context, or minimum normative content. The principle of separation needs to engage these normative issues, but should not get into controversial issues of social policy. The state should be neutral regarding religious discourse in order to provide and safeguard the space for debate and contestation within and among religious and cultural communities and social movements.

This conception of the separation of religion and the state can unite diverse communities of belief and practice into one political community only when its moral claims are limited to a minimum. Separation alone is also unable to address the objections or reservations that religious believers may have about specific principles of secular governance. In other words, the minimal normative content that makes the separation of religion and state conducive to inter-religious coexistence, pluralism, and the support of a space of civic reason diminishes its capacity to legitimize itself as universal without reference to some other moral source.

Here is the main point to take away from this discussion: separation of religion and the state means that no specific understanding of religious doctrine can be directly enforced as state policy—but that condition alone is not sufficient to address religious believers' need to express the moral implications of their faith in the public domain. For that reason, I emphasize that the separation of religion and the state is necessary but insufficient, unless we also acknowledge and regulate the political role of religion. This requirement is not as difficult to achieve as it may seem, because the religious and the secular are interdependent concepts.[23] Politics and religion do not operate in distinct realms; the one continually informs and is informed by the other.

The Constitutional and Legal Framework of Religious Freedom

The part of the First Amendment concerning the free exercise of religion was initially limited to the federal level, and did not apply to the states. In due course, however, the various freedoms under the First Amendment (religion, speech, press, assembly, petition) were progressively applied to the state level through the Fourteenth Amendment, which provided that "no state shall deprive any person of life, liberty, or property, without due process of law."[24] To illustrate the judicial application of this formula, let's consider polygamy—as an issue that might arise among American Muslims, because polygamy is permitted by Sharia.

Mormon polygamy was under federal jurisdiction in the 1880s, when Utah was a US territory. This controversy started when Congress outlawed polygamy in all US territories, disqualifying polygamists from holding political office, voting, or sitting on juries, and then passed laws to confiscate Latter-day Saints (LDS) Church property if Mormons did not cease the practice of polygamy. In *Reynolds v. United States* (98 U.S. 145, 1878), a Mormon man was convicted of polygamy in violation of a federal statute. He challenged the law on the grounds that it violated his right to free exercise of religion, arguing that he had a duty as a male Mormon to practice polygamy when circumstances permitted. The Supreme Court interpreted the Free Exercise Clause very narrowly in this case, holding that while the First Amendment prohibited Congress from regulating thoughts, Congress could still regulate actions, even religious ones. As Chief Justice Waite put it, "Congress was deprived of all legislative power over mere opinion, but was left free to reach actions which were in violation of social duties or subversive of good order" (*Reynolds v. United States* 98 U.S. 145, at 164, 1878).

This reasoning was used again in *Davis v. Beason* (133 U.S. 333, 1890), when the Court upheld a statute in the Idaho Territory that required voters to swear an oath that they neither engaged in polygamy nor were members of an organization that promoted polygamy. In this case, a Mormon was appealing a conviction for falsely swearing the oath, on the grounds that the law violated the First Amendment. The Court applied the same reasoning in *The Late Corporation of the Religion of Jesus Christ of Latter-Day Saints v. United States* (136 U.S. 1, 1890), a case in which the Mormon Church challenged the law that allowed the US Government to confiscate property of the Church until Mormons ceased practicing and advocating polygamy. The Court held that the law did not violate the Free Exercise Clause. Criminal prohibitions on polygamy are currently not a violation of the Free Exercise Clause, and polygamy remains illegal in all 50 states.[25]

Religious Beliefs versus Religious Actions

The Supreme Court broke away from that earlier reasoning in *Cantwell v. Connecticut* (310 U.S. 296, 1940), where the Court found a law of the State of Connecticut—requiring religious proselytizers to apply for a certificate from the local government—to be unconstitutional, because it authorized the local government to determine whether the activity is religious or not. The Supreme Court found this law to be censorship of religion, in violation of the First and Fourteenth Amendments. Before *Cantwell*, the Supreme Court was consistent in ruling that the First Amendment protected religious beliefs, but not religious actions. In *Cantwell*, the Court held that religious actions, too, were protected by the First Amendment (and by the Fourteenth Amendment, which applied the clause to the states). On the facts of this case, however, the Court held that it is not unconstitutional for a state, by general and nondiscriminatory legislation, to regulate the times, the places, and the manner of soliciting upon its streets.

In other words, whereas freedom of belief is absolute, religious actions could be subject to limitations. Thus, in *Poulos v. State of New Hampshire* (345 U.S. 395, 1953), the Court upheld a law that required licenses for any displays on public property. Licenses for religious displays in public parks were not granted to any group, as a matter of policy. When a group of Jehovah's Witnesses applied for a license to use the park for a religious meeting, they were denied on the basis of the policy that no religious meetings were allowed in the parks. Despite that denial, the group held their meeting, and the group's leader was arrested. Although the Jehovah's Witnesses challenged the law as infringing on their right to free exercise of religion and freedom of speech, the Court upheld the ordinance on the grounds that this law is nondiscriminatory among religious groups, and is merely regulating the time, place, and manner of exercise. The reasoning here, it seems to me, is that the time, place, and manner of exercising a right can be problematic if left totally unregulated, like when a demonstration is held on a busy street at the peak of rush hour.

The Supreme Court described the key distinction between *Poulos* and cases like *Cantwell* by first confirming that First Amendment rights can be the subject of reasonable nondiscriminatory regulation by governmental authority, in order to preserve peace, order, and tranquility. In *Poulos* the law was not discriminatory, because officials had no discretion when considering whether to grant a permit; therefore, it did not violate the First Amendment, as opposed to *Cantwell*, in which discretion was allowed.

This same principle has been applied consistently in similar cases. In *Watchtower Society v. Village of Stratton* (536 U.S. 150, 2002), for instance, proselytizers were required to register, but the law was discriminatory, because it permitted citizens to opt out of being subjected to solicitation only by Jehovah's Witnesses and no other religious group. The law was ruled by the Supreme Court to be unconstitutional, because it applied to only one group of religious proselytizers.

Constitutional Protection and "Free Exercise"

Constitutional protection applies to *all belief*, including religious belief in general, and not just specific religions. For example, *Torcaso v. Watkins* (367 U.S. 488, 1961) was a challenge to a Maryland law that required individuals to swear an oath professing a belief in God in order to hold certain government positions. An atheist, nominated for the position of notary public, refused to swear the oath. The Court held that the law violated the Establishment Clause, stating:

> We repeat and again reaffirm that neither a State nor the Federal Government can constitutionally force a person "to profess a belief or disbelief in any religion." Neither can constitutionally pass laws or impose requirements which aid all religions as against nonbelievers, and neither can aid those religions based on a belief in the existence of God as against those religions founded on different beliefs. (*Torcaso* v. *Watkins*, 367 U.S. 488, 495, 1961, footnotes omitted)

In *Sherbert v. Verner* (374 U.S. 398, 1963), a Seventh-day Adventist was fired for refusing to work on Saturdays, which is their Sabbath day. The woman was denied unemployment benefits, despite the fact that workers whose Sabbath was Sunday were not denied the same benefits when fired for refusing to work on Sunday. The clear discrimination in this case constituted a violation of the Free Exercise Clause. This case also introduced the standard that the government cannot limit someone's free exercise unless it has a "compelling government interest" and the law in question is narrowly tailored to furthering that interest.

The principle in *Sherbert* that unemployment benefits cannot be denied to those who refuse to work on the Sabbath was expanded by several cases, such as *Frazee v. Illinois Department of Employment Security* (489 U.S. 829, 1989). In this case, a man refused a temporary job offer because it might have required him to work on Sunday, in violation of his religious beliefs. This man did not worship on Sunday and was not a member of an established religion. He was merely a Christian who thought it was wrong to work on Sunday. Under Illinois law, personal belief was not enough for those seeking unemployment benefits after refusing to work on the Sabbath, and individuals seeking unemployment benefits were required to have been a member of a group that worships on that day. The Court held that Frazee's refusal was based on a sincerely held religious belief, and he was entitled to invoke First Amendment protection.

The relevant issue in *Wisconsin v. Yoder* (406 U.S. 205, 1972) was whether a state can compel Amish children to attend school, even though attending past the eighth grade was inconsistent with Amish religious doctrine. The Supreme Court considered this principle to be an important part of the Amish religious belief, stating that "the traditional way of life of the Amish is not merely a matter of personal preference, but one of deep religious conviction, shared by an organized group, and intimately related to daily living" (*Wisconsin v. Yoder*, 406 U.S. 205, at 216, 1972). The Court also said that "however strong the State's interest in universal compulsory education, it is by no means absolute to the exclusion or subordination of all other interests" (*Wisconsin v. Yoder*, 406 U.S. 205, at 215, 1972). Ultimately the Court decided that the free exercise rights of the Amish families as well as the fundamental right of the parents to raise their children outweighed the governmental interest in educating children. Therefore, an exception to the mandatory schooling laws was granted to the Amish community.

In *Goldman v. Weinberger* (475 U.S. 503, 1986), the Court considered how the Free Exercise Clause applies to members of the military. In this case a Jewish man, an officer and a psychologist in the Air Force, wore his yarmulke with his uniform. He was allowed to do this for several years, but eventually he was ordered to remove the yarmulke because it violated the military dress code. Refusing to comply, the man sued the Secretary of Defense on the grounds that being ordered to remove his yarmulke violated his right to free exercise. The military claimed that allowing accommodations for religious apparel such as yarmulkes would reduce discipline. The Court agreed, holding that "the First Amendment does not require the military to accommodate such practices in the face of its view that they would detract from the uniformity sought by the dress regulations" (*Goldman v. Weinberger,* 475 U.S. 503, at 509–510, 1986).

In *Lyng v. Northwest Indian Cemetery Protective Association* (485 U.S. 439, 1988), the government wanted to build a road between two California towns. The prospective path of the road ran through a site that various Native American tribes used for religious purposes. The Native American tribes sued the federal government on the grounds that building a road through the sacred area infringed on their right to free exercise. Privacy and peacefulness, they maintained, were required for the religious activities the tribes engaged in on this land. The Court held that "[w]hatever rights the Indians may have to the use of the area, however, those rights do not divest the Government of its right to use what is, after all, its land" (*Lyng v. Northwest Indian Cemetery Protective Association,* 485 U.S. 439, at 453, 1988). Essentially, because this government action did not prohibit religious beliefs or actions and was not discriminatory, it was constitutional, even though it burdened the free exercise of the Native American tribes.

The relevant issue in *Jimmy Swaggart Ministries v. Board of Equalization of California* (493 U.S. 378, 1990) was the constitutionality of imposing sales and use taxes on religious material. The plaintiff sold religious materials to residents in California, where the sale was subject to a 6 percent sales tax and a 6 percent use tax, and then sought a refund for the taxes—on the grounds that they infringed on the organization's right to free exercise. The Court held that "religious activity may constitutionally be subjected to a generally applicable income or property tax akin to the California tax at issue" (*Jimmy Swaggart Ministries v. Board of Equalization of California,* 493 U.S. 378, at 394, 1990). The California law was constitutional, because it "applies neutrally to all relevant sales regardless of the nature of the seller or purchaser, so that there is no danger that appellant's religious activity is being singled out for special and burdensome treatment" (*Jimmy Swaggart Ministries v. Board of Equalization of California,* 493 U.S. 378, at 395–396, 1990).

Besides illustrating constitutional protection as it applies to the free exercise of religion in the United States, the preceding cases also demonstrate the difficulty of predicting outcomes in different situations. We should recall, however, that predictability and consistency are not ends in themselves, and that they may in fact indicate rigidity and stagnation. It is good and healthy for a legal system and its judiciary to reach different or unexpected outcomes sometimes, because that is a sign of maturity and development.

The key matter of principle for our purposes is that there should be no discrimination among different religions. Whatever standards apply to *any* American religion apply to *all* American religions—equally, openly, and consistently. One may disagree with the Supreme Court's interpretation of the First Amendment or with its application to the facts at hand, but the reasons for such disagreement will not include discrimination among different religions. A petition by a Muslim will be treated no differently than one by a Christian.

American Muslims must learn how US constitutional and legal systems work, what legal and material resources can launch constitutional challenge to situations that Muslims find objectionable or problematic, and ways in which Muslims can promote solidarities and alliances with other communities that are likely to be sympathetic with or supportive of their cause. American Muslims should realize, too, that building up the necessary knowledge, experience, and resources takes time, as well as a genuine commitment to religious pluralism and acceptance of difference. I should not expect others to stand in solidarity with me in my time of crisis unless I am prepared to stand in solidarity with them when their own crisis strikes.

Applications to American Muslims' Concerns

The constitutional and legal framework outlined here applies equally to all issues of concern for all communities; therefore, any number of issues could serve to illustrate how that framework functions. For this section, I've chosen three issues—employment discrimination, prison accommodations, and education (both religious and secular)—as examples to explore; I don't mean to imply that they are significant for all American Muslims.

I will treat the matter of education in more detail, both because it holds broad significance for all communities and, especially, because it has particular implications for the preservation and development of Muslim identity.

Employment Discrimination

Employment discrimination on the basis of religion is governed by the Equal Employment Opportunities Act, also known as Title VII, which states:

It shall be an unlawful employment practice for an employer

    a) to fail or refuse to hire or to discharge any individual, or otherwise to discriminate against any individual with respect to his compensation, terms, conditions, or privileges of employment, because of such individual's race, color, religion, sex, or national origin; or

    b) to limit, segregate, or classify his employees or applicants for employment in any way which would deprive or tend to deprive any individual of employment opportunities or otherwise adversely affect his status as an employee, because of such individual's race, color, religion, sex, or national origin (42 U.S.C. § 2000e-2(a)(1) to-2(a)(2)).

Title VII also requires employers to reasonably accommodate an employee's religious practice, so long as it does not place an "undue hardship" on the employer. The law is violated if an employee is either treated less favorably than other employees or is subjected to adverse employment actions because of his or her religious beliefs.[26]

A plaintiff (the employee) who wishes to claim employment discrimination must establish a *prima facie* case, in order to avoid having his or her claim summarily dismissed. If the plaintiff does establish this case, the burden falls on the defendant (the employer) to establish a *prima facie* case as well, by proving either that the employer's actions were not discriminatory or that the employer had made a good faith effort to accommodate the plaintiff's religious practices.

As stated by the Ninth Circuit Court of Appeals in *Heller v. EBB Auto Co.* (8 F.3d 1433, 1438, 9th Cir. 1993), the specific criteria are as follows:

First, the employee must establish a *prima facie* case by proving that…

- he had a bona fide religious belief, the practice of which conflicted with an employment duty;
- he informed his employer of the belief and conflict; and…
- the employer threatened him with or subjected him to discriminatory treatment, including discharge, because of his inability to fulfill the job requirements.

The *prima facie* case does not include showing that the employee made any effort to compromise his or her religious beliefs or practices before seeking an accommodation from the employer.

Second, if the employee proves a *prima facie* case, the employer must establish that it initiated good faith efforts to accommodate the employee's religious practices.

An example of a successful claim of employment discrimination is *E.E.O.C. v. Alamo Rent-A-Car LLC* (432 F. Supp. 2d 1006, D. Ariz. 2006). In this case, a Muslim woman, Ms. Nur, claimed that she had a religious duty to wear a headscarf during the holiday of Ramadan. She requested an accommodation for this religious duty, and was told she would "be allowed to wear a head covering at work in the back of the office, but that she would need to remove the head covering while at the rental counter. Alamo did not excuse Ms. Nur from working at the rental counter during Ramadan" (*E.E.O.C. v. Alamo Rent-A-Car LLC,* 432 F. Supp. 2d 1006, 1009, D. Ariz. 2006). The district court held that "Alamo's proposal would have failed to accommodate Ms. Nur's religious conflict, and was not a reasonable accommodation" (*E.E.O.C. v. Alamo Rent-A-Car LLC,* 432 F. Supp. 2d 1006, 1013, D. Ariz. 2006). Because Alamo did not offer a reasonable accommodation to the plaintiff's religious conflict, to avoid liability the defendants had to show that accommodating the plaintiff would cause an undue burden. The court granted summary judgment for the plaintiff, because the defendants merely claimed that allowing the plaintiff to wear her headscarf would have resulted in an undue burden, without providing any evidence to support that claim (*E.E.O.C. v. Alamo Rent-A-Car LLC,* 432 F. Supp. 2d 1006, 1017, D. Ariz. 2006).

In contrast, *Webb v. City of Philadelphia* (562 F.3d 256, 3d Cir. 2009) illustrates an unsuccessful claim. In this case a Muslim police officer, Ms. Webb, repeatedly wore her *hijab* to work despite the fact that it was not allowed, and she was sent home for this violation of the dress code. When she was given a thirteen-day suspension for this repeated violation, she filed a lawsuit alleging, among other things, a Title VII violation. The Third Circuit Court of Appeals found that the plaintiff did establish a *prima facie* case of discrimination: "Webb's religious beliefs are sincere, her employer understood the conflict between her beliefs and her employment requirements, and she was disciplined for failing to comply with a conflicting official requirement. Thus, the burden shifts, and the City must establish that to reasonably accommodate Webb (that is, allow her to wear a headscarf with her uniform) would constitute an undue hardship" (*Webb v. City of Philadelphia,* 562 F.3d 256, 261, 3d Cir. 2009).

The Court found that accommodating the plaintiff's religious beliefs would have caused an undue burden to the city: "In the City's view, at stake is the police department's impartiality, or more precisely, the perception of its impartiality by citizens of all races and religions whom the police are charged to serve and protect. If not for the strict enforcement of Directive 78, the City contends, the essential values of impartiality, religious neutrality, uniformity, and the subordination of personal preference would be severely damaged to the detriment of the proper functioning of the police department" (*Webb v. City of Philadelphia,* 562 F.3d 256, 261, 3d Cir. 2009). The Court of Appeals affirmed judgment for the defendant.

Prison Accommodations

Muslims face many issues regarding prison accommodations, such as female inmates who wish to wear headscarves, *halal* food accommodations, and prayer requirements. A single federal statute, with necessary adjustments, applies to all prison situations: 42 U.S.C. § 2000cc-1.

A good illustration of the application of this statute is the case of *Khatib v. County of Orange* (639 F.3d 898, 9th Cir. 2011), which concerned a Muslim woman who was forced to remove her *hijab* in front of male officers. Khatib was taken into custody after her probation was revoked, and was ordered by the police officer to remove her headscarf. When she explained that her religious beliefs prohibit her from taking off her headscarf, the officer told her the male officers would remove the headscarf for her if she did not do so herself. To avoid being touched by the male officers, which would have been another violation of her religious beliefs, Khatib removed her *hijab*. Her probation was reinstated later that day, and she was released.

Khatib then filed a complaint alleging that forcing her to remove the *hijab* was a violation of the Religious Land Use and Institutionalized Persons Act (RLUIPA). The district court found in favor of the county, the Ninth Circuit reversed and remanded, holding that RLUIPA applies to the action of forcing the woman to remove her *hijab*, meaning that it would be justified only if the county was pursuing a compelling governmental interest and was using the least restrictive means to accomplish that interest.

In *Sutton v. Rasheed* (323 F.3d 236, 3d Cir. 2003), the Third Circuit Court of Appeals considered a case in which high-risk inmates were denied the religious texts of Nation of Islam because a prison official deemed them not religious. In what was known as the "Special Management Unit" (SMU), where there were various levels, the inmates at level IV and V were allowed only one "Bible, Quran, or equivalent" (*Sutton v. Rasheed,* 323 F.3d 236, 241–242, 3d Cir. 2003). At level III, inmates were allowed two additional religious texts; and at level II, four additional religious texts.

When the plaintiffs were moved from level IV down to levels III and II, however, they were not allowed to have their Nation of Islam books, because the Muslim chaplain for the prison had determined that those were not religious texts. The plaintiffs brought in an expert to testify to the validity of their beliefs, and the expert testified that the books were essential religious texts of the Nation of Islam. The Third Circuit found the prison practice to be a violation of the plaintiff's rights, but affirmed summary judgment for the defendants regarding damages, because the prison had already ceased the practice and was now allowing inmates to have access to these texts in the SMU.

Another example involves the difference between Shia and Sunni Muslims, and whether they are allowed to worship separately in prison. Since Shia Muslims are a small minority among American Muslims, prison chaplains who have been hired to lead Muslim inmates in worship tend to be Sunnis. In a number of lawsuits, Shia Muslims claimed that their religious beliefs dictated the need for a separate Jumah service (Friday congregational prayer). They also complained of discrimination and conversion attempts by the Sunni chaplains. Applying the balancing test used by the Supreme Court in *Turner v. Safley* (482 U.S. 78, 1987), the courts in these cases rejected requests of Shia inmates for a separate Jumah service because that request was reasonably overweighed by legitimate concerns of prison officials.[27]

Education: Secular and Religious

Although education is not a fundamental right under the Constitution (*San Antonio Independent School District v. Rodriguez,* 411 U.S. 1, 35, 1973), every state constitution now provides for the right of education.[28] As a state constitutional right, education must be available to *all citizens on an equal basis and without discrimination (Brown v. Board of Education,* 347 U.S. 483, 493, 1954). Despite wide variations in the practice of the states, there are some common features. For instance, public education must be provided throughout the state free of charge, financed through taxes. Individual school systems/districts are controlled and governed by the local public school board, yet the system throughout the state is considered a cohesive unit under the law.[29]

Subject to variation among states, general education is compulsory, and it is guided by a rational state interest, because education is seen as necessity for public safety and the free exercise of fundamental rights. The courts also recognize, however, that parents have the right to shape the intellectual and religious development of their children. Accordingly, parents may choose to satisfy state compulsory education laws through private schools, as long as those schools meet the state's standards (*Pierce v. Society of Sisters*, 268 U.S. 510, 1925). If the parents fail to meet the minimum requirements set by the state, the state will be able to step in and more directly control the education of the child (*Johnson v. Charles City Community Schools Board of Education*, 368 N.W. 2D 74, Iowa 1985).

In accordance with the "disestablishment of religion" requirement in the First Amendment, the state cannot support or promote any religion, coerce a person to attend or refrain from attending a religious service, or in any way support a religious institution or activity (*Everson v. Board of Education*, 330 U.S. 1, 1947). In matters of religion, state action—in order to be constitutional—must have a secular purpose and must function in ways that would have primarily secular effects. Through the Establishment Clause cases, *secular* has come to mean "in and of this world" or "non-religious," rather than "un-religious" or "anti-religious."[30]

To ensure the neutrality of the state in matters of religion in general, the Supreme Court created a three-pronged test in *Lemon v. Kurtzman* (403 U.S. 602, 1971):

1. The statute or policy must have a secular legislative purpose;
2. Its primary effect must be one that neither inhibits nor enhances religion, and
3. It must not foster excessive entanglement with religion.

All three elements of this test have been both frequently relied upon and controversial. It is not possible to elaborate much here, but for basic clarity, I would add that the third test means that the law in question should not require or permit the state to interfere in the internal doctrine and organization of religious institutions or groups.

Within Public Schools

As applied to education, this test means that public schools may not make any accommodation for religious instruction during the school day on school grounds, even if all religions are represented and parental consent has been obtained (*Illinois ex rel. McCollum v. Board of Education*, 333 U.S. 203, 1948). At the same time, the state must allow students and employees the freedom and time to practice their own religious beliefs, even if those practices are to occur during school hours, provided those practices do not violate another part of the First Amendment or impede the state's ability to safeguard rights of individuals.

Thus, on the one hand, religious classes provided by public schools during school hours and in public buildings for voluntary attendance by students are unconstitutional (*Doe v. Human,* 725 F. Supp. 1499, W.D. Ark. 1989). On the other hand, parents/students may petition a public school for release during school hours to attend either religious education or practices, which are not paid for by public funds and do not occur in public school buildings (*Zorach v. Clauson,* 343 U.S. 306, 1952). This arrangement, while fulfilling compulsory education standards, permits a dual-enrollment program in which private (religious) school students may enroll in public schools (and vice versa) on a part-time basis, in order to take advantage of programs or services not available at one institution or the other (*Morton v. Board of Education of City of Chicago,* 216 N.E.2d 305, Ill. App. Ct. 1966; and *Snyder v. Charlotte Public School District, Eaton County,* 365 N.W.2d 151, Mich. 1984).

If a public school allows nonsectarian student groups (those not affiliated with or limited to a particular religious group) to organize and hold meetings on school grounds during school hours, then it must also grant student religious clubs the same permission (*Widmar v. Vincent,* 454 U.S. 263, 1981; and Equal Access Act of 1984, 20 U.S.C. § 4071, 1984). In such situations, student religious clubs should be able to meet in the public building immediately before or after school hours, and to use religious texts as part of their meetings, provided such meeting times and spaces are made available to all student groups, and school personnel do not participate in or endorse student religious groups (*Board of Education of Westside Community Schools v. Mergens,* 496 U.S. 226, 1990). Students are also permitted to use lunchtime for religious club meetings, because lunch is noninstructional time (*Ceniceros v. San Diego Unified School District,* 66 F. 3d 1535, 9th Cir. 1995).

Student groups may not discriminate against other students by preventing them from joining or participating in any given group, but groups are allowed to discriminate in choosing who may hold a leadership position that is important to maintaining the group's purpose or identity. Religious student groups may restrict leadership positions in order to facilitate the purpose of the group (*HSU v. Roslyn Union Free School District No.* 3, 85 F. 3d 839, 2nd Cir. 1996).

Applying these rulings to Muslim students gives those students the right, for example, to organize prayer groups during school hours, provided the groups do not meet during instructional time; to distribute literature to other students concerning the Muslim religion; and to lobby for an accurate presentation of Islam in historical and cultural context. One of the difficulties that Muslim students will continue to face, however—and which is impossible to legislate against—is the pressure that they may feel from other students or school personnel to assimilate into what they may perceive as a Christian society.[31] The state may help here, for example, by giving teachers and school administrators training in promoting pluralism. Similar objectives may be pursued through reaching out to parents and community leaders to socialize their children into pluralistic values.

Charter Schools and Parochial/Private Schools

Other possibilities for Muslim parents include establishing either charter schools or parochial/private schools. A charter school is created by a contract between the state and the organizing body, outlining the goals and methods by which the school will educate its students. These schools may cater to specific communal interests, such as the arts or music, provided they also satisfy the educational requirements of the state. While independent in curriculum and structure, some charter schools can be government-funded and remain free to students. Since they are public institutions, charter schools cannot discriminate in the selection of faculty, staff, or students on the basis of religion, or impose religious or religiously motivated policies (such as Muslim dress for girls).

As public institutions, usually operating in public facilities, charter schools must follow the same rules as public schools regarding such policies as refusing to allow religious instruction in the building during school hours or by employees of the school. Additionally, a charter school may rent shared facilities with a private/religious school, so long as the charter school is organized and operated independently of the private school. Students may be dual-enrolled in a charter school and a private school, a right that traditional public school students also enjoy.[32]

So how does a charter school function differently from a traditional public school, yet within the First Amendment constraints?

According to one case study,[33] a charter school was created by East African elders and community members who wished their children to be educated in an environment that reinforced their religious and cultural values. They wanted to provide a school where students could practice their religion and cultural traditions without being ostracized by other students. Thus the school offers official breaks throughout the day, during which prayer is allowed, including weekly congregational prayer (*Jumah*) on Friday afternoon. To accommodate this weekly congregational prayer, the school day ends early on Fridays, so that the praying does not occur during operational hours; and all students are invited—but not required—to attend. *Halal* meals are served in the cafeteria. There is no dress code; girls are allowed to wear the full veil (*hijab*); and physical education and health classes are separated by gender.

A second possibility for religiously and culturally sensitive education is the private/parochial school. Because these schools are private, most (if not all) of the First Amendment restrictions on prayer, religious practice, and dress do not apply. In order to be established and accredited, however, private schools must still meet the minimum educational requirements, as specified in the compulsory educational system of the state. Private schools generally are required to incorporate as not-for-profit entities, to attain all business and educational operating licenses, and to register with the Internal Revenue Service. If a private school fulfills the state's interest in general education, it can obtain federal funding under specific guidelines.[34] Permitted state support for parochial schools includes providing transportation for parochial students as well as free textbooks (books on regular school subjects, not religious texts; *Cochran v. Louisiana State Board of Education,* 281 U.S. 370, 1930; and *Everson v. Board of Education,* 330 U.S. 1, 1947). The *Lemon* case, however, modified the discussion about private schools. Its three-pronged test, applied to the question of federal funding for private schools, determined that such funds could not be used for teachers' salaries or compensation in any way, because of the teachers' role in providing a sectarian education. Other federal funding possibilities in private education that have been found to pass the *Lemon* test appear in the following cases:

- *Mueller v. Allen* (463 U.S. 388, 1983): allowed tax benefits for parents of parochial school children.
- *Agostini v. Felton* (521 U.S. 203, 1997): allowed Title I teachers to offer remedial services, guidance, and job counseling to the qualifying students in parochial schools.
- *Mitchell v. Helms* (530 U.S. 793, 2000): allowed federal funds for acquisition of instructional and educational materials for parochial schools. The "neutrality principle," as applied to parochial schools, holds that if aid is "religiously neutral," then the state is not responsible for how the parochial school chooses to use it.[35]
- *Zelman v. Simmons-Harris* (536 U.S. 639, 2002): allowed funds from voucher programs to be used by parochial schools.

These cases are noted briefly here not only to illustrate the range of matters on which state funding for parochial schools is allowed, but also to show the fluidity and dynamism of the field. In other words, there is room to "negotiate" and "mediate" competing concerns, and there is the possibility of shifting judicial opinion, provided that it is done within the broad parameters of the First Amendment and its core requirements.

Homeschooling

The third and final possibility for religious education is homeschooling. Parents do not have a fundamental right to homeschool their children; each state sets its own regulations for homeschooling. Parents wishing to educate their children at home must still satisfy the educational requirements set by the compulsory education system of the state in which they live. No fixed formula and no rigid regulations exist, but parents may be able to satisfy the state requirements by keeping a record of attendance, hours of study, and grades; using nationally standardized testing material; ensuring that those who will be conducting the homeschooling are properly certified; and placing limits on the numbers of children that may be homeschooled together (*Null v. Board of Education of County of Jackson,* 815 F. Supp. 937, S. D. W.Va. 1993).

I would caution that the kinds of constitutional and legal safeguards briefly illustrated here are futile in the long run unless they are supported by strong cultural legitimacy for constitutionalism and the rule of law. Cultural legitimacy is necessary for any critical mass of citizens who seek to generate and sustain sufficiently strong civic engagement in constitutional governance under the rule of law.

Citizens need to trust each other, and to expect that the claims others make in discourse about public policy are at least made in good faith and within a reasonable margin of error. If citizens make wild claims about other citizens, with reckless disregard for the truth, they tend to undermine trust and mutual respect in society at large. Once those qualities are lost—or seriously diminished—by excessive misrepresentations and hate-mongering, recovering the necessary conditions for social cohesion and political stability will be extremely difficult.[36]

Two recent controversies, namely, the Park 51 Islamic center in New York City and the Islamic center in Murfreesboro, Tennessee, are matters of serious concern because of the manner in which public discourse was conducted, regardless of the final outcome of the planning permit process. In the first case, the Park 51 Islamic center project was confronted by an extremely reckless, hate-promoting campaign of irrational and groundless allegations against Islam and Muslims.[37] Although there was no challenge to the planning permission in a court of law,[38] and although the controversy seems to have subsided by the time of writing, the damage done to the integrity of public discourse may persist.

The controversy in Murfreesboro, Tennessee, was litigated in *Estes v. Rutherford County Regional Planning Commission*, in which the plaintiffs opposed the county's decision to approve site plans for the construction of an Islamic center. The judge ruled that the county government did not give proper notice of the public meeting in which the construction was to be approved. Other claims—dismissed by the judge—included that Islam was not a legitimate religion to be protected by the First Amendment, and that mosque proponents were part of a secret plot to overthrow the Constitution of the United States. Rutherford County voted to appeal the judge's ruling that they did not give adequate public notice.[39]

The construction of the Islamic Center of Murfreesboro opened for Friday prayers on August 10, 2012, in time for the end of Ramadan Islamic holiday (*Id al-Fitr*).[40] However, litigation continued when the US Department of Justice filed a lawsuit in District Court, alleging that the county violated the Religious Land Use and Institutionalized Persons Act. Moreover, the struggle over this particular Islamic Center may give a distorted picture of the life of Muslims in the State of Tennessee. "Over the same period [of litigation and protests], new mosques have opened in Memphis, Chattanooga, Nashville and other cities with little or no controversy."[41]

"Islamic" Family Law and American State Law

As noted earlier, we need to give family law issues special attention not only because they may raise different kinds of concerns among American Muslims, but because they also reflect a dilemma under the First Amendment. As a religious normative system, Islamic family law cannot be enforced by state courts, yet the coercive authority of the state may be needed to support community-based dispute resolution over issues like termination of marriage and custody of children. There are several underlying reasons for this dilemma.[42]

First, family law affects every Muslim—man, woman, and child. What's more, family law concerns the most intimate and religiously significant relationships, namely, sexual relations and parenting. Both of these facts point toward the need for regulation and adjudication of family law disputes, but any such regulation must be flexible. Dispute resolution in these areas usually comes through mediation and arbitration. But since mediation and arbitration happen in the privacy of people's homes and with the consent of the parties, it cannot easily be monitored. In contrast, when disputes are resolved through the application of legally binding rules, conflict resolution becomes a matter of adjudication by state courts, even if it involves some degree of arbitration. The key difference between these two methods of resolution is the nature of the sanction that supports the process: Is that sanction consensual and private, or coercive and official?

The second reason for focusing on family law is the fact that this field is the subject of the most detailed and categorical regulation by the Quran and Sunna of the Prophet. Clearly, these norms have been applied or practiced through community-based processes throughout Islamic history. The exceptional status of Islamic family law was continued and reinforced by British, French, Dutch, and other colonial administrators during European colonial rule over Muslim lands.

As a general rule, the colonial administrators replaced Sharia norms with secular European codes in all fields *except* family law. At the same time, colonial administrations centralized the administration of justice in the hands of official judges controlled by the state. Both aspects of that colonial policy were continued by "native" governments after independence from colonial rule. This created the impression among Muslims and observers alike that family relations for Muslims must be governed by Sharia, as enforced by the coercive authority of the state.

Thus the third reason for special attention to this field is that many Muslims believe that Sharia norms regarding such matters as marriage, divorce, and custody of children should be "enforced" by statutory and/or judicial law of the state as applied by official state courts. This belief appears to be prevalent in most Muslim-majority countries, such as Egypt, Iran, and Pakistan, as well as in countries where Muslims constitute a significant minority, such as India and Israel. We should note that both India and Israel, which are otherwise regarded as "secular states," enforce religious family law for *all* religions. Whatever the Hindus and Sikhs in India and the Jews in Israel may think of these policies, their enforcement by secular, democratic states reinforces the belief that Sharia family law, too, must be enforced by state courts.

One of the questions I am raising, however, is this: When an outcome is coercively enforced by inherently secular courts of the state, will that outcome be compliant with Sharia at all?[43] If a family law norm is applied by state courts, that means that it has become secular state law, and is *not* simply Sharia any longer. The fact that the act of theft is both a crime and a sin does not mean that both characterizations are the same.

A recent example may help clarify this important point: A Muslim wife can "buy" the right to repudiate a marriage by paying the husband an agreed sum of money or property (called *khul'* in Arabic). This method of terminating a marriage has always been part of Sharia and is practiced in some Muslim-majority countries, but was not available to Egyptian women until 2000. In other words, the right of the wife to terminate a marriage in this way is now enforced by Egyptian courts because the state allowed it, and not because it is part of Sharia.[44]

According to Sharia's own standards, American judges are neither competent nor authorized to enforce Sharia norms. In any case, there are no calls for this regulation among American Muslims, and no prospects of success for such a call, since it would be coming from less than one percent of the population of the country.

Here's another question, one that is more immediate for our purposes here: How is any of this discussion relevant to American Muslims, who live in a country where it is constitutionally impossible for religious law to be enforced by state courts? The demographics and profile of American Muslims make it extremely unlikely that there can be any call for "enforcement of Sharia" by American courts. As I have argued in detail elsewhere,[45] it is neither possible nor desirable to enforce Sharia norms through the coercive authority of the state. Whatever the state does is by definition secular, and ceases to be religious by the very act of enforcing it by state courts.

Nevertheless, I believe that traditional interpretations of Sharia confront American Muslims (and Muslims everywhere today) with a complex set of dilemmas. On the one hand, it could be argued that some Sharia norms need to be enforced by the state because they relate to property rights under Sharia law of inheritance or succession, which must be registered and protected by the state. The coercive authority of the state is needed to enforce and follow through with administrative and financial outcomes of disputes. For instance, the financial entitlements of a wife after a divorce need to be enforced when the husband fails to comply, and property rights of the heirs in the distribution of a deceased person's estate need to be officially registered and protected.

On the other hand, the nature of the modern state, along with the current conditions under which Muslims in pluralistic and complex societies live, do not permit the legitimate and systematic enforcement of Sharia. Since there is no agreement among Muslims, even in a limited local community, on the interpretation of Sharia, state enforcement will have to select one view to the exclusion of other views that may be equally legitimate. This historical reality is reflected not only in the main Sunni/Shia divide, but also in the difference within and between various Sunni and Shia schools of jurisprudence (*mad-hahib*).[46]

It can be argued, too, that since most American Muslims are either immigrants or of immediate immigrant descent, the association between family law and Islamic identity is too strong in their minds to be simply replaced by the secular family law of the individual US state where they live. I am not suggesting here that those American Muslims should be exempt from conforming to the law of the state—that is neither permitted by American law nor desirable, in my view. Even traditional Sharia norms obligate Muslims to abide by the law of the land. Rather, my point is that the persistence of social or cultural association between Sharia and family law may persist in the socialization of children and community-based mediation or arbitration of marital disputes that are determined at a private and informal level.

This legal reality may be more familiar to African American Muslims than to those who are immigrants or of immigrants' descent. Those in the latter group, who are more accustomed to the association of state family law with Sharia, may worry about how subsequent generations of children from Muslim parents can remain Muslim if their most intimate relations are exclusively governed by secular law. Can they manage to practice a sufficient level of fidelity to Sharia in their communities while submitting to the secular family law of the state?

Numerous possible answers emerge, alongside further questions:

- Should state courts enforce rulings of private arbitration when the disputing parties believe the ruling to be the result of applying Sharia, just as they would enforce the outcome of any secular arbitration?
- If private arbitration or mediation happens and is voluntarily observed in the communities, should the state intervene to protect women/children in that setting?
- What happens when applicable state or federal US law is seen by a Muslim person or family as totally in opposition to their view of Sharia?
- If secular law always prevails over Sharia norms, what does it mean to be Muslim at all?
- Can the person or family "opt out" of secular law by free and voluntary choice, or does the state still have the right to intervene to protect its interests in family law?
- How can the state do that without violating the privacy and sanctity of family relations?

These questions, of course, are not new for other American religious communities, and they have been the subject of mediation and compromise over the years. What may be new are the implications of the Islamic law dimension of family law, regardless of whether American courts can or will apply it. It may therefore be helpful to review the main principles of what might called "Islamic family law."

Overview of Islamic Family Law

Although I am using the term "Islamic family law" here because it is familiar to readers, I would prefer to avoid it. The phrase "Islamic family law" is misleading—a contradiction in terms—because it implies that an Islamic norm is or can be state law and simultaneously remains religious.

In my view, *state law is always secular.* When it enacts or enforces a Sharia norm, that is the result of the political will of the state, not the religious authority of Islam. This difference in the source of authority underlying the sanction means that religious norms cannot remain religious when enacted into state law. An overlap between Sharia norms and state law does not mean that the act is characterized in the same way under both Sharia and secular law. As in the example I used earlier, theft is both a crime and a sin, but the *religious classification* of the act as a sin under Sharia is completely different and separate from its *legal classification* as a crime, and vice versa.

A caveat: The following principles present Islamic family law as it has been and continues to be widely accepted among Muslims today, and not what any of those principles might become through re-interpretation in the future. I fully accept the possibility of such reforms, but find it confusing to mix, in the familiar phrase, "what the law *is,* with what the law *ought to be.*"

Marriage

Under Islamic family law, the key to marriage and all its consequences is that marriage is a contract. As such, the marriage contract must satisfy the following essential "pillars:"

- the concurrence of an offer and acceptance...
- between two legally competent parties who are qualified to be married to each other...

- exchanged through a clear and categorical formulation that affirms the mutual consent of the parties...
- in the presence of at least two competent witnesses to attest to and publicize the fact that the marriage contract was validly concluded.

A dower (*mahr*) is a required gift by the husband to the wife, due at the time of contract, though its payment or delivery can be postponed by agreement of the parties. This "obligatory gift" is a necessary consequence (but not a requirement) of the validity of the marriage contract.

Additionally, all the principles of *any* contract under Islamic law apply to every marriage contract: for example, requirements of legal competence to conclude a contract; the clarity and unequivocal nature of the language or formula; and the stipulation that an offer cannot be withdrawn once accepted. It is also imperative that the consensual nature of the contractual obligation must be ensured; that is, the parties clearly have understood and have freely consented to the formation of a contract.

In marriage, another requirement is that the man and woman are not already related to each other in any of the ways that preclude the possibility of marriage. These legal bars to marriage can be classified as either permanent or temporary. The reasons for a *permanent* bar to marriage include specific blood relations: the parties are not related as mother, father, or grandparent, as aunt or uncle on either side, or as sister or brother (whether half or full).

Specific relationships based on marriage relations (in-laws) create another permanent bar to marriage: for example, the mother of a wife, the wife of a father or grandfather if divorced by her husband, or the former wife of a son. Thus, a father cannot marry the former wife of his son, and a son cannot marry the former wife of his father. It is permissible, however, to marry the former wife of a brother.

Five situations pose a *temporary* bar to marriage. A man cannot marry, for instance, a married woman during her waiting period (*idda*)[47] after divorce or the death of her husband, but he can marry her once the waiting period ends. A Muslim man can marry a woman who is a believer in what Sharia accepts as divine scripture, mainly the Bible. Thus a Muslim man can marry a Christian or Jewish woman (known as People of the Book), but not, for example, a Buddhist. A Muslim woman can marry only a Muslim man. Marriage is permitted, however, once the religious barrier ends (e.g., a Christian man converts to Islam). It could be argued that the possibility of marrying a Christian or a Jew should be open to a Muslim woman as it is open to a Muslim man, but that is not the accepted view of Sharia at present, though it may happen in practice.[48]

The consequences of marriage include the following:

- The wife is entitled to the dower gift (*mahr*), according to the terms agreed upon with the husband or, if necessary, decreed by court or arbitration. If no amount was agreed upon, each school of Islamic jurisprudence has rules for determining the amount and conditions for its payment to the wife. This gift is the exclusive personal property of the wife, and she is not required to spend any of it on maintaining the household.
- Each spouse is entitled to inherit from the estate of the other upon the spouse's death, according to the applicable rules of inheritance.
- The wife is entitled to maintenance (food, shelter, clothing, and other material support) by the husband, without spending any of her own money or property. In exchange, the husband is entitled to obedience by his wife. These mutual obligations are interdependent, so that the husband is not entitled to obedience if he fails to provide appropriate maintenance, and the wife is not entitled to maintenance if she refuses to be obedient to the husband.

Termination of Marriage

The phrase "termination of marriage" is used here to refer to the variety of ways in which a marriage can end, some of which do not fit the modern notion of "divorce." As a general rule, but subject to many significant disagreements among schools and scholars of Islamic jurisprudence on various aspects of this process, a marriage can be terminated in any of the following ways:

1. Unilateral repudiation by the husband (*talaq*).
2. Repudiation by the wife (*talaq*) under delegation by the husband. In other words, the husband delegates to his wife the power to repudiate her husband unilaterally. This is called *talaq al-tafwid*. Once a husband has given such delegation to his wife, he cannot revoke the authorization unilaterally; and if *talaq* is exercised by the wife, meaning she repudiates her husband, that *talaq* constitutes a final termination of the marriage.
3. Mutual agreement on termination of marriage, upon payment of compensation by the wife to the husband.
4. Judicial decree, which can be based on a range of grounds; for example, annulment (called *faskh*, *tafriq*, or *tatliq*) for legal reasons such as defects in the contract, lack of social compatibility (*kafaa*) between the spouses,

inadequacy of dowry (*mahr*), or a legal cause, such as physical harm, incompatibility of the spouses, or failure of the husband to provide maintenance.

Repudiation by the husband (*talaq*) is first effected as a tentative termination of marriage that can be revoked by the husband unilaterally (without a new contract or payment of dower) within a three-month waiting period (*idda*), but becomes final after that time. Final termination of a marriage can be either "minor" (where remarriage is possible with a new contract) or "major" (where remarriage is not possible, unless the woman marries another man and that marriage is terminated in the normal course of events).

The finality and consequences of judicial termination of marriage vary under different schools of Islamic jurisprudence. Under the Maliki school, for instance, judicial termination due to the husband's failure to provide for his wife results in a revocable termination (the marriage can be resumed without a new contract) during the *idda* period, once the husband's ability to provide for his wife is established. In the Shafii and Hanbali schools, this same situation results in minor finality. The Hanafi school does not permit judicial termination for the husband's failure to provide, so the marriage continues and the husband remains financially responsible for the amount due to the wife. This debt can be executed against the husband's property or, if the husband lacks financial means to pay, he can be sent to prison.

Child Custody and Family Maintenance

In Islamic law, paternity of children is established through the application of several principles. There is a very strong but rebuttable presumption that a child is the legitimate offspring of the marriage, if the apparent parents were married at the time of conception of the child. If the presumption of legitimacy is totally untenable, for example, if the spouses could not have had intercourse within a time frame that permits the possibility of pregnancy, the father may still claim the child as the offspring of the marriage. If a child cannot be deemed the offspring of a valid marriage, then the child is deemed to be illegitimate. In that case, the child can be identified only by his or her mother, alone. The stigma of illegitimacy is normally severe in Islamic societies, but if the mother becomes the only "lawful" parent, she will have all the rights of the father.

Under traditional Islamic family law, the modern legal concept of custody does not exist. Instead, there are two types of child/parent relationships:

1. Material care for the child (*hadana*), which is presumed to belong to the mother from birth up to a specific age, as determined by each school (e.g., age seven for boys and age nine for girls, according to some scholars). After the specified age, the material care of the child shifts to the father.

2. The moral well-being of the child and supervision over his or her property and financial affairs (*wilaya*) always belongs to the father, even while the child is still under the material care (*hadana*) of the mother. The fact that the father has the authority to supervise (*wilaya*) the property and financial affairs of the child, however, does not affect the legal capacity (*ahliya*) of the child to make contracts, dispose of property, and so on. Legal capacity is governed by another set of presumptions according to the child's age progression, from a passive capacity to have inheritance or gifts before birth, to a limited capacity from birth to full capacity at puberty.

Again, we should recall that there are many differences of opinion on these matters among various schools of Islamic jurisprudence.

Besides the obligations of the husband/father for the maintenance of his wife and children, Islamic law also sets maintenance obligations among members of the wider family and other relatives. This obligation depends on such factors as degree of relationship and material status of relatives, whereby the obligation is most strongly owed to parents and destitute relatives and is weakest for distant relatives or those who have no urgent need for assistance. Whether or not the state provides legal remedies for failure to provide extended family support, the obligation under Islamic law remains binding.

As this brief review shows, most principles of Islamic family law are reasonable and humane, except the few but serious elements of discrimination against women. Those elements are normally minimized in practice through preference of some views over others within the various schools, and through selective borrowing (*takhayur*) from among those schools. As we will see later regarding the enforcement of *mahr* agreements as regular contracts, some aspects of Islamic family law can be applied by American courts when those elements are consistent with relevant state or federal law and public policy. Of course, such application may take place only as a matter of secular law, which will never be as a matter of Sharia as such.

This possibility might be acceptable regarding the contractual nature of marriage and its consequences, where the outcome is simply American law of contract. It would be totally unacceptable to American courts to terminate a marriage through unilateral repudiation by the husband or the exclusive right of a Muslim husband to the custody of children. Yet perceptions of Sharia and "country of origin" cultural practices among immigrant Muslims may create serious tensions with American law. The problem regarding a religious versus a civil end of marriage is familiar from the Jewish principle of *get*, whereby a Jewish wife may be divorced as a matter of civil law and remain married as a matter of Jewish law.

Custody of Children in American Law

Family law in the United States is almost entirely governed by states (*Sosna v. Iowa,* 419 U.S. 393, 404, 1975). There are also a few relevant federal statutes and uniform acts, proposed by the Uniform Law Commission (ULC), that reflect national thinking in the field and trends toward uniformity. Section 3 of the federal *Defense of Marriage Act* (DOMA) provides that "in determining the meaning of any Act of Congress…the word 'marriage' means only a legal union between *one man and one woman* as husband and wife."[49] This definition of marriage does not describe polygamy, so if any state were to recognize a polygamous marriage, that union would not be considered a marriage for federal purposes (1 U.S.C. § 7). Among draft bills proposed by the ULC is the Uniform Premarital Agreement Act (UPAA), which has been adopted by more than twenty states. According to the Defense of Marriage Act, "UPAA is designed to permit people contemplating marriage to arrange for their property according to their exact desires, provided that the agreement is entered fairly and with full understanding of its contents."[50] This legislation also establishes guidelines as to when agreements are unenforceable, and it eliminates the normal requirement of consideration for a binding contract. It also can be applied to *mahr* agreements as prenuptial agreements.[51]

The federal Uniform Child Custody and Jurisdiction Act (UCCJA) was proposed by the ULC in 1968 and subsequently enacted in all fifty states, the District of Columbia, and the Virgin Islands. In response to some criticism of that act, the ULC proposed the Uniform Child Custody Jurisdiction and Enforcement Act (UCCJEA) in 1997. The UCCJEA has been passed in forty-nine states, the District of Columbia, and the Virgin Islands.[52]

While family law is governed almost exclusively by states, some constitutional protections prevent states from legislating in certain areas regarding the family. For example, substantive due process protection under the Fifth and Fourteenth Amendments is related mostly to privacy issues, including the right to marry, the right to reproduce, and the right to rear one's children. *Parents have a fundamental right to direct their children's upbringing and education.* In *Pierce v. Society of Sisters* (268 U.S. 510, 1925), the Court considered an Oregon law that required "every parent, guardian, or other person having control or charge or custody of a child between 8 and 16 years to send him 'to a public school for the period of time a public school shall be held during the current year' in the district where the child resides; and failure so to do is declared a misdemeanor" (*Pierce v. Society of Sisters,* 268 U.S. 510, 530, 1925). The Court found this law to be a violation of the Due Process Clause of the Fourteenth Amendment, because it violated the right of parents to raise their children.

Individuals have a fundamental right to marry. In *Zablocki v. Redhail* (434 U.S. 374, 1978), a Wisconsin man was denied a license to marry, on the grounds that he owed a significant amount of money in child support. The court claimed that "The Constitution does not specifically mention freedom to marry, but it is settled that the 'liberty' protected by the Due Process Clause of the Fourteenth Amendment embraces more than those freedoms expressly enumerated in the Bill of Rights....And the decisions of this Court have made clear that freedom of personal choice in matters of marriage and family life is one of the liberties so protected" (*Zablocki v. Redhail,* 434 U.S. 374, 392–393, 1978). A state can still impede the right of its citizens to marry, but only when those regulations can survive strict scrutiny, because they are interfering with a fundamental right.

Families have a fundamental right to live together. In *Moore v. City of East Cleveland* (431 U.S. 494, 1977), an extended family was prohibited from living together by a local zoning ordinance. The Court held this ordinance unconstitutional, claiming that "the Constitution prevents East Cleveland from standardizing its children and its adults by forcing all to live in certain narrowly defined family patterns" (*Moore v. City of East Cleveland,* 431 U.S. 494, 506, 1977).

This last right—for an extended family to live together—might be helpful for immigrant Muslims who tend to have this cultural tradition, along with the right to direct the upbringing and education of their children. The right to marry and the general prohibition of discrimination, however, are at odds with the principle of Islamic law that bars marriage on grounds of religion, in addition to discrimination against Muslim women in this regard.

With fifty state family law systems, it is not possible to review them here, or to compare any of them to the wide range of Islamic family law views regarding custody of children. Instead, my limited objective for now is to illustrate the sort of tension that might arise between American law and religious/ cultural understandings of gender relations and parenting of children among some American Muslims.

Granted that the law of the state and relevant federal law will be applied by the courts and social services, as should be the case, what does that mean to

Muslims and their children? What are the religious and sociological implications of American custody law for American Muslims, in the long run?

Factors in Determining Custody

As an example, here are the main principles that apply to the custody law of the State of Georgia, of which I am a citizen. The relevant provision of the Georgia Code can be summarized as follows:[53]

In all cases in which the custody of any child is at issue between the parents, there shall be no *prima-facie* right to the custody of the child in the father or mother. There shall be no presumption in favor of any particular form of custody, legal or physical, nor in favor of either parent...the judge...may grant sole custody, joint custody, joint legal custody, or joint physical custody as appropriate.

The judge may take into consideration all the circumstances of the case,... in determining to whom custody of the child should be awarded. The duty of the judge in all such cases shall be to exercise discretion to look to and determine solely what is for *the best interest of the child* and what will best promote the child's welfare and happiness and to make his or her award accordingly.

In determining the best interest of the child, the judge may consider any relevant factor including, but not limited to:

- the love, affection, bonding, and emotional ties existing between each parent and the child; the capacity and disposition of each parent to give the child love, affection, and guidance and to continue the education and rearing of the child;
- each parent's knowledge of and familiarity with the child and the child's needs;
- the capacity and disposition of each parent to provide the child with food, clothing, medical care, day-to-day needs, and other necessary basic care, with consideration made for the potential payment of child support by the other parent;
- the stability of the family unit of each of the parents and the presence or absence of each parent's support systems within the community to benefit the child;
- the mental and physical health of each parent;
- each parent's employment schedule and the related flexibility or limitations, if any, of a parent to care for the child;
- each parent's past performance and relative abilities for future performance of parenting responsibilities.

Islamic Family Law in Communities and before American Courts

The strategy I am proposing is that Islamic family law be practiced in communities according to shared understandings of Sharia, as it has been through the centuries. There is nothing new or unusual about this strategy, because it is happening continually in all communities and at different levels. Marital arrangements, divorce settlements, and disputes over property and custody of children are always negotiated and mediated within families and communities. People do not rush into litigation until they are convinced that they have exhausted other possibilities. This tendency is not surprising, because litigation is expensive, emotionally draining, and socially costly. Going to court is also contingent on having a legal cause of action, and it is always risky, as one may lose.

Still, I am proposing community-based practice not as a proactive strategy of religious self-determination, but rather as simply an inevitable reality. In this light, I propose that community-based practice should be made subject to two major and complex caveats.

First, it must respect the fundamental rights of all concerned, and be fully and truly consensual. Since it is unconstitutional in the United States for state courts to coercively enforce the outcome of mediation and arbitration in communal settings, parties must comply voluntarily with such outcomes. Compliance is unlikely to happen unless the process is entirely voluntary, but that requirement is difficult to verify, because persuasion and coercion often overlap in subtle ways.

Second, the above requirements, and also the substantive norms upon which mediation and arbitration are conducted, must be legitimized and supported by an internal Islamic discourse. In particular, discrimination against women and the general patriarchal framework that upholds traditional interpretations of Sharia must be eliminated on the basis of Islamic arguments. Otherwise, the system cannot be legitimate. I have discussed elsewhere the approach and methodology that I find most promising for achieving these objectives, but I am willing to accept an alternative methodology that can achieve the same objectives.

These principles are already familiar and authoritative in the United States in relation to Jewish family law, especially in the State of New York. In *Avitzur v. Avitzur* (58 N.Y.2d. 108, N.Y 1983), for instance, a husband and wife were granted a civil divorce. Since they had married according to Jewish law, in addition to their civil marriage under the laws of the State of New York, they had originally signed a *ketubah* in which the husband promised to grant his wife a religious divorce (*get*). Otherwise, the couple would remain married under Jewish law and the woman could not remarry. But the husband refused to follow through, and the woman was left in a state of marital limbo. The New York Court of Appeals ordered the husband to grant his wife the *get*, as he had agreed in his pre-marriage agreement. This was not an impermissible entanglement between religion and state, because the *ketubah* acts as a secular contract to which the defendant must adhere. The outcome of this case was later codified in New York Domestic Relations Law, Article 13, §253, Removal of Barriers to Remarriage, of 1992 (N.Y. Dom. Rel. Law §253, McKinney).

An example involving Muslim parties is *Odatalla v. Odatalla* (810 A.2d 93, Ch.Div. 2002), where a Muslim couple seeking a divorce disputed whether their *mahr* agreement was enforceable in New Jersey court. The husband in this case had agreed to $10,000 deferred *mahr* and argued that it was unenforceable. The New Jersey Superior Court disagreed, claiming: "It is this court's opinion that it can specifically enforce the terms of a Mahr Agreement provided it meets certain conditions. The first requirement is that the agreement can be enforced based upon 'neutral principles of law' and not on religious policy or theories. The 'neutral principles of law' approach was clearly explained in *Jones v. Wolf*" (*Odatalla v. Odatalla*, 810 A.2d 93, 95–96, 9ch.Div. 2002). "Furthermore, the Mahr Agreement is not void simply because it was entered into during an Islamic ceremony of marriage. Rather, enforcement of the secular parts of a written agreement is consistent with the constitutional mandate for a 'free exercise' of religious beliefs, no matter how diverse they may be. If this Court can apply 'neutral principles of law' to the enforcement of a Mahr Agreement, though religious in appearance, then the Mahr Agreement survives any constitutional implications" (*Odatalla v. Odatalla*, 810 A.2d 93, 96–97, Ch.Div. 2002). The court enforced the *mahr* agreement and awarded the wife the $10,000, claiming "the Mahr Agreement in the case at bar is nothing more and nothing less than a simple contract between two consenting adults" (*Odatalla v. Odatalla*, 810 A.2d 93, 98, Ch.Div. 2002).

This approach, however, is not always available to or clear for an American court to apply.[54] *In re Marriage of Shaban* (88 Cal. App. 4th 398 Cal. App. 4th Dist. 2001), for instance, a former husband tried to enforce a *mahr* agreement as if it were a prenuptial agreement. This *mahr* agreement also stated that the parties intended their marriage to be governed by Islamic law. The husband attempted to use an expert witness to clarify the meaning of the *mahr* agreement. The court would not accept this witness, claiming that "[a]n agreement whose only substantive term in any language is that the marriage has been made in accordance with 'Islamic law' is hopelessly uncertain as to its terms and conditions. Had the trial judge allowed the expert to testify, the expert in effect would have written a contract for the parties" (*In re Marriage of Shaban*, 88 Cal. App. 4th 398, Cal. App. 4th Dist. 2001).

Regardless of whether a state recognizes an Islamic marriage, it typically will recognize a marriage and/or divorce if it is valid in the jurisdiction where the marriage was performed.[55] "Divorce by *talaq* carries no weight in U.S. courts on its own; however, in most cases, American courts uphold such divorces when they are obtained abroad, so long as certain other procedural requirements are satisfied."[56] Some Muslim men have tried to take advantage of this system by traveling to countries where *talaq* is allowed, so they can perform *talaq* on their wives and have the divorce recognized by American courts. These attempts, however, have not been successful: "American courts have uniformly refused to recognize such opportunistic *talaqs*, holding that to do so would violate state and federal constitutional provisions of equal protection and due process."[57]

The issue of state courts' enforcement of religious arbitration awards became controversial in Canada. In 2003, the Islamic Institute of Civil Justice, a small Muslim organization in Ontario, Canada, proposed offering arbitration for private businesses and family matters in accordance with both Islamic legal principles and Ontario's Arbitration Act of 1991. The Ontario Arbitration Act of 1991 allowed for religious, as well as nonreligious, arbitration in private matters. Since the act came into effect in 1992, Jewish and Christian groups set up arbitration boards that ruled in accordance with their religious principles. These arbitrations were legally binding, as long as they did not violate existing Canadian law.[58]

This proposal resulted in an intense debate on the introduction of "Sharia law" in Ontario. Numerous interest groups in the community perceived Sharia as threatening to equality for women and expressed the fear that women would be unable to address unfair decisions made by religious rulings. Amendments to the Arbitration Act were proposed, focusing on institutionalized oversight and education on the principles of religious arbitration and Canadian family law. The proposed amendments were ignored, however, and the debate finally ended early in 2006, when the provincial premier amended the Ontario Arbitration Act to disallow all forms of religious arbitration.

Following this controversy, Julie Macfarlane conducted in-depth interviews with Muslim scholars, community leaders, social workers, and divorced men and women throughout the United States and Canada. Approximately

75 percent of the data collected is from respondents in the United States, while 25 percent is from Canadian respondents.[59]

Before reviewing some of the findings of this study, it should first be emphasized that "neither Islamic marriage nor divorce has any legal effect in North America. A marriage license and a civil legal decree are required to be legally effective. Otherwise the actions are forms of private ordering which have no formal legal status."[60] Any discussion or examination of "Islamic" marriage, divorce, and related issues in the United States and Canada would be only as a matter of cultural and social practice that may be extremely important for the community of Muslims to maintain, but has no legal significance from the state's point of view.

We should also distinguish between Islamic family law within the United States and questions of recognition and enforcement of foreign legal actions. The latter is usually referred to as matter of conflict of laws (or private international law), to be accepted by American courts as a matter of comity between nations, or in reciprocity. In such cases, the legal issue is about the status of foreign law and judgments, regardless of whether that law is religious, customary, or secular.

For our purposes, the question is about the status of Islamic family law when applied to events happening within any of the jurisdictions of the United States, or among parties who are subject to those jurisdictions. When we frame the issue in those specific terms, we find that the important difference between American and Islamic family law is that the latter "has no concept of matrimonial property, a very different approach to spousal support after divorce, and different traditions regarding child support."[61]

The principles of Islamic marriage and divorce are refracted through the judgments of the imams who, in practice, substitute for Islamic judges in North America. The imams are highly pragmatic in the application of Islamic law principles, adapting them to many different circumstances.[62]

Macfarlane found a persistent problem in the Muslim community: some Muslim men appear to believe that *mahr* is merely symbolic. Despite the fact that it is written in the marriage contract (*nikah*), they may refuse to pay it. They may regard it as a part of ritual, without moral or legal meaning. This reluctance to keep the promise made is exacerbated by the approach of the courts in the United States and Canada, which historically have been reluctant to enforce the *mahr*, deeming the *nikah* a contract for a religious purpose and therefore—unlike a prenuptial agreement—unenforceable. This approach has led some imams to develop *nikah* worded so as to minimize the religious aspects of the ceremony and to emphasize instead its contractual nature.

In North America, sympathetic imams will offer, as a practical matter, to approve divorce for women in situations where a woman cannot secure the permission of her husband, often describing this as *khula* (divorce initiated by the woman). Although imams are not judges, they are trying to help women who are caught in "limping marriages" with husbands who refuse to participate in discussion of divorce. The only other option would be to send the woman to a Muslim country and get a judge to annul her marriage. In Macfarlane's view, the emergence of regional panels of imams who will consider and award annulments is a sign of movement away from ad hoc decision-making by individual imams and toward a more structured form of extrajudicial annulment.[63]

Macfarlane calls for premarital counseling in the development of the marriage contract, to check the rising level of marital breakdown within the Muslim community. As a result, a network of resources has aimed to promote and assist with premarital counseling, both in the development of the *nikah* and in other shared understandings between the couple. For instance, in 2008 the Healthy Marriage Initiative introduced the Healthy Marriage Community Covenant, asking imams to commit to at least three sessions of premarital counseling with a couple before conducting a *nikah*.[64]

The influence of the imams, especially where there is little extended family to assist, is extremely important in settling the expectations for the consequences of divorce. It is also interesting to note that some imams explicitly encourage divorcing couples to adopt a civil law framework. Another indication of the imams' tendency to work within the family law system of the state is that when they are advising Muslim parties on the appropriate level of payment, they use the child support guidelines of the state where they live. In a few cases, shared custody of children was negotiated, despite the fact that there is no provision for shared custody under Islamic law. Macfarlane's study clearly confirms that divorcing couples can reach agreement that blends Islamic and civil law outcomes.[65]

The areas of contention in studies like Macfarlane's relate to several factors: the legal standing of Islamic marriage and divorce in North America; recognition of agreements reached between spouses in relation to either marriage or divorce; and the recognition of marriages and divorces that take place in a Muslim country.

Normally there is no difficulty in recognizing a marriage that is legal under foreign law. In divorce situations, where the wife and/or children live in the United States, American courts may be called upon to resolve disputes about matters such as division of property and child support. In these cases,

American courts may apply the principle of "comity" to recognize as legal a procedure conducted according to rules of another jurisdiction.[66]

It is not uncommon for American Muslim spouses, when one or both persons live in the United States, to seek an overseas divorce from a Muslim court. Around 10 percent of the divorces Macfarlane describes took this route. In the majority of the divorce cases in Macfarlane's study, Islamic divorce was sought in addition to—not as a substitute for—civil divorce.

A number of jurisdictions in Canada and courts in the United States recognize the outcomes of religious arbitrations, such as those conducted by the Jewish Bet Din and by Christian ecclesiastical courts. In the United States, the Federal Arbitration Act (FAA) recognizes and enforces the outcomes of religious arbitration. Some states incorporate FAA provisions into their law or provide their own process of empowering the courts to both review and enforce the outcome of a family dispute that is freely and voluntarily referred to private arbitration, using an agreed-upon set of principles (e.g., New York and Florida).[67]

Do Muslims want Sharia law imposed in North America? Many assume that as the Muslim population has expanded, so has the call for implementation of Sharia in North America. In fact, however, Macfarlane's study as well as public statements by Muslim leaders reveal virtually no interest in or support for the formal, legal recognition of family law.

Muslims, Macfarlane found, understand that their private choices of Muslim marriage and divorce processes are separate from the formal legal system. None of her 212 respondents—including imams, legal scholars, Muslim lawyers, and others working in the legal system—suggested that the courts should directly apply Islamic law to Muslims (or non-Muslims).

Only three out of forty-two imams and others interviewed by Macfarlane expressed a desire for a separate, legally competent, Islamic tribunal. Here is the majority belief, as she reports it:

> Canadian [or U.S.] civil courts are not a part of Islamic beliefs—but as citizens, we have to obey the laws. The Canadian [or U.S.] laws always override the Sharia....Several imams spoke out against the idea of a separate Islamic tribunal system, arguing that the goal should be integration, not competing systems. One imam pointed out the importance of maintaining the same standards for all: "It would be better to integrate elements of Islamic family law into the court system than to have a separate Sharia court...this would be safer for both men and women... however, the court system needs...to accommodate the needs of the Muslim community."[68]

Macfarlane also concluded that North American Muslims' use of the secular legal system for registering marriage, decreeing civil divorces, and resorting to court for contentious matters clearly shows that seeking an Islamic marriage or divorce in addition to a secular civil one does not reflect an antagonism toward local laws and norms: "Using *nikah* for marriage or an imam for divorce does not mean that these men and women are rejecting the state legal system, but that they are supplementing it with their own customs and traditions."[69] American Muslims are acting in this regard in the exact manner as Christians do when they have a "church wedding."

As with other chapters in this book, the preceding review of the legal environment within which American Muslims can exercise their religious self-determination is not intended to be exhaustive. The purpose of this chapter is to present an overview of some of the possibilities and experiences of American citizens and their communities, without being prescriptive or inhibiting of what American Muslims can do. Moreover, it is not for me, of course, to try to prescribe or predict the outcome of the processes (in the plural) of religious self-determination, which I see as necessarily emerging out of the activities of Muslims in their communities and in their relationships to other communities.

In accordance with this approach, the final chapter of this book will be confined to a summary and reflections on the main themes and insights presented in the book as a whole. As an American Muslim, I prefer to see the answer to the question "What is an American Muslim?" as a constant work in progress, to which all self-identifying Muslims will contribute, over time.

5

Imagined and Re-Imagined Communities: Looking Forward

AS I STATED at the beginning of this book, I am *not* concerned here with defending Islam and American Muslims against negative stereotyping or charges of being "un-American." If there is anything a Muslim should do to "defend" Islam, it is to be the best Muslim he or she can be, which is what this book seeks to facilitate. Regarding "Americanness," there is no uniform or monolithic measure of national identity other than citizenship. Every Muslim who is a citizen of the United States already bears the only identity that all Americans share.

As we affirm citizenship, our multiple and overlapping identities will continue to evolve, interact, and cross-fertilize. And the more actively we embrace our citizenship, the more we will be able to contribute to the process of defining what it means to be American. Integral to that contribution is to strive in solidarity with other citizens to secure that sense of national belonging that enables all the other ways of belonging we seek.

While individual autonomy is both the means and end of religious self-determination, all persons affirm and experience their identities in community with others. The multiple and overlapping identities of American Muslims are experienced by persons in their communities, not as isolated, solitary, or detached individuals.

Yet acting as a community carries certain risks. One is that elites may appropriate the collective voice and will of a community. Others include the marginalization of women and the repression of religious and cultural dissidents and members of heterogeneous groups who self-identify as Muslims. But this does not mean that it is possible or desirable to dispense with the communal dimension of our lives. The idea and ideal of community are seductive and susceptible to abuse precisely because community is foundational to our humanity and integral to our religious self-determination.

We are likely to surrender our personal happiness, freedom, and privacy and to sacrifice our material well-being for the sake of our communities, and we tend to accept this exchange as legitimate and fair. A Muslim woman, for instance, may choose to remain single after a civil divorce because she believes herself to be still married under Sharia law and assumes that this is demanded of her by her community. She may be willing to suffer loss without even exploring the possibilities of a legitimate Islamic resolution of her predicament for fear of exposing her family and community to shame or ridicule.

The exploration of possibilities for the reconciliation of the needs and aspirations of individual Muslim women and men with the legitimate interests of their communities is part of what I mean by religious self-determination, as discussed earlier. Although this should be undertaken through internal debate and contestation within communities of Muslims, that should also happen within the broader social and political context of those communities. This multilayered contextual approach calls for the re-imagining of communities, as I will try to clarify here.

It is in this light that we should understand the actual or perceived anxieties of American Muslims about moral disintegration and loss of community. Much of our social and political action is driven by such concerns. The powerful social impulse to avoid moral degradation that undermines our communities shapes gender relations within the family, the socialization of our children, and our choice of leaders, from the local to the national level. American Muslims must critically consider the basis of such anxieties.

What we fear may, in fact, be part of a healthy and necessary process of change and, as such, may be more in the best interest of individuals and their communities than the continuation of the status quo. For instance, when change in our traditional homelands is driven by environmental factors like persistent floods or prolonged drought, or the emergence or decline of some industry or trade, the question should be how best to adapt rather than to stubbornly hold on to old ways that are no longer sustainable. The best adaptation may involve change in gender relations within our families and local communities because women are getting more education and working outside their homes to help support their families.

When we migrate from our traditional homelands to nearby urban centers or foreign lands in pursuit of better economic opportunities or freedom from political violence, our attitudes toward other social and religious communities must adapt accordingly. Otherwise, we would defeat the purpose of our migration, or create more disintegration, both within our communities and outside them. But notions of migration, integration, or disintegration are metaphors that we use for shifts in structural or spatial formations of our social relationships. What I mean by these remarks can apply to varieties of permanent or temporary forms of social and economic mobility, both locally and globally.

Human societies have evolved through such processes of change and adaptation throughout history. To actively participate in this evolution is, I believe, to act in accordance with the Quranic principle of *al-amr bil ma'ruf wa al-nah 'an al-munkar*—enjoining what is right and combating what is wrong.[1] This is a recurring theme in the Quran for identifying who is a Muslim (3:110, 114; 22:41), as well as instructing Muslims in what to do (3:104; 31:17). The meaning and implications of this phrase have been the subject of rich scholarship and reflection throughout Islamic history.[2]

Adapting to change, however, requires maintaining a proper balance of the ends and means of being Muslim, through religious self-determination. This balance must be struck as Muslims "imagine" and "re-imagine" their communities in different contexts, in response to changing socioeconomic relations within our communities and in their relations to other communities. These are difficult and risky processes because the possibilities for the re-imagination of "being Muslim" require us to abandon the security of the anchor of our familiar cultural awareness and social experience. But abandoning the security of familiarity is happening anyway; the question is how to do so intelligently and deliberately.

How Are Communities Imagined and Re-Imagined?

Change is a universal and permanent fact of life. All Americans are changing all the time, as are all Muslims, both individually and communally. The identities that we seek to assert or preserve are changing "as we speak"—even as we attempt to assert or preserve them. By the time we achieve an identity that we have been seeking, it is no longer in the precise state it was when we began seeking it. Therefore, our perception of what an identity is must include ways in which it is changing. And therefore we must ask an essential question: How should we *intend* change to happen to us—in which direction, and to which ends?

Benedict Anderson famously said that nations are imagined communities in which members hold mental images of their affinities, without ever meeting or knowing each other, let alone living in intimate daily relations. The imagination of a nation is premised on exclusive membership and is never inclusive of humanity at large. The nation is also imagined as a community of deep solidarity and fraternity, regardless of the realities of inequality and exploitation.³ However, how the community is imagined does not remain static over time—there is always some degree of re-imagining.

This territorial conception of nationalism is the premise on which the post-colonial "nation-state" rests, though there is much less basis for it in other parts of the world than in Europe, where it originated. I am not concerned here with the imagined nation as such, whether the claim is true or false for all the citizens of a state, or whether the concept is coherent for all parts of the world. My focus is on the usefulness of the concept of imagined community for presenting my argument for the need to *re-imagine* American Muslim communities. Assuming that any community of Muslims is an imagined community, the question for our purposes is what the qualities or values of a community of Muslims are imagined to be, and to what extent there is agreement on this topic among members of a given community.

When we speak of community, we mean a subjectively conceived idea or ideal that is real and necessary for all of us, despite the difficulty of defining, quantifying, or verifying its existence. What each community is imagined to be is within the imagination of each member of that community. My question here is about the values and human relationships that are projected onto the imagined community. For instance, how are gender relations within the family and community perceived? What priority is given to the values of social justice and sharing of political power within the imagined community, and in relation to other communities in the larger polity? I am not suggesting that any community will necessarily live up to what it is imagined to be, but that its ideal form can be invoked in calling for change or reform.

The idea of an imagined community can be seen to have persisted throughout Islamic history in the idealized notion of the universal community of Muslims (*umma*). Although that ideal never materialized in terms of statehood—there was never a centralized political authority within a fixed territory governing all Muslims—the myth persisted precisely because of the appeal of the ideal of social and political unity among diverse communities of Muslims. As discussed in chapter 3, it is not possible to speak of a single, monolithic community of American Muslims, neither of African American Muslims, nor of American Muslims of immigrant origins.

To the extent that there are various imagined communities of American Muslims, they should be re-imagined in relation to the Quranic principle of enjoining what is right and combating what is wrong within the American context. This context is the framework within which what is right and wrong can concretely be evaluated. I expect there is already some re-imagining happening among various communities, and my call is for members of each community to more deliberately and strategically pursue values and human relationships that are best suited to their particular context.

What I am proposing is not new or peculiar to Muslims, as re-imagining of communities is integral to their being imagined in the first place. As briefly illustrated in chapter 2, Catholics, Jews, and Mormons have all re-imagined their communities over time. The limited question is how this process might evolve among American Muslims. It is not, of course, for me to prescribe the outcomes, but it is my right and obligation as an American Muslim to contribute to public reflection about the process.

The primary role in the re-imagining of community is that of proactive "agents of social change." By this term I mean those motivated and engaged social actors who take the initiative in seeking to influence the direction of change in favor of individual freedom and social justice, instead of being passive subjects of change; I mean local actors who realize that God's purpose in this life is achieved through the agency of human beings. I am talking here about local actors who live the life of their communities and enjoy their confidence, while remaining open to influence by wider social currents of positive change through the protection of human rights and promotion of cross-cultural cooperation. While the internal, grassroots location of these agents enables them to effect social change, it is their humane consciousness that guides the direction of the change they bring about in their communities.

Muslim Virtual Communities

Another aspect of the concept of imaged community is how, where, and among whom the imagination of community happens. For instance, the idea of *virtual community* has emerged with the growth of the Internet. Assuming that the term "community" in Anderson's sense is appropriate in this context, the relevant question is whether this mode of communing and communicating can be part of the process of re-imagining American Muslim communities. It seems to me that this possibility and its potential contribution to the transformation and adjustments that Muslim communities are experiencing everywhere is relevant to the main question of this book: *What is an American Muslim?* Since there is no possibility of keeping old imagined communities, if we ever had them, what are the parameters of our imagination of communities that an American Muslim can have?

Virtual communities are not actual communities by the literal meaning of the term. A traditional community would require people to "commune," to share and/or compete for space, resources, attention, and identity. Virtual communities are "the social aggregations that emerge from the Net when enough people carry on those public discussions long enough, with sufficient human feeling, to form webs of personal relationships in cyberspace."[4]

This definition is a good starting point because it notes that human feeling is necessary to the formation of a virtual community. A community cannot exist without a social or quasi-social element. Also, the discussions are "public," but the anonymity that the virtual world affords often strains the definition. When virtual communities emerged in the 1990s, it was probably true that they formed by gradual accretion of ideas and participants. With the advent of Facebook, college students were able to form groups based on just about anything that interested them, out of thin air, and conduct conversations based on those affinities. They created a virtual community based on people's desire to have a virtual community, rooted in real-life affinity at first (that is, the school one attended became his or her de facto virtual community) but eventually spreading well beyond the initial boundaries of so-called real life.

A later definition of virtual communities cites "computer-mediated communication (CMC)" that enables people to locate and interact with people with shared interests.[5] Whether those communities come to exist through gradual accretion and conversation, or are produced with the intention of developing a dialogue, the essential characteristic of virtual communities is the digitally mediated nature of the communication. This, of course, affects the speed with which affinities are found and nurtured, as well as the personal human feeling (or lack thereof) that accompanies virtual communities.

Muslim virtual communities are likewise groups of people and/or subgroups, united by common identity, affinity, or interest(s), which are presumably somehow "Muslim" or concerned about being Muslim. They can be ad hoc communities or intentionally designed ones; they can be freestanding or developed within larger communities. It is not possible or necessary to review all the variety of virtual communities that may be affiliated with being Muslim or to discuss whether or how they are relevant. In fact, the inquiry into the "Muslim" qualifier is problematic, as it is bound to lead to questions regarding the criteria of being Muslim and how and by whom those criteria are determined and applied. There are no satisfactory answers to such questions, and no way of verifying their validity, especially in the digital environment.[6]

My limited purpose here is to note the phenomenon and illustrate some of its varieties.

For example, the Center for the Study of Muslim Networks (CSMN) of Duke University is a meta-network that seeks to gather and coordinate among many other subgroups and affinity communities, but it is itself a subgroup of a greater university and academic department of religious studies. CSMN "is located in Durham, North Carolina…but will extend outwards to encompass Islamic networks throughout the world…CSMN will have three broad but complimentary objectives: (1) to rethink Islam by focusing on the role of networks in Muslim societies; (2) to foster inclusive, sustained dialogue between international activists, artists, and scholars of the Muslim world, and their US counterparts; and (3) to expand humanistic engagement with the benefits, as also the pitfalls, of technological appeals to cross-cultural norms and values."[7]

Here one can see that the CSMN is an intentional, subcommunal virtual community that exists under the aegis of Duke and various other universities. There is a clear connection between the virtual community being created and the "real-life" communities that undergird it. Further, this is an intentional community. It has a purpose that is clearly stated, and in this way it can approximate real-life community values and shared visions. Community members can talk among themselves about what it means to be Muslim. They do not merely talk about what it means to be Muslim *online*. Such a topic may arise, but it would not be the point of the community. The CSMN is trying to accomplish something beyond mere conversation among affinity partners. It is a conversation with real-world applications.

A more relevant example of a virtual Muslim community for our purposes here is "Muslim Women Online," a large virtual world wherein Muslim women interact with and support one another. This is an online community that sustains real-world relationships, rather than people projecting virtual online lives, as in the preceding example. Women across the world can find one another through this network with astounding speed and can empathize with one another in very tangible ways. This aspect makes this entity as close to a legitimate community without the communal element as any I have been able to find. The emotion of empathy, the sharing of an identity, and the consistent reflection thereon and building thereof are the pertinent elements that make a virtual community into a real community. There is also "the possibility of transformation of an on-line relation to an off-line relation…'just as community ties that began in-person can be sustained through email, on-line ties can be reinforced and broadened through in-person meetings'…."[8]

The traditional understanding of communities as tied to physical locations is not present in the arena of virtual communities. Rather, the "space" occupied is digital, and the communities develop around interests or affinities. What makes them communal is that they unite individuals around a particular personality identity and not a particular geographic or political identity. The groups may unite around a geographic or political identity as well, but this is true of many online communities.

Virtual communities, in their original formations, did not necessarily "do" anything more than afford opportunities for conversations among people with a unifying interest who are otherwise separated, either physically or socially. As the online world has evolved, intentional virtual communities can and do exist to accomplish goals, which can be either real-world goals or completely digital goals, as in the case of CSMN. CSMN appears to do this through rapid and easy communication among conversation partners who otherwise would never be able to meet and interact.

Since virtual communities lack the physical closeness of real-life communities, communication is essential—it is the substance, the source, and the medium of virtual communities. In the final analysis, however, it is difficult to see how a virtual community can help Muslims achieve religious self-determination and embrace their citizenship without being rooted somehow in a real-life community as well. There may well be virtual communities with governance structures—most have "moderators" who condition conduct based around certain general codes of online conduct, but in general, the democratization of technology prevents great amounts of stratification in virtual communities.

Muslim virtual communities are Muslim because they say they are, and because of the type of communication they foster. Intentional communities like CSMN are founded on some presumably Islamic principles, though some of them may be more inclusive than others in their view of what it means to be Muslim. The online communities of Muslim women are formed because all participants self-identify as Muslim. Their communication will be an outgrowth of these twin identities, which the participants claim to share.

Framework and Context

The short question that is the title of this book can be seen in terms of multiple interacting questions: *What is an American? What is a Muslim? And what is an American Muslim?* Further, it raises another query: *Why ask this question, and why in this particular way?* One may also wonder: *Who is asking, and for what purpose?*

As American Muslims, we are rightly concerned with preserving our Islamic identity through—and not at the expense of—our US citizenship, but we must make certain that whatever identity we seek to preserve should be *worth preserving* according to our own expectations. Religious identity or any other kind of identity is only a means to an overarching end of upholding human dignity and advancing the well-being of the individual person.

In this book I have developed a particular view of religious self-determination for American Muslims, without attempting to impose specific outcomes. I do not claim to be neutral, and neutrality, of course, is not an end in itself. The argument I am trying to advance favors proactive citizenship and rejects the false dichotomy between majority and minority based on any identity (religious identity, in this case). Still, I have not been explicit about my own particular objective for two reasons. First, the analysis and argument presented here is more about a particular attitude and approach to public engagement that allows for the expression and development of a variety of views and positions, instead of seeking to advance my own. Second, since I see my argument as applicable to a range of racial, cultural, and other formations of identity, there are too many factors that I should take into account in arriving at my own view, let alone presuming to speak on behalf of American Muslims at large.

The Major Themes: "Beyond Minority Politics" and Religious Self-Determination

Two main themes drive this book: (1) the need for American Muslims to move "beyond minority politics," and (2) the quest for religious self-determination. Both themes represent intentional choices we must make and responsibilities we must assume in the inevitable process of change. Both themes convey ways in which we can enhance our ability to influence the direction of change; they are also possible outcomes of that process. The work of moving beyond minority politics must engage the "human agency" of those who are the subjects of change. Religious self-determination infuses that change, directing its content and its progress.

Among the many ways in which these two main themes can be examined in relation to American Muslims, I would highlight a few.

First, I have sought to separate the multiple and overlapping identities that different communities of Americans tend to share, on the one hand, from national identity (as indicated by citizenship) on the other. My citizenship, while enabling me to define and assert the identities I choose to have, is not contingent on any of those identities. Yet at the same time, certain conceptions of religious identity can raise tensions that are problematic for citizenship. Islamic identity, for instance, is not inherently problematic for the modern citizenship of a pluralistic democratic state like the United States, but some conceptions of an Islamic identity can be ambivalent about the modern secular state.

Second, I have examined the complex and evolving meaning of citizenship of the United States, with its historically harsh policies of racial exclusion. Because this book places a high value on freedom of religion, I have had to be especially careful to avoid simplistic assumptions about the origins and development of this principle of American pluralism. The struggles of Catholic, Jewish, and Mormon citizens for inclusion and equality in the United States are particularly instructive for Muslims, though each group's evolution from exclusion to inclusion has its own particularities. I have examined the tensions within the concept of religious freedom, and how that concept evolves from myth to the reality of separation between religion and the state, even while they remain politically connected.

Third, I have highlighted the significant variety of American Muslims and their diverse experiences of citizenship, two facets that defy either simple classification or a credible prediction of outcomes. Highlighting some of the tensions within the multiple communities of American Muslims, I have also examined the ambiguities that arise around the practice of religious and secular leadership. My goal was to urge us to confront tendencies of denial and apologia by assuming responsibility for our understanding and practice of Islam—instead of abdicating responsibility in the guise of "defending Islam" against criticism. There is no reason to be apologetic about Islam, a world religion that has sustained numerous civilizations through fifteen centuries of global history. There are many errors, however, that we as Muslims need to correct in our understanding and practice of our religion.

I then discussed the constitutional and legal framework of religious self-determination in relation to traditional interpretations of Sharia. I examined the mediation of tensions between the separation of religion and the state and the rights and obligations of parents regarding children. Further, I highlighted the constitutional and legal resources that are available to American Muslims when they take a more proactive view of their citizenship. I am not suggesting that American Muslims never take such a view; I'm only calling for a more active approach, one that recognizes and internally critiques the theological and sociological tensions within various communities of American Muslims.

Self-determination involves, in all cases, both external and internal factors. For instance, it includes what one makes of her own self-determination as well as what a person needs to do in order to assert that self-determination publicly. "Self-transformation," another facet, involves changing our attitudes and beliefs, our social institutions and habitual behavior—both to exercise self-determination now and to enhance our ability to exercise self-determination in the future. My call for moving "beyond minority politics" looks two ways: we must stop perceiving ourselves as a minority, and we must not accept being so perceived by others. Making this shift in attitude requires an internal exercise of self-determination. Strengthened by that internal exercise, we are better able to resist being perceived as "outsiders."

Many factors contribute to the successful exercise of self-determination, but I am particularly concerned about the part that the human subject must do for herself: what the "self" needs to be and do in order to realize the "determination" it wishes to have. The *subjects* of change must be the ones to determine what this process of self-transformation should entail for them, including the objectives and strategies of self-transformation that will help them engage in the process with strong motivation and conviction. Since means are integral to their ends, and vice versa, determining the priorities and methods of self-transformation is integral to the purpose itself.

The Role of American Law in Religious Self-Determination

American law, of course, does not involve itself in Islamic theology. What it does do is create a space for Muslims to freely debate Islamic reform. It is in fact able to protect the space for free debate precisely because it is constitutionally prevented by the First Amendment of the Constitution of the United States from supporting or opposing any view of religion. American law as such has nothing to say on the exile of Muslim women to small, dark, segregated spaces in mosques. When such discrimination happens in the context of a mosque, the civil authorities—whether at the local, state, or federal level—will not intervene against what might otherwise be unlawful discrimination against women. As stipulated by the Supreme Court of the United States in *Lemon v. Kurtzman* (403 U.S. 602 1971), noted earlier, state authorities should not intervene in matters of doctrine or internal organization of any religious community. It is difficult to think of an alternative way to balance the fundamental right of freedom of religion with the obligation of the state to protect citizens.

For instance, as reported by Margot Badran, a group of Muslim women publicly protested their exclusion from the main prayer space in the major mosque on Massachusetts Avenue in Washington, D.C. The chairman of the board of the mosque called the police, who listened to both sides of the dispute and then supported the right of the board to exclude the Muslim women from that part of the mosque. Badran pointed out to the officer in charge the irony of the refusal of the police to protect these women against discrimination and exclusion from a place of worship on grounds of gender, and so openly under police protection in the nation's capital. The officer responded that the mosque is a private place, and that the board elected by the community of Muslims who pray regularly in that mosque has the right to eject anyone who does not observe the rules set by the board.[9] Similar episodes are reported from all over the United States.[10]

Although state and federal law in the United States does not intervene in disputes over the doctrine or internal organization of a religious community, it does protect the right of Muslim women and their supporters to protest their exclusion from religious spaces. The right of protesters to organize so as to advocate changing the membership of the board of a mosque or religious center is also protected by law. The board of a mosque, for instance, should be representative of the community and should serve the community's interests, as determined by the members of the community at large. If a group of members wishes to change how the board is administering the affairs of the mosque, they should campaign among the community to change membership of the board. This principle of democratic self-governance is necessary for religious self-determination because state officials have neither the competence nor the authority to adjudicate religious disputes among believers.

However, intervention by the state is not the only way to protect women against discrimination. And even if state intervention were constitutionally permissible, it might not be the best or most sustainable means of protection, in any case. When discrimination is deeply rooted in the socialization of children and daily gender relations in social life, the community is unlikely to provide either the political will or material resources needed to secure the dignity of women or their equality to men. Those seeking to influence the way the community should be re-imagined should be able to deploy the theological arguments in favor of equality for women. It is particularly important that advocates of change must not only understand the anxieties of their community, but also be able to incorporate in their strategies effective and culturally sensitive responses. The combination of knowledge, skills, and approaches I am suggesting are represented by those I call advocates of social change.

Re-Imagining American Muslim Communities—A Tentative Contribution

As an American Muslim, my purpose in this book is to contribute to advancing self-transformation among American Muslims at large, and also to help in setting priorities and deploying effective approaches to religious self-determination. The premise of the following tentative proposal for debate is simply that we should question our assumptions among ourselves, and should clarify our arguments before we are caught unprepared for the questions of our children, which are bound to come, probably sooner than we expect.

To begin, I think we should question our assumptions and preconceived notions of what it means to be a Muslim. Let's make a practice of examining more carefully whatever is presented as *the* (in categorical singular terms) Islamic position on any issue, such as the exclusion of women from the main area of worship in mosques or the denial of equality between men and women in family relations. Typically, we take for granted the "accepted" positions that we have held unthinkingly for years. Instead we must learn to ask ourselves: What are the bases of that position?

For instance, on what theological basis, and from what sociological justification, do we deny women access to the main space in mosques, when Muslim men and women are living totally integrated lives all the time? A man and woman may share the same public transport coming to the mosque for the Friday prayers, but when they arrive, the man goes into the main space for prayers and the woman goes to the basement—out of sight, in the house of God!

How can we regulate our family affairs in accordance with an understanding of Sharia that we can live by and defend morally? Why should custody of children, for example, be the exclusive prerogative of fathers (or other male relatives on the father's side upon the death of the father), and never of mothers, regardless of the moral character of either parent? Why should the father, and never the mother, be entrusted with determining all matters of the material and moral upbringing of the child, including control over the financial affairs of a minor child?

All such matters are presumed to be settled once and for all, to be complied with in private, within families and communities, regardless of what state authorities may or may not do. Yet, the premise of this assumption will probably be challenged as more Muslim spouses and parents begin to resort to state courts for relief against what they feel are unjust outcomes of Sharia in family law matters. Increasingly, I expect, Muslim women and men will begin to question how gender relations and the well-being of children are regulated, almost clandestinely, within families and communities. Being raised in a questioning culture and educated in a critical school environment, young Muslims in particular will begin to question the premise of the supremacy of Sharia norms. They will soon begin to ask: How did such norms come to be Sharia in the first place?

For instance, young Muslims will notice the obvious unfairness of the presumption that the custody of children always vests in the father, grandfather, or other male relative of the child, regardless of their competence or suitability in comparison to that of female relatives. Is it true, as their parents seem to accept, that this presumption is immutable as a matter of religious doctrine? How can religious doctrine be so clearly unjust and fail to consider how socioeconomic context and cultural practice are bound to change over time?

My own answer for such questions, for which I believe to be religiously accountable, is that Islamic religious doctrine is historically contextual, a product of human interpretation, and not immutable or divine as such. Accordingly, I would first oppose the application of any Sharia norm as the positive law of the state, as explained in chapter 1. Second, I would oppose the community-based practice of dated human interpretations of Sharia that are no longer appropriate in today's context. As I have argued elsewhere, there is a valid and coherent alternative methodology for the interpretation of Sharia norms today.[11] Let me briefly explain.

Every possible understanding of Sharia is always a human interpretation, and never divine as such. While the Quran and Sunna (Hadith) are the divine sources of Islam according to Muslim belief (which I personally share), the meaning and implementation of these sources for everyday life are always the product of human interpretation and action in a specific historical context. It is simply impossible to know and apply Sharia in this life except through the agency of human beings. Any view of Sharia known to Muslims today, even if unanimously agreed upon, necessarily emerged out of the opinions of human beings about the meaning of the Quran and Sunna, as accepted by many generations of Muslims and the practice of their communities. In other words, the opinions of Muslim scholars became established as binding Sharia norms through the consensus of believers over many centuries, not by the spontaneous decree of a ruler or will of a single group of scholars.

Since it is not possible to verify the validity of any view of Islam independently from competing views among believers, constant debates and discussion are necessary for believers to decide which view they accept. We are
responsible before God only for the views we hold and actions we perform,
and nothing else. It is the accumulation over time of agreements in favor of
one view or another, *not* a declaration of doctrine by some religious institution or group, which claims to establish the authority of some views as "orthodox" among Muslims.

It is simply not possible for any human being or institution to adjudicate
among competing views, or to decide by majority vote, on the religious truth
or fallacy of any view. A parliament or congress can make "secular" state law,
but it cannot establish the Islamic binding authority of a principle or norm.
There is no act or moment when any principle or rule becomes established as
Islamic.

Judgments about what is religiously permissible or prohibited (*halal* or
haram), or what is required or merely permitted (*wajb* or *mubah*) need to
be made by believers. Whatever Sharia norms a Muslim accepts according to
the interpretation he or she accepts—for instance, whether a transaction is
permissible, or is prohibited because it involves impermissible usury (interest on a loan, *riba* in Arabic)—are always determined by believers personally.
State law may prohibit usury as unfair, harmful to the economy, or contrary to
sound social policy, but that prohibition does not constitute the Sharia sin of
usury (*riba*). State legislation must be based on "civic reason," that is, reasons
and processes of reasoning which enable all citizens to debate, accept, or reject
a proposed law or policy without reference to religious belief or lack of it.[12]

There are many issues on which Muslims widely agree. Moreover, since
Muslims are free to choose in all matters of religion, and coercion is rejected
as a matter of principle (see, e.g., verses 2:256; 10:99; and 88:21-22 of the
Quran), those who disagree even on issues on which there is overwhelming
agreement are entitled to their dissent. In fact, the stronger the agreement
among believers on an issue, the more important it is to respect the right to
dissent, because it will be harder to exercise that right against a view that is
widely accepted. Any dissident view is the valid religious position for those
who believe in it, and it may become widely accepted by others if debate is
allowed. Islam started as a dissent from the polytheism of seventh-century
Arabia, and every orthodox view of Islam started as a dissident view in relation to the preexisting dominant belief.

It is also important to note here that the theological and methodologi-
cal aspects of traditional interpretations of Sharia, known as *usul al-fiqh*, were

themselves the product of the same process of human interpretation and consensus-building. The accurate text of the Quran and valid reports of Sunna of the Prophet were the subject of consensus among generations of Muslims. Neither the Quran nor Sunna mentions or defines what came to be known among Muslims as *usul al-fiqh*, which were subsequently established by Muslim scholars during the second and third centuries of Islam.[13] Those generations of Muslim scholars who constructed traditional interpretations of Sharia for their communities were willing to accept religious responsibility for their choices.

The problem today may be that present-day Muslims do not appreciate the human nature of the earlier process and tend to mystify it beyond the possibility of human reconsideration. I agree that contesting established interpretations of Sharia is a serious matter that should not be undertaken lightly, but it is equally problematic to fail to do so when it is necessary. Worrying about misleading oneself or others is a valid concern of honest piety, but it only means that Muslims should try their best to verify the validity and relevance of the sources they are relying on, and the reasonableness and viability of the interpretations they are proposing. We are responsible for trying our best, not for getting the "correct" answer, which human beings can't know for certain in any case. That is why Muslim scholars said that knowledge of Sharia is always "suppositional" (*zaniy*); it is what any Muslim, after careful consideration and reflection, supposes to be true.[14] If generations of Muslims agree, a consensus emerges over one view or another, and it then becomes part of the tradition. But an interpretation is not binding for any Muslim until he or she accepts it as such.

I realize that the process of conformity with religious norms is never that simple and straightforward, and I appreciate that the powerful forces of social conformity are often overwhelming. We are already strongly socialized into accepting established norms of Sharia as immutable, and we risk being ostracized by our own families and immediate community if we oppose those norms. But I also see that it is not possible to abdicate responsibility for what I believe to be Sharia, whether positively by observing it in practice, or negatively by trying to avoid making up my mind about any issue. Failing to take a position on an issue is in fact a position; one does not avoid religious responsibility by remaining undecided or by deferring to the views of others. When I follow the opinions of those I accept as religious leaders, I remain fully responsible for what I accept and act upon, just as those whose views I follow also remain responsible for their views.

It is also important to note that there is no way of abdicating responsibility because we must decide and act on all sorts of ethical and practical issues that continually confront us in our daily lives, whether we like it or not. For instance, the issue of custody of children, raised earlier, is bound to arise within our own families and communities wherever we happen to live, and we will be required to take a position and be responsible for whatever position we take or fail to take. We will have to either accept or question the traditional assumption of male custody and act accordingly, whether by claiming custody for our own children, or resisting the claims of others for that responsibility.

When a dispute concerns the children of other members of our families or community, we must still take a position and defend it openly. This is an integral part of our religious right and obligation to "enjoin what is right and combat what is wrong" (Quran 3:104, 110, 114; 22:41; 31:17), as noted earlier. This is how communities of Muslims are realized and sustained, anywhere in the world, regardless of what the state or the wider society do or fail to do, whether Muslims are the demographic minority or majority of the population.

If the Islamic norm-setting process is to continue to take place by consensus, as has always been the case among Muslims (and I see no alternative to this), then how should that process work today? Who is entitled to participate in such debates, and what value is to be attributed to various views? Since there is no agreed-upon procedure or prior determination of such matters, those who self-identify as Muslim should just express their views, and others who also self-identify as Muslims should debate those views and decide for themselves whether to accept or reject them. There is simply no valid way of vetting who is or is not a Muslim, and no way of telling which is the correct or wrong view on any issue, except through debate and free acceptance or rejection among all those who self-identify as Muslims. This is what I am doing now and for which I am religiously responsible, and I believe that all Muslims who encounter my views should make up their own minds and act accordingly.

Since it is a matter of *persuasion*—and never coercion—then voices that are relatively more persuasive will have more influence on participants in debates than other voices do. But the participants themselves must decide which voice is persuasive and what degree of influence it should have on their thinking. Moreover, popularity is not equivalent to validity of religious views. Religious truth to each believer is what she or he believes it to be; it cannot be the outcome of majority vote or imposition by others.

Clearly, then, the best way of coming to a conclusion on an Islamic view of any subject is through fair and open public debate that enables all self-identifying Muslims to participate and decide for themselves. Whatever position one takes is only the human judgment of that person or group of people, and never an official view of Islam itself as it is known and upheld by God (Quran 43:3 and 4). This process and its safeguards are the fundamental core values of being a citizen of the United States, that is, of the only way to be an American.

I have given some examples in this book of the sorts of challenges that we, American Muslims, should rise to meet, and have briefly presented my own view of how we can do that by exercising our religious self-determination. Our citizenship in the United States protects our right to freely debate any issues we wish, but it cannot do that for us. Whatever one believes the United States to be, whether good or bad, no one can deny that freedoms of religion, belief, and expression are constitutionally, legally, politically, and, most important, culturally protected in this country. The cultural foundation is the most important for these and all other freedoms enjoyed by the citizens of the United States because that is where the constitutional, legal, and political bases are founded and secured.

To conclude, an American Muslim is a citizen of the United States who happens to be a Muslim, as she or he may happen to be a Christian, Jew, Hindu, or an adherent of any religion or belief. This is not to imply a hierarchy of political identity over religious faith, but simply a matter of context. There is no competition or incompatibility between religious identity and citizenship, like being American and Muslim or Muslim and American, as the context indicates. If the context is religious, then the person may be a Muslim (or of other religion or belief) who happens to be a citizen of the United States. There is only interdependence and mutual support between religion and citizenship, especially in the United States through centuries of constitutional jurisprudence and politics of the First Amendment. Asserting my American citizenship entitles and enables me to exercise my religious self-determination as a Muslim, which in turn leads me to uphold the values of justice and equality on which my citizenship must be founded. This is also an integral part of my religious right and an obligation to "enjoin what is right and combat what is wrong," noted earlier. For that I am calling on all American Muslims to embrace faith and citizenship.

Notes

CHAPTER 1

1. The Charter of Medina refers to a series of agreements drafted by the Prophet to regulate peaceful coexistence and relationships among all of the significant tribes and clans of Medina (Yathrib) including Muslims, Jews, Christians, and pagans. Serjeant, R. B., "Sunnah Jami'ah, Pacts with the Yathrib Jews, and the Taḥrīm of Yathrib: Analysis and Translation of the Documents Comprised in the So-called 'Constitution of Medina,'" *Bulletin of the School of Oriental and African Studies* 41 (1978): 1–42; Yildirim, Yetkin, "Peace and Conflict Resolution in the Medina Charter," *Peace Review* 18, no. 1 (2006).

    I am not suggesting that those documents collectively known as the Charter of Medina were a "constitution" or that they provided "citizenship" in the modern sense of these concepts. Still, I do believe that the terms of those agreements were the historically contextual equivalent of a constitution and citizenship in the modern context. Consider that the Magna Carta of 1215 and English Bill of Rights of 1689 are the basis of the unwritten conventions that constitute the constitution of the United Kingdom today.

2. An-Na'im, Abdullahi Ahmed, *Islam and the Secular State: Negotiating the Future of Sharia.* Cambridge, MA: Harvard University Press, 2008, 1.

3. Abraham, Margaret, Esther Ngan-ling Chow, Laura Maratou-Alipranti, and Evangelia Tastsoglou, "Rethinking Citizenship with Women in Focus," in Abraham, Margaret, Esther Ngan-ling Chow, Laura Maratou-Alipranti, and Evangelia Tastsoglou, eds. *Contours of Citizenship: Women, Diversity and Practices of Citizenship.* Farnham, UK, and Burlington, VT: Ashgate Publishing, 2010, 1–21, at 12.

4. Spivak, Gayatri Chakravorty, *Can the Subaltern Speak? Reflections on the History of an Idea.* Edited by Rosalind C. Morris. New York: Columbia University Press, 2010; Burman, Erica, "Experience, Identities and Alliances: Jewish Feminism and

Feminist Psychology." In *Shifting Identities Shifting Racisms: A Feminism and Psychology Reader*, edited by Kum-Kum Bhavnani and Ann Phoenix, 155–178. London: Sage Publications, 1994; Essed, Philomena, "Contradictory Positions, Ambivalent Perceptions: A Case Study of a Black Woman Entrepreneur." In *Shifting Identities Shifting Racisms: A Feminism and Psychology Reader*, edited by Kum-Kum Bhavnani and Ann Phoenix, 99–118. London: Sage Publications, 1994.

5. Faulks, Keith, *Citizenship*. New York: Routledge Press, 2000; Pocock, J. G. A., "The Ideal of Citizenship since Classical Times," *Queen's Quarterly* 99, no. 1 (1992): 35–55.

6. Faulks 2000, 20; Pocock 1992, 40.

7. Riesenberg, Peter, *Citizenship in the Western Tradition: Plato to Rousseau*. Chapel Hill: University of North Carolina Press, 1992, 99.

8. Wells, Charlotte Catherine, *Law and Citizenship in Early Modern France*. Baltimore: Johns Hopkins University Press, 1995, 80, 103.

9. Faulks 2000, 23–25.

10. *Ibid.*, 32.

11. Kymlicka, Will, and Wayne Norman, "Return of the Citizen: A Survey of Recent Work on Citizenship Theory," *Ethics* 104, no. 2 (1994): 352–381; Marshall, Thomas Humphrey, *Citizenship and Social Class and Other Essays*. Cambridge: Cambridge University Press, 1950.

12. Cairns, Alan C., John C. Courtney, Peter MacKinnon, Hans J. Michelmann, and David E. Smith, eds., *Citizenship, Diversity and Pluralism: Canadian and Comparative Perspectives*. Montreal and London: McGill-Queen's University Press, 1999, 4–21.

13. Reid, Alan, Judith Gill, and Alan Sears, eds., *Globalization, the Nation-State and the Citizen: Dilemmas and Directions for Civics and Citizenship Education*. London: Routledge, 2010, 5–12.

14. Kymlicka, Will, *Multicultural Odysseys: Navigating the New International Politics of Diversity*. Oxford: Oxford University Press, 2007.

15. Modood, Tariq, Anna Triandafyllidou, and Richard Zapata-Barrero, eds., *Multiculturalism, Muslims and Citizenship: A European Approach*. London and New York: Routledge, 2006.

16. Anzulovic, Branimir, *Heavenly Serbia: From Myth to Genocide*. New York: New York University Press, 1999.

17. Ritzer, George F., ed., *Encyclopedia of Social Theory*. London: Sage Publications, 2004, 394–395.

18. Dryzek, John S., and Patrick Dunleavy, *Theories of the Democratic State*. Basingstoke, UK: Palgrave Macmillan, 2009.

19. Chatterjee, Partha, *Empire and Nation: Selected Essays*. New York: Columbia University Press, 2010, 164.

20. Tan, Sor-hoon, ed., *Challenging Citizenship: Group Membership and Cultural Identity in a Global Age*. Burlington, VT: Ashgate Publishing, 2005.

21. See, for example, Human Rights Watch, "France: Renewed Crackdown on Roma," August 10, 2012, at http://www.hrw.org/news/2012/08/10/france-renewed-crackdown-roma.

22. Mansbach, Richard W., and Kirsten L. Taylor, "Identity Politics: Nationalism and Ethnicity." In *Introduction to Global Politics*, edited by Richard W. Mansbach and Kirsten L. Taylor. London and New York: Routledge, 2007, 703–705.

23. Berger, Benjamin L., "The Cultural Limits of Legal Tolerance." In *After Pluralism: Reimagining Religious Engagement*, edited by Courtney Bender and Pamela E. Klassen. New York: Columbia University Press, 2010, 98–123.

24. *Ibid.*

25. *Ibid.*, 110–111.

26. An-Na'im 2008, 1.

27. For instance, the states of Norway and Canada tend to be more oriented toward providing for social services than the United States or most of its constituent states. Although I personally prefer the position of the state of Canada, I accept that the position of the states of the United States can also be legitimate in response to the democratic demands of their citizens.

28. *Ibid.*, 92–101.

29. Gill, Graeme, *The Nature and Development of the Modern State.* New York: Palgrave Macmillan, 2003, 2–4.

30. An-Na'im 2008, 1.

31. Hallaq, Wael, "Can the Shari'ah Be Restored?" In *Islamic Law and the Challenges of Modernity*, edited by Yvonne Y. Haddad and Barbara F. Stowasser, 21–53. Walnut Creek: Altamira Press, 2004.

32. Vikør, Knut S., *Between God and the Sultan: A History of Islamic Law.* Oxford: Oxford University Press, 2005, 141–145.

33. Awwa, Muhammad Salim, *Punishment in Islamic Law; A Comparative Study.* Indianapolis: American Trust Publications, 1982.

34. Chatterjee 2010, 225–226.

35. Jakobsen, Janet R., "Ethics after Pluralism." In *after Pluralism: Reimagining Religious Engagement*, edited by Courtney Bender and Pamela E. Klassen. New York: Columbia University Press, 2010, 32.

36. Tamanaha, Brian, "Understanding Legal Pluralism: Past to Present, Local to Global," *Sydney Law Review* 30 (2007): 375–411, at 391–396.

37. Woodman, Gordon R., "Ideological Combat and Social Observation: Recent Debate about Legal Pluralism, *Journal of Legal Pluralism* 42 (1998): 21–59, at 45.

38. Michaels, Ralf, "The Re-Statement of Non-State Law," *Wayne Law Review* 58 (2005): 1209–1259, at 1222.

39. Tamanaha 2007, 394.

40. An-Na'im Abdullahi Ahmed, "Religious Norms and Family Law: Is It Legal or Normative Pluralism?" *Emory International Law Review* 25, no. 2 (2011): 785–809.

41. An-Na'im 2008, 12–15.

CHAPTER 2

1. Karst, Kenneth L., "Paths to Belonging: The Constitution and Cultural Identity," *North Caroling Law Review* 64 (1986): 306–309.

2. *Ibid.,* 304–305.

3. Pickus, Noah, *True Faith and Allegiance: Immigration and American Civic Nationalism.* Princeton, NJ: Princeton University Press, 2005, 112–123.

4. Karst 1986, 316–318.

5. Bellamy, Richard, *Citizenship: A Very Short Introduction.* Oxford: Oxford University Press, 2008, 17.

6. *Ibid.,* 12.

7. Preuss, Ulrich K., "The Ambiguous Meaning of Citizenship." Paper presented at the Center for Comparative Constitutionalism, University of Chicago Law School, December 1, 2003. Unpublished paper available at http://ccc.uchicago.edu/docs/preuss.pdf, viewed September 6, 2011, 13.

8. *Ibid.,* 14–15.

9. *Ibid.,* 16–17.

10. Schuck, Peter H., "The Reevaluation of American Citizenship," *Yale Law School Faculty Scholarship Series.* Paper 1696 (1997). Viewed May 21, 2012, at http://digitalcommons.law.yale.edu/fss_papers/1696.

11. *Congressional Globe*, 39th Cong., 1st Sess. 144 (1866): 2890–2897.

12. Gerber, David A., and Alan M. Kraut, eds., "Becoming White: Irish Immigration in the Nineteenth Century." In *American Immigration and Ethnicity: A Reader*, 161–168. New York: Palgrave Macmillan, 2005.

13. Aleinikoff, T. Alexander, "Theories of Loss of Citizenship," *Michigan Law Review* 84 (1986): 1471–1503, at 1473–1474.

14. *Ibid.,* 1475–1478.

15. Saito, Natsu Taylor, "Alien and Non-Alien Alike: Citizenship, 'Foreignness,' and Racial Hierarchy in American Law," *Oregon Law Review*, 76 (1997): 261, 262–263.

16. *Ibid.,* 268–271.

17. *Ibid.,* 281.

18. *Ibid.,* 309.

19. Orgad, Liav, and Theodore Ruthizer, "Race, Religion and Nationality in Immigration Selection: 120 Years after the Chinese Exclusion Case," *Constitutional Commentary* 26 (2010): 237–239, 247–248.

20. Faulks, Keith, *Citizenship.* London: Routledge, 2000, 4–7.

21. Karst 1986, 337–338.

22. Jacoby, Susan, *Freethinkers: A History of American Secularism.* New York: Henry Holt, 2004, 26–28.

23. Dreisbach, Daniel L., *Thomas Jefferson and the Wall of Separation Between Church and State.* New York: New York University Press, 2002, 148.

24. Curry, Thomas J., *The First Freedoms: Church and State in America to the Passage of the First Amendment.* Oxford: Oxford University Press, 1986, 195–196.

25. Witte, John, Jr., *Religion and the American Constitutional Experiment: Essential Rights and Liberties.* Boulder: Westview Press, 2000, 96.

26. Lambert, Frank, *The Founding Fathers and the Place of Religion in America.* Princeton: Princeton University Press, 2003, 281.

27. Feldman, Noah, *Divided by God: America's Church-State Problem—And What We Should Do about It.* New York: Farrar, Straus and Giroux, 2005, 59–60.

28. *Ibid.,* 61.

29. *Ibid.,* 62–63.

30. *Ibid.,* 65–66.

31. *Ibid.,* 71–72.

32. *Ibid.,,* 67–68.

33. *Ibid.,* 82.

34. *Ibid.,* 85.

35. Demerath, N. J., III, and Rhys H. Williams, "Separation of Church and State? A Mythical Past and Uncertain Future," *Society* 21, no. 4 (1984): 3–10.

36. Jacoby 2004, 153.

37. Feldman 2005, 145–146.

38. Lienesch, Michael, *In the Beginning: Fundamentalism, the Scopes Trial, and the Making of the Antievolution Movement.* Chapel Hill: University of North Carolina Press, 2007.

39. Witte 2000, 150.

40. Corbett, Michael, and Julia Mitchell Corbett, *Politics and Religion in the United States.* New York: Garland Publishing, 1999, 23.

41. Bellah, Robert N., "Civil Religion in America," *Daedalus* 96, no. 1 (1967): 1–21, 12.

42. Mason, Patrick Q., *The Mormon Menace: Violence and Anti-Mormonism in the Postbellum South.* London: Oxford University Press, 2011, 172.

43. Moore, R. Laurence, *Religious Outsiders and the Making of Americans.* Oxford: Oxford University Press, 1986, 6.

44. *Ibid.,* 19.

45. *Ibid.,* 20.

46. Portes, Alejandro, and Rubén G. Rumbaut, *Immigrant America: A Portrait.* Third Edition, Revised, Expanded, and Updated. Berkeley: University of California Press, 2006, 119.

47. *Ibid.,* 121–124.

48. Glazier, Jack, *Dispersing the Ghetto: The Relocation of Jewish Immigrants across America.* New York: Cornell University Press, 1998, 2.

49. Portes and Rumbaut 2006, 124.

50. Pyle, Ralph E., and James D. Davidson, "The Origins of Religious Stratification in Colonial America," *Journal for the Scientific Study of Religion* 42, no. 1 (2003): 57–75, 60.

51. *Ibid.,* 60–63.

52. Pyne, Tricia T., "The Politics of Identity in Eighteenth-Century British America: Catholic Perceptions of Their Role in Colonial Society," *U.S. Catholic Historian* 15, no. 2 (1997): 1–14.

53. Jenkins, Philip. *The New Anti-Catholicism: The Last Acceptable Prejudice.* Oxford: Oxford University Press, 2003, 23.

54. *Ibid.,* 25.

55. Tumbleson, Raymond D., *Catholicism in the English Protestant Imagination: Nationalism, Religion and Literature 1600–1745.* Cambridge: Cambridge University Press, 1998.

56. Higham, John, *Strangers in the Land: Patterns of American Nativism, 1860–1925.* Piscataway, NJ: Rutgers University Press, 1955.

57. Ignatiev, Noel, *How the Irish Became White.* London: Routledge, 1995.

58. Jenkins 2003, 23.

59. *Ibid.,* 30.

60. Morris, Charles, *American Catholic, the Saints and Sinners Who Built America's Most Powerful Church.* New York: Vintage Books, 1998, 99–111; McLoughlin, Emmett, *American Culture and Catholic Schools.* New York: Lyle Stuart, 1960.

61. Greeley, Andrew M., *The Catholic Experience: An Interpretation of the History of American Catholicism.* Garden City, NY: Doubleday, 1969, 33.

62. Fisher, James Terence, *Communion of Immigrants: A History of Catholics in America.* Oxford: Oxford University Press, 2007, 77.

63. *Ibid.,* 83.

64. Greeley 1969, 34.

65. Jenkins 2003, 31.

66. *New York Times* 1924.

67. Dumenil, Lynn, "The Tribal Twenties: 'Assimilated' Catholics' Response to Anti-Catholicism in the 1920s," *Journal of American Ethnic History* 11, no. 1 (1991): 21.

68. Jenkins 2003, 36.

69. Blanshard, Paul, *American Freedom and Catholic Power.* Boston: Beacon Press, 1958, 125, 79.

70. *Time Magazine* 1983.

71. Greeley 1969, 284.

72. *Ibid.,* 286.

73. Farber, Eli, "America's Earliest Jewish Settlers, 1654–1820." In *The Columbia History of Jews and Judaism in America*, edited by Marc Lee Raphael, 21–46. New York: Columbia University Press, 2008, 24–26.

74. *Ibid.,* 36.

75. *Ibid.,* 37.

76. Ashton, Dianne, "Expanding Jewish Life in America, 1826–1901." In *The Columbia History of Jews and Judaism in America*, edited by Marc Lee Raphael, 47–69. New York: Columbia University Press, 2008, 50.

77. *Ibid.*, 50.

78. *Ibid.*, 51–55.

79. *Ibid.*, 60.

80. Glazier 1998, 6.

81. Goldstein, Eric L., "The Great Wave: Eastern European Jewish Immigration to the United States, 1880-1924." In *The Columbia History of Jews and Judaism in America*, edited by Marc Lee Raphael, 70–92. New York: Columbia University Press, 2008, 70.

82. *Ibid.*

83. *Ibid.*, 76.

84. *Ibid.*, 70–74.

85. Glazier 1998, 94.

86. *Ibid.*, 9.

87. *Ibid.*, 10.

88. *Ibid.*, 33.

89. Philipson, David, "Jews and Industries," *Menorah* 4, no. 1 (1888): 100 at 107.

90. Newman, William M., and Peter L. Halvorson, "An American Diaspora? Patterns of Jewish Population Distribution and Change, 1971–1980," *Review of Religious Research* 31, no. 3 (1990): 186.

91. *Ibid.*, 192.

92. King, Ryan D., and Melissa F. Weiner, "Group Position, Collective Threat, and American Anti-Semitism," *Social Problems* 54, no. 1 (2007): 47–77, 47.

93. Handlin, Oscar, "American Views of Jews at the Opening of the Twentieth Century." In *Anti-Semitism in the United States*. Edited by Leonard Dinnerstein. New York: Holt Rinehart Winston, 1971, 48–57.

94. Glock, Charles Y., "The Churches and Social Change in Twentieth-Century America," *The Annals of the American Academy of Political and Social Science* 527 (1993): 67–83.

95. Prell, Riv-Ellen, "Triumph, Accommodation, and Resistance: American Jewish Life from the End of World War II to the Six-Day War." In *The Columbia History of Jews and Judaism in America*, edited by Marc Lee Raphael, 114–141. New York: Columbia University Press, 2008, 119.

96. *Ibid.*, 121.

97. *Ibid.*, 135.

98. Glock 1993, 73.

99. The Anti-Defamation League website at http://www.adl.org/about-adl/#.UXqg-BsrJKAc. Viewed April 26, 2013.

100. Wenger, Beth S., "Rites of Citizenship: Jewish Celebrations of the Nation." In *The Columbia History of Jews and Judaism in America*, edited by Marc Lee Raphael, 366–384. New York: Columbia University Press, 2008.

101. Albert Vorspan, "Blacks and Jews," in Nat Hentoff, *et al.*, *Black Anti-Semitism and Jewish Racism*. New York: R. W. Baron, 1969, 190–226, 190.

102. Hanks, Maxine, and Jean Kinney Williams, *Mormon Faith in America*. Edited by J. Gordon Melton. New York: Infobase Publishing, 2003, 118.

103. Gordon, Sarah Barringer, "Blasphemy and the Law of Religious Liberty in Nineteenth-Century America," *American Quarterly* 52, no. 4 (2000): 682–719, 706–708.

104. *Ibid.*, 706.

105. Durham, W. Cole, Jr., and Brett G. Scharffs, *Law and Religion: National, International and Comparative Perspectives*. New York: Aspen Publishers, 2010, 207–208.

106. Gordon 2000, 709.

107. Miller 2003, 9–24, 17.

108. Hanks and Williams 2003, 117. The community's success in achieving this goal may be symbolized by the fact that Mitt Romney was the chosen candidate of the Republican Party for the highest elected office of president of the United States in the 2012 general elections. On the other hand, his Mormon faith may have counted against him with some voters.

109. Mauss, Armand L., "Sociological Perspectives on the Mormon Subculture," *Annual Review of Sociology* 10, no. 1 (1984): 437–460, at 440.

110. *Ibid.*, 446.

111. Corbett and Corbett 1999, 106–107.

112. Richey, Russell E., and Donald G. Jones, "The Civil Religion Debate." In *American Religion*, edited by Russell E. Richey and Donald G. Jones, 3–18. New York: Harper & Row, 1974, 3–18.

113. Bellah 1967, 13.

114. Wald, Kenneth, *Religion and Politics in the United States*. New York: St. Martin's Press, 1987, 142.

115. *Ibid.*, 188.

116. Corbett and Corbett 1999, 124–126.

117. Bellah, Robert N., and Phillip E. Hammond, *Varieties of Civil Religion*. San Francisco: Harper & Row, 1980, 8–10.

118. *Ibid.*, 12–13.

119. *Ibid.*, 16–17.

120. Moore 1986, vii–viii.

121. Bellah and Hammond 1980, 141.

122. *Ibid.*, 144.

CHAPTER 3

1. Hurvitz, Nimrod, *The Formation of Hanbalism: Piety into Power*. New York: Routledge Curzon, 2002.

2. McCloud, Aminah Beverly, *African American Islam*. New York: Routledge, 1995.

3. Karim, Jamillah Ashira, "Between Immigrant Islam and Black Liberation: Young Muslims Inherit Global Muslim and African American Legacies," *Muslim World*

95, no. 4 (2005): 497–513; Chande, Abdin, "Islam in the African American Community: Negotiating Between Black Nationalism and Historical Islam," *Islamic Studies* 47, no. 2 (2008): 221–241.

4. Karim 2005.

5. Chande 2008, 227.

6. Berg, Herbert, "Mythmaking in the African American Muslim Context: The Moorish Science Temple, the Nation of Islam, and the American Society of Muslims," *American Academy of Religion* 73, no. 3 (2005): 685–703.

7. McCloud 1995; Turner, Richard Brent, *Islam in the African-American Experience.* Bloomington: Indiana University Press, 2003; Jackson, Sherman A., *Islam and the Blackamerican: Looking toward the Third Resurrection.* Oxford: Oxford University Press, 2005.

8. Smith, Jane I., *Islam in America.* New York: Columbia University Press, 1999, 50–53; Leonard, Karen, "American Muslims and Authority: Competing Discourses in a Non-Muslim State," *Journal of American Ethnic History* 25, no. 1 (2005): 5–6.

9. Peek, Lori, "Becoming Muslim: The Development of a Religious Identity," *Sociology of Religion* 66, no. 3 (2005): 215; Smith 2003, 5–6.

10. Peek 2005, 215.

11. GhaneaBassiri, Kambiz, *A History of Islam in America: From the New World to the New World Order.* New York: Cambridge University Press, 2010, 263, 294; Pew Research Center, "Muslim Americans: Middle Class and Mostly Mainstream." May 22, 2007. Retrieved August 3, 2011. http://pewresearch.org/pubs/483/muslim-americans; 1.

12. Bukhari, Zahid H., "Demography, Identity, Space: Defining American Muslims." In *Muslims in the United States: Demography, Beliefs, Institutions,* edited by Philippa Strum and Danielle Tarantolo, 7–20. Washington, DC: Woodrow Wilson International Center for Scholars, 2003, 7–20.

13. Moore, Kathleen M., "Muslims in the United States: Pluralism under Exceptional Circumstances," *The Annals of the American Academy of Political and Social Sciences* 612, no. 1 (2007): 14–16.

14. Pew Research Center. "Muslim Americans: Middle Class and Mostly Mainstream." May 22, 2007. Retrieved August 3, 2011. http://pewresearch.org/pubs/483/muslim-americans; 12.

15. Pew Research Center. "The Future of the Global Muslim Population: Projections from 2010 to 2030." January 27, 2011. http://www.pewforum.org/Global-Muslim-Population.aspx.

16. Project MAPS 2004: Muslims in the American Public Square and Zogby International. *Muslims in the American Public Square: Shifting Political Winds & Fallout from 9/11. Afghanistan, and Iraq.* Retrieved July 31, 2008. http://www.zogby.com/AmericanMuslims2004.pdf.

17. D'Appollonia, Ariane Chebel, *Frontiers of Fear: Immigration and Insecurity in the United States and Europe.* Ithaca, NY: Cornell University Press, 2012, 175–178.

18. Baghy, Ishan, *A Portrait of Detroit Mosques: Muslim Views on Policy, Politics and Religion*. Clinton Township, MI: Institute for Social Policy and Understanding, 2004.

19. Moore 2007, 122.

20. Pew Research Center. "The Future of the Global Muslim Population: Projections from 2010 to 2030." January 27, 2011. http://www.pewforum.org/Global-Muslim-Population.aspx, 23. Cf. GhaneaBassiri 2010, 296–300.

21. Pew Research Center 2011; Pew Research Center 2007.

22. Pew Research Center 2011, 23–29; Pew Research Center 2007, 20–23.

23. Pew Research Center 2011, 27–28.

24. GhaneaBassiri, 2010, 324–326.

25. Pew Research Center 2007, 26–27.

26. http://www.pluralism.org/research/profiles/display.php?profile=74465.

27. There is no agreed definition of jihad among Muslims, neither historically nor at the present time. Questions about who may exercise *jihad*, against whom, when, and whether by peaceful means or through the use of force, have always been extremely controversial among Muslims. See, for example, Abdullahi Ahmed An-Na'im, "Islamic Ambivalence to Political Violence: Islamic Law and International Terrorism," in Abdullahi Ahmed Ahmed An-Na'im, ed., *Muslims and Global Justice* (Philadelphia: University of Pennsylvania Press, 2011), 35–64, at 51-60. This chapter was first published as an article in *German Yearbook of International Law* 31 (1988): 307–336.

28. Momen, Moojan, *An Introduction to Shi'i Islam: The History and Doctrines of Twelver Shi'ism*. New Haven: Yale University Press, 1987, 176–181.

29. O'Connor, Kathleen Malone, "The Islamic Jesus Messiahhood and Human Divinity in African American Muslim Exegesis," *Journal of the American Academy of Religion* 66, no. 3 (1998): 504.

30. McCloud 1995, 40.

31. Curtis, Edward E., IV, "African American Islamization Reconsidered: Black History Narratives and Muslim Identity," *Journal of the American Academy of Religion* 73, no. 3 (2005): 659.

32. Berg 2005, 688.

33. Curtis 2005, 680.

34. *Ibid.*, 661.

35. Berg 2005, 685–703; Chande 2008, 221–241.

36. Turner, Richard Brent, "What Shall We Call Him? Islam and African American Identity," *The Journal of Religious Thought* 51, no. 1 (1994): 25–53.

37. Aidi, Hishaam, "Jihadis in the Hood: Race, Urban Islam, and the War on Terror," *Middle East Report* 224 (2002): 39–40.

38. Chande 2008, 224.

39. Turner 2003, xxix, and generally xxv–xxx.

40. McCloud 1995, 118.

41. *Ibid.*, 126.

42. *Ibid.*, 167.

43. *Ibid.*, 63.

44. *Ibid.*, 157.

45. *Ibid.*, 147.

46. Karim, Jamillah, "Through Sunni Women's Eyes: Black Feminism and the Nation of Islam." In *Black Routes to Islam*, edited by Manning Marable and Hishaam D. Aidi, 155–166. New York: Palgrave Macmillan, 2009, 156.

47. *Ibid.*, 157.

48. *Ibid.*, 161.

49. *Ibid.*, 161.

50. Rouse, Carolyn, "Engaged Surrender: African American Women and Islam." Berkeley: University of California Press, 2004, 216.

51. *Ibid.*, 213.

52. Ahmad, Imad-ad-Dean, "Islamic Religion and American Culture." Presented at the Association of Muslim Social Scientists 32nd Annual Conference at Indiana University, Bloomington, Indiana, Sept. 26–28, 2003.

53. Pew Research Center 2007, 19.

54. *Ibid.*, 20.

55. *Ibid.*, 21.

56. *Ibid.*, 30.

57. *Ibid.*, 38.

58. *Ibid.*, 48.

59. *Ibid.*, 49.

60. Elliot, Andrea, "Between Black and Immigrant Muslims, an Uneasy Alliance," *New York Times*, March 11, 2007.

61. *Ibid.*

62. Takim, Liyakat, "The Indigenization and Politicization of American Islam," *Politics and Religion Journal* 5, no. 1 (2011): 115–116.

63. Senzai, Farid, "Engaging American Muslims: Political Trends and Attitudes." *Institute for Social Policy and Understanding*. April 2012. http://ispu.org/pdfs/ISPU%20Report_Political%20Participation_Senzai_WEB.pdf: 6.

64. Karim 2005.

65. Wadud, Amina, "American Muslim Identity: Race and Ethnicity in Progressive Islam." In *Progressive Muslims: On Justice, Gender, and Pluralism,* edited by Omid Safi, 270–285. Oxford: One World, 2003.

66. Chande 2008, 222.

67. Jackson 2005, 4.

68. *Ibid.*

69. *Ibid.*

70. *Ibid.*, 5.

71. *Ibid.*, 6.

72. Hallaq, Wael B., *Shari'a: Theory, Practice, Transformations*. Cambridge: Cambridge University Press, 2009, 98–100.

73. Coulson, Noel J., *A History of Islamic Law*. Edinburgh: Edinburgh University Press, 1964, 102.

74. An-Na'im, Abdullahi Ahmed, *Islam and the Secular State: Negotiating the Future of Sharia*. Cambridge, MA: Harvard University Press, 2008.

75. Leonard 2005, 9.

76. *Ibid.,* 8.

77. *Ibid.,* 10.

78. Jackson 2005, 6.

79. Leonard 2005, 9, 11–12.

80. Barzegar, Abbas, "The Emerging Latino Muslim Community in America," *The Pluralism Project, Harvard University*. 2003. http://pluralism.org/reports/view/197; http://www.amila.org.

81. http://www.zaytunacollege.org/global/404/.

82. Leonard 2005, 21.

83. *Ibid.*

84. Taha 1987.

85. An-Na'im, Abdullahi Ahmed, "Mahmud Muhammad Taha and the Crisis in Islamic Law Reform: Implications for Interreligious Relations," *Journal of Ecumenical Studies* 25, no. 1 (1988): 1–21.

86. Leonard, Karen Isaksen, *Muslims in the United States: The State of Research*. New York: Russell Sage Foundation, 2003, 175–176.

87. Pew Research Center 2011, 33–35; Pew Research Center 2007, 32–33.

CHAPTER 4

1. Jacoby, Susan, *Freethinkers: A History of American Secularism*. New York: Metropolitan Books, 2004, 26–28.

2. Corbett, Michael, and Julia Mitchell Corbett, *Politics and Religion in the United States*. New York: Garland Publishing, Inc., 1999, 83–84.

3. Corbett and Mitchell 1999, 48.

4. Bellah, Robert N., "Civil Religion in America," *Dædalus, Journal of the American Academy of Arts and Sciences* 96, no. 1 (1967): 1–21, at 12. As noted later, however, many state governments in the United States did support churches financially.

5. Corbett and Mitchell 1999, at 106–107.

6. Wimberley, Ronald C., and William H. Swatos, Jr., "Civil Religion." In William H. Swatos, Jr., editor, *Encyclopedia of Religion and Society*, Hartford Institute of Religion Research, Hartford Seminary. Viewed May 1, 2013, at http://hirr.hartsem.edu/ency/civilrel.htm.

Reference to Bellah's article is to Robert Bellah 1967, in addition to other articles cited later in this chapter in which he developed the concept of civil religion.

7. Wuthnow, Robert, "Divided We Fall: America's Two Civil Religions," *The Christian Century* 105 (1988): 395–399.

8. Bellah 1967, 13.

9. Demerath, N. J., and R. H. Williams, "A Mythical Past and Uncertain Future," *Society* 21, no. 4 (1984): 3–10, at 5.

10. Wald, Kenneth, *Religion and Politics in the United States.* New York: St. Martin's Press, 1987, 183.

11. Demerath and Williams 1984, 4.

12. Wald 1987, 188.

13. Corbett and Mitchell 1999, 124–126.

14. Wood, James, "Abridging the Free Exercise Clause," *Journal of Church & State* 32, no. 4 (1990): 741–752, 742.

15. Corbett and Mitchell 1999, 23.

16. An-Na'im, Abdullahi Ahmed, *Islam and the Secular State.* Cambridge, MA: Harvard University Press, 2008.

17. Gill, Graeme, *The Nature and Development of the Modern State.* New York: Palgrave Macmillan, 2003, at 2–4.

18. Gill 2003, 17.

19. *Ibid.*, 19.

20. Minkenberg, Michael, "The Policy Impact of Church-State Relations: Family Policy and Abortion in Britain, France and Germany," *West European Politics* 26, no. 1 (2003): 195–217, at 209–210.

21. Brock, Rita Nakashima, "The Fiction of Church and State Separation: A Proposal for Greater Freedom of Religion," *Journal of the American Academy of Religion* 70, no. 4 (2002): 855–862.

22. Freedman, Jane, "Secularism as a Barrier to Integration? The French Dilemma," *International Migration* 42, no. 3 (2004): 5–27, at 6, 8.

23. Asad, Talal, "Religion, Nation-State, Secularism." In *Nation and Religion*, edited by Peter van der Veer and Hartmut Lehmann, 178–196. Princeton: Princeton University Press Press, 1999, at 192.

24. Cornell University Law School, "First Amendment: An Overview." Legal Information Institute. Last modified August 19, 2010. http://www.law.cornell.edu/wex/first_amendment.

25. Hagerty, Barbara Bradley, "Some Muslims in U.S. Quietly Engage in Polygamy." National Public Radio. Last modified May 27, 2008. http://www.npr.org/templates/story/story.php?storyId=90857818.

26. Solieman, Ishra, "Born Osama: Muslim-American Employment Discrimination," *Arizona Law Review* 51 (2009): 1069–1096.

27. Beaudry, Jennifer K., "Islamic Sectarianism in United States Prisons: The Religious Right of Shi'a Inmates to Worship Separately from Their Fellow Sunni Inmates," *Hofstra Law Review* 35 (2007): 1833–1864.

28. Cornell University Law School, "Education Law: An Overview." Legal Information Institute. Accessed September 16, 2012. http://www.law.cornell.edu/wex/education.

29. Moes, Matthew, "Education Law and Muslim Students." *Capella University, School of Education*. Accessed July 10, 2012. http://www.theisla.org/filemgmt_data/admin_files/EducationLaw%26Muslims.pdf.

30. Smith, Steven D., "Constitutional Divide: The Transformative Significance of School Prayer Decisions," *Pepperdine Law Review* 38 (2011): 945–1020.

31. Moes 2012, 14–17.

32. *Ibid.*, 23.

33. Basford, Letitia, Sarah Hick, and Martha Bigelow, "Educating Muslims in an East African US Charter High School." http://religiouscharterschools.blogspot.cmo/2007/10/educating-muslims-in-east-african-us.html. October 15, 2007, at 4.

34. Moes 2012, 19.

35. Alexander, Kern, and M. David Alexander, *American Public School Law*. Belmont: Wadsworth Group, 2001.

36. Lee, Simon, *The Cost of Free Speech*. London: Faber and Faber, 1990; Levin, Abigail, *The Cost of Free Speech: Pornography, Hate Speech, and Their Challenge to Liberalism*. Basingstoke: Palgrave Macmillan, 2010.

37. Bruinius, Harry, "Mosque Debate: Behind America's Anxiety over Islam," *The Christian Science Monitor*. Last modified September 3, 2010. http://www.csmonitor.com/USA/Society/2010/0903/Mosque-debate-Behind-America-s-anxiety-over-Islam.

38. Whitted, Alex R., "Park51 as a Case Study: Testing the Religious Land Use and Institutionalized Persons Act," *Indiana Law Review* 45 (2011): 249–274.

39. Loller, Travis, "Murfreesboro Mosque Ruling Raises Questions," Associated Press. Last modified June 11, 2012. http://www.courier-journal.com/article/DN/20120611/NEWS03/306110040/?nclick_check=1.

40. *New York Times,* Editorial, August 19, 2012. "Ramadan in Murfreesboro." *New York Times*, viewed September 18, 2012, at http://www.nytimes.com/2012/08/20/opinion/ramadan-in-murfreesboro-tenn.html.

41. Associated Press, September 17, 2012, viewed September 18, 2012, at http://www.wdam.com/story/19558684/news-minute-here-is-the-latest-tennessee-news-from-the-associated-press.

42. An-Na'im, Abdullahi A., ed., *Islamic Family Law in a Changing World: A Global Resource Book*. London: Zed Books, 2002, 1–22.

43. An-Na'im, Abdullahi A., "The Compatibility Dialectic: Mediating the Legitimate Coexistence of Islamic Law and State Law," *Modern Law Review* 73, no. 1 (2010): 1–29.

44. Fawzy, Essam, "Muslim Personal Status Law in Egypt." In Lynn Welchman, ed. *Women's Rights & Islamic Family Law: Perspectives on Reform*. London: Zed Books 2004, 15–91.

45. An-Na'im 2008.

46. Rahman, Fazlur, *Islam*. Chicago: University of Chicago Press, 1979; Weiss, Bernard G., *The Spirit of Islamic Law*. Athens: University of Georgia Press, 1998; Hallaq, Wael B., *Authority, Continuity and Change in Islamic Law*. Cambridge: Cambridge University Press, 2001.

47. *Idda* is the waiting period a wife must observe before she can remarry. *Idda* is normally three months after termination of marriage and four months and ten days after death of husband. There is no parallel waiting period for a husband after termination of marriage or death of his wife. The commonly accepted rationale for observing *idda* by the wife is to ensure that she is not pregnant from the former or deceased husband.

48. An-Na'im, Abdullahi Ahmed, ed., *Inter-Religious Marriage among Muslims*. New Delhi: Global Media Publications, 2005.

49. Eclavea, Romualdo P., "Marriage," *American Jurisprudence*, 2nd ed. 52 (2012). On June 26, 2013, the Supreme Court handed a decision in United States v. Windsor (133 S. Ct. 2675, 2013), declaring Section 3 of the Defense of Marriage Act (DOMA) unconstitutional "as a deprivation of the liberty of the person protected by the Fifth Amendment." I am not discussing that decision here because that would be too much of a digression into issues that are not relevant for our purposes here. It may also be too early to attempt a summary of the ruling and implications of that case at the time of writing.

50. Uniform Law Commission, Premarital Agreement Act Summary. Access September 17, 2012. http://uniformlaws.org/ActSummary.aspx?title=Premarital%20 Agreement%20Act.

51. Sizemore, Chelsea A., "Enforcing Islamic Mahr Agreements: The American Judge's Interpretational Dilemma," *George Mason Law Review* 18 (2011): 1085–1116.

52. Uniform Law Commission, Premarital Agreement Act Summary. Access September 17, 2012. http://uniformlaws.org/ActSummary.aspx?title=Premarital%20 Agreement%20Act.

53. O.C.G.A. § 19-9-3 (2012).

54. Oman, Nathan B., "How to Judge Shari'a Contracts: A Guide to Islamic Marriage Agreements in American Courts," *Utah Law Review* (2011): 287–334, at 290.

55. Eclavea 2012 § 65.

56. Thompson, Emily L., and F. Soniya Yunus, "Choice of Laws or Choice of Culture: How Western Nations Treat the Islamic Marriage Contract in Domestic Courts," *Wisconsin International Law Journal* 25 (2007): 361–395, at 382.

57. Oman 2011, 312–313.

58. Korteweg, Anna C., "The Sharia Debate in Ontario: Gender, Islam, and Representations of Muslim Women's Agency," *Gender & Society* 22, no. 4 (2008): 434–454.

59. Macfarlane, Julie, *Islamic Divorce in North America: A Shari'a Path in a Secular Society*. New York: Oxford University Press, 2012, xvi.

60. *Ibid.*, 211.

61. *Ibid.*

62. *Ibid.*, xviii.

63. *Ibid.*, 37–38.

64. *Ibid.*, 50.

65. *Ibid.*, 178–179.

66. *Ibid.*, 212.

67. *Ibid.*, 213.

68. *Ibid.*, 215.

69. *Ibid.*

CHAPTER 5

1. Taha, Mahmoud Mohamed, *The Second Message of Islam*. Syracuse, NY: Syracuse University Press, 1987, 62–112; Taha, Mahmoud Mohamed, *Risalat al-Salah* (Treaties on Prayers) in Arabic, 4th ed. Omdurman, Sudan, published by the author, 1969, 8–22.

2. Cook, Michael, *Commanding Rights and Forbidding Wrong in Islamic Thought*. Cambridge: Cambridge University Press, 2000.

3. Anderson, Benedict, *Imagined Communities: Reflections on the Origin and Spread of Nationalism*, rev. ed. New York: Verso, 1991, 5–7.

4. Lapechet, Jaye, "Virtual Communities: The 90s Mind Altering Drug or Facilitator of Human Interaction?" Berkeley: University of California [no date]. Viewed April 27, 2013, at http://besser.tsoa.nyu.edu/impact/s94/students/jaye/jaye_asis.html#fn5.

5. Ridings, Catherine M., and David Gefen, "Virtual Community Attraction: Why People Hang Out Online." Viewed April 27, 2013, at http://jcmc.indiana.edu/vol10/issue1/ridings_gefen.html#s1.

6. See, for example, the self-described virtual Muslim world "Muxlim Pal." Setrakian, Lara, "A New Muslim (Virtual) World," ABC News, December 10, 2008. Viewed April 27, 2013, at http://abcnews.go.com/International/story?id=6433768&page=1.

7. CSMN, Center for the Study of Muslim Networks (CSMN) of Duke University. Viewed April 27, 2013, at https://web.duke.edu/muslimnets/csmn_about.html.

8. Bastani, Susan, "Muslim Women Online," April 24, 2001. Viewed April 27, 2013, at http://homes.chass.utoronto.ca/~wellman/publications/muslimwomen/MWN1.PDF.

9. Badran, Margot, "Ejected from God's House." *Al-Ahram Weekly*, 2010, 988, http://weekly.ahram.org.eg/2010/988/op14.htm. Viewed August 23, 2012.

10. Rezk, Rawya, "Muslim Women Seek More Equitable Role in Mosques," *The Columbia Journalist, Religion and Ethics News Weekly,* November 12, 2004. Episode no. 81. Viewed August 23, 2012, at http://www.pbs.org/wnet/religionandethics/week811/cover.html.

11. An-Na'im, Abdullahi Ahmed, *Toward an Islamic Reformation: Civil Liberties, Human Rights and International Law.* Syracuse, NY: Syracuse University Press, 1990.

12. An-Na'im, Abdullahi Ahmed, *Islam and the Secular State: Negotiating the Future of Shar'ia.* Cambridge, MA: Harvard University Press, 2008.

13. Hallaq, Wael B., *Authority, Continuity and Change in Islamic Law.* Cambridge: Cambridge University Press, 2001.

14. Ibn Rushd (Averroes), *Fasl al-Maqal bayn al-Shar 'a wa al-Hikmah min Itsal* (The Decisive Treatise Determining the Connection between the Law and Wisdom), trans. Charles E. Butterworth. Provo, UT: Brigham Young University Press, 2001.

Bibliography

Abraham, Margaret, Esther Ngan-ling Chow, Laura Maratou-Alipranti, and Evangelia Tastsoglou, "Rethinking Citizenship with Women in Focus," in Abraham, Margaret, Esther Ngan-ling Chow, Laura Maratou-Alipranti, and Evangelia Tastsoglou, eds. *Contours of Citizenship: Women, Diversity and Practices of Citizenship*. Farnham, UK, and Burlington, VT: Ashgate Publishing, 2010, 1–21.

Afroyim v. Rusk, 387 U.S. 253, 268. (U.S. 1967).

Ahmad, Imad-ad-Dean. "Islamic Religion and American Culture." Presented at the Association of Muslim Social Scientists 32nd Annual Conference at Indiana University, Bloomington, Indiana, September 26–28, 2003.

Aidi, Hishaam. "Jihadis in the Hood: Race, Urban Islam, and the War on Terror." *Middle East Report* 224 (2002): 36–43.

Aleinikoff, T. Alexander. "Theories of Loss of Citizenship." *Michigan Law Review* 84 (1986): 1471–1503.

Alexander, Kern, and M. David Alexander. *American Public School Law*. Belmont: Wadsworth Group, 2001.

Anderson, Benedict. *Imagined Communities: Reflections on the Origin and Spread of Nationalism*, rev. ed. New York: Verso, 1991.

An-Na'im, Abdullahi A. "The Compatibility Dialectic: Mediating the Legitimate Coexistence of Islamic Law and State Law." *Modern Law Review* 73, no. 1 (2010): 1–29.

An-Na'im, Abdullahi Ahmed, ed. *Inter-Religious Marriage among Muslims*. New Delhi: Global Media Publications, 2005.

An-Na'im, Abdullahi Ahmed. *Islam and the Secular State: Negotiating the Future of Sharia*. Cambridge, MA: Harvard University Press, 2008.

An-Na'im, Abdullahi A., ed. *Islamic Family Law in a Changing World: A Global Resource Book*. London: Zed Books, 2002.

An-Na'im, Abdullahi Ahmed. "Mahmud Muhammad Taha and the Crisis in Islamic Law Reform: Implications for Interreligious Relations." *Journal of Ecumenical Studies* 25, no. 1 (1988): 1–21.

An-Na'im, Abdullahi Ahmed. "Religious Norms and Family Law: Is It Legal or Normative Pluralism?" *Emory International Law Review* 25, no. 2 (2011): 785–809.

An-Na'im, Abdullahi Ahmed. *Toward an Islamic Reformation: Civil Liberties, Human Rights and International Law.* Syracuse, NY: Syracuse University Press, 1990.

Anzulovic, Branimir. *Heavenly Serbia: From Myth to Genocide.* New York: New York University Press, 1999.

Asad, Talal. "Religion, Nation-State, Secularism." In *Nation and Religion*, edited by Peter van der Veer and Hartmut Lehmann, 178–196. Princeton: Princeton University Press, 1999.

Ashton, Dianne. "Expanding Jewish Life in America, 1826–1901." In *The Columbia History of Jews and Judaism in America*, edited by Marc Lee Raphael, 47–69. New York: Columbia University Press, 2008.

Associated Press. September 17, 2012, viewed September 18, 2012, at http://www.wdam.com/story/19558684/news-minute-here-is-the-latest-tennessee-news-from-the-associated-press.

Awwa, Muhammad Salim. *Punishment in Islamic Law; A Comparative Study.* Indianapolis: American Trust Publications, 1982.

Badran, Margot. "Ejected from God's House." *Al-Ahram Weekly*, 2010, 988, http://weekly.ahram.org.eg/2010/988/op14.htm, viewed 23 August 2012.

Baghy, Ishan. *A Portrait of Detroit Mosques: Muslim Views on Policy, Politics and Religion.* Clinton Township, MI: Institute for Social Policy and Understanding, 2004.

Baldwin, James. *Black Anti-Semitism and Jewish Racism.* Edited by Nat Hentoff. New York: R. W. Baron, 1969.

Barzegar, Abbas. "The Emerging Latino Muslim Community in America." *The Pluralism Project, Harvard University.* 2003. http://pluralism.org/reports/view/197.

Basford, Letitia, Sarah Hick, and Martha Bigelow. "Educating Muslims in an East African US Charter High School." http://religiouscharterschools.blogspot.cmo/2007/10/educating-muslims-in-east-african-us.html. October 15, 2007.

Bastani, Susan. "Muslim Women Online." 24 Apr 2001. http://homes.chass.utoronto.ca/~wellman/publications/muslimwomen/MWN1.PDF.

Beaudry, Jennifer K. "Islamic Sectarianism in United States Prisons: The Religious Right of Shi'a Inmates to Worship Separately from Their Fellow Sunni Inmates." *Hofstra Law Review* 35 (2007): 1833–1864.

Bellah, Robert. *Beyond Belief.* New York: Harper & Row, 1970.

Bellah, Robert N. "Civil Religion in America." *Dædalus, Journal of the American Academy of Arts and Sciences* 96, no. 1 (1967): 1–21.

Bellah, Robert N., and Phillip E. Hammond. *Varieties of Civil Religion.* San Francisco: Harper & Row, 1980.

Bellamy, Richard. *Citizenship: A Very Short Introduction.* Oxford: Oxford University Press, 2008.

Bennett, David H. *The Party of Fear: From Nativist Movements to the New Right in American History*. New York: Random House, 1995.

Berg, Herbert. "Mythmaking in the African American Muslim Context: The Moorish Science Temple, the Nation of Islam, and the American Society of Muslims." *American Academy of Religion* 73, no. 3 (2005): 685–703.

Berger, Benjamin L. "The Cultural Limits of Legal Tolerance." In *After Pluralism: Reimagining Religious Engagement,* edited by Courtney Bender and Pamela E. Klassen, 98–123. New York: Columbia University Press, 2010.

Blanshard, Paul. *American Freedom and Catholic Power.* Boston: Beacon Press, 1958.

Brock, Rita Nakashima. "The Fiction of Church and State Separation: A Proposal for Greater Freedom of Religion." *Journal of the American Academy of Religion* 70, no. 4 (2002): 855–862.

Bruinius, Harry. "Mosque Debate: Behind America's Anxiety over Islam." *The Christian Science Monitor.* Last modified September 3, 2010. http://www.csmonitor. com/USA/Society/2010/0903/Mosque-debate-Behind-America-s-anxiety-over-Islam.

Bukhari, Zahid H. "Demography, Identity, Space: Defining American Muslims." In *Muslims in the United States: Demography, Beliefs, Institutions*, edited by Philippa Strum and Danielle Tarantolo, 7–20. Washington, DC: Woodrow Wilson International Center for Scholars, 2003.

Burman, Erica. "Experience, Identities and Alliances: Jewish Feminism and Feminist Psychology." In *Shifting Identities Shifting Racisms: A Feminism and Psychology Reader*, edited by Kum-Kum Bhavnani and Ann Phoenix, 155–178. London: Sage Publications, 1994.

Cairns, Alan C., John C. Courtney, Peter MacKinnon, Hans J. Michelmann, and David E. Smith, eds. *Citizenship, Diversity and Pluralism: Canadian and Comparative Perspectives.* Montreal and London: McGill-Queen's University Press, 1999.

Camilleri, Joseph A., Anthony P. Jarvis, and Albert J. Paolini, eds. *The State in Transition: Reimagining Political Space.* Boulder, CO: Lynne Rienner Publishers, 1995.

Cantwell v. Conn., 310 US 296 (U.S. 1940).

Chande, Abdin. "Islam in the African American Community: Negotiating Between Black Nationalism and Historical Islam." *Islamic Studies* 47, no. 2 (2008): 221–241.

Chatterjee, Partha. *Empire and Nation: Selected Essays*. New York: Columbia University Press, 2010.

Congressional Globe. 39th Cong. 1st Sess. 144 (1866).

Cook, Michael. *Commanding Rights and Forbidding Wrong in Islamic Thought*. Cambridge: Cambridge University Press, 2000.

Corbett, Michael, and Julia Mitchell Corbett. *Politics and Religion in the United States*. New York: Garland Publishing, 1999.

Cornell University Law School. "Education Law: An Overview." Legal Information Institute. Accessed September 16, 2012. http://www.law.cornell.edu/wex/education.

Cornell University Law School. "First Amendment: An Overview." Legal Information Institute. Last modified August 19, 2010. http://www.law.cornell.edu/wex/
first_amendment.

Coulson, Noel J. *A History of Islamic Law.* Edinburgh: Edinburgh University
Press, 1964.

"Crowds Reach Capital for Holy Name Rally; Coolidge Will Address Mass Meeting on
Sunday Afternoon—Sessions Open with Mass Today." *New York Times.* September
17, 1924.

CSMN, Center for the Study of Muslim Networks of Duke University. https://web.
duke.edu/muslimnets/csmn_about.html.

Curry, Thomas J. *The First Freedoms: Church and State in America to the Passage of the
First Amendment.* Oxford: Oxford University Press, 1986.

Curtis, Edward E., IV. "African American Islamization Reconsidered: Black History
Narratives and Muslim Identity." *Journal of the American Academy of Religion* 73,
no. 3 (2005): 659–684.

D'Appollonia, Ariane Chebel. *Frontiers of Fear: Immigration and Insecurity in the
United States and Europe.* Ithaca, NY: Cornell University Press, 2012.

Davis v. Beason, 133 U.S. 333 (U.S. 1890).

Demerath, N. J, and R. H. Williams. "A Mythical Past and Uncertain Future." *Society*
21, no. 4 (1984): 3–10.

Dreisbach, Daniel L. *Thomas Jefferson and the Wall of Separation Between Church and
State.* New York: New York University Press, 2002.

Dryzek, John S., and Patrick Dunleavy. *Theories of the Democratic State.* Basingstoke,
UK: Palgrave Macmillan, 2009.

Dumenil, Lynn. "The Tribal Twenties: 'Assimilated' Catholics' Response to
Anti-Catholicism in the 1920s." *Journal of American Ethnic History* 11, no. 1 (1991):
21–49.

Durham, W. Cole, Jr., and Brett G. Scharffs. *Law and Religion: National, International
and Comparative Perspectives.* New York: Aspen Publishers, 2010.

Eclavea, Romualdo P. "Marriage." *American Jurisprudence,* 2nd ed. 52 (2012).

Elk v. Wilkins, 112 U.S. 94 (U.S. 1884).

Elliot, Andrea. "Between Black and Immigrant Muslims, an Uneasy Alliance." *New York
Times,* March 11, 2007.

Epperson v. Ark., 393 US 97 (U.S. 1968).

Essed, Philomena. "Contradictory Positions, Ambivalent Perceptions: A Case Study of
a Black Woman Entrepreneur." In *Shifting Identities Shifting Racisms: A Feminism
and Psychology Reader,* edited by Kum-Kum Bhavnani and Ann Phoenix, 99–118.
London: Sage Publications, 1994.

Everson v. Bd. of Educ., 330 U.S. 1 (U.S. 1947).

Farber, Eli. "America's Earliest Jewish Settlers, 1654–1820." In *The Columbia History of
Jews and Judaism in America,* edited by Marc Lee Raphael, 21–46. New York: Columbia University Press, 2008.

Faulks, Keith. *Citizenship*. London: Routledge, 2000.

Fawzy, Essam. "Muslim Personal Status Law in Egypt." In *Women's Rights and Islamic Law: Perspectives on Reform*, edited by Lynn Welchman, 15–92. London: Zed Books, 2004.

Feldman, Noah. *Divided by God: America's Church-State Problem—And What We Should Do about It*. New York: Farrar, Straus and Giroux, 2005.

Fisher, James Terence. *Communion of Immigrants: A History of Catholics in America*. Oxford: Oxford University Press, 2007.

Freedman, Jane. "Secularism as a Barrier to Integration? The French Dilemma." *International Migration* 42, no. 3 (2004): 5–27.

Gerber, David A., and Alan M. Kraut, eds. "Becoming White: Irish Immigration in the Nineteenth Century." In *American Immigration and Ethnicity: A Reader*, 161–168. New York: Palgrave Macmillan, 2005.

GhaneaBassiri, Kambiz. *A History of Islam in America: From the New World to the New World Order*. New York: Cambridge University Press, 2010.

Gill, Graeme. *The Nature and Development of the Modern State*. New York: Palgrave Macmillan, 2003.

Glazier, Jack. *Dispersing the Ghetto: The Relocation of Jewish Immigrants across America*. New York: Cornell University Press, 1998.

Glock, Charles Y. "The Churches and Social Change in Twentieth-Century America." *The Annals of the American Academy of Political and Social Science* 527 (1993): 67–83.

Goldstein, Eric L. "The Great Wave: Eastern European Jewish Immigration to the United States, 1880–1924." In *The Columbia History of Jews and Judaism in America*, edited by Marc Lee Raphael, 70–92. New York: Columbia University Press, 2008.

Gordon, Sarah Barringer. "Blasphemy and the Law of Religious Liberty in Nineteenth-Century America." *American Quarterly* 52, no. 4 (2000): 682–719.

Greeley, Andrew M. *The Catholic Experience: An Interpretation of the History of American Catholicism*. Garden City, NY: Doubleday, 1969.

Hagerty, Barbara Bradley. "Some Muslims in U.S. Quietly Engage in Polygamy." National Public Radio. Last modified May 27, 2008. http://www.npr.org/templates/story/story.php?storyId=90857818.

Hallaq, Wael B. *Authority, Continuity and Change in Islamic Law*. Cambridge: Cambridge University Press, 2001.

Hallaq, Wael. "Can the Shari'ah Be Restored?" In *Islamic Law and the Challenges of Modernity*, edited by Yvonne Y. Haddad and Barbara F. Stowasser, 21–53. Walnut Creek: Altamira Press, 2004.

Hallaq, Wael B. *Shari'a: Theory, Practice, Transformations*. Cambridge: Cambridge University Press, 2009.

Handlin, Oscar. "American Views of Jews at the Opening of the Twentieth Century." In *Anti-Semitism in the United States,* edited by Leonard Dinnerstein. New York: Holt Rinehart Winston, 1971: 48–57.

Hanks, Maxine, and Jean Kinney Williams. *Mormon Faith in America*, edited by J. Gordon Melton. New York: Infobase Publishing, 2003.

Higham, John. *Strangers in the Land: Patterns of American Nativism, 1860–1925*. Piscataway, NJ: Rutgers University Press, 1955.

Hurvitz, Nimrod. *The Formation of Hanbalism: Piety into Power*. New York: Routledge Curzon, 2002.

Ibn Rushd (Averroes), *Fasl al-Maqal bayn al-Shar ʿa wa al-Hikmah min Itsal* (The Decisive Treatise Determining the Connection between the Law and Wisdom). Trans. Charles E. Butterworth. Provo, UT: Brigham Young University Press, 2001.

Ignatiev, Noel. *How the Irish Became White*. London: Routledge, 1995.

Immigration and Nationality Act of 1952, Chapter 2. §311, 66 Stat. 163, 239. (1952).

Jackson, Sherman A. *Islam and the Blackamerican: Looking toward the Third Resurrection*. Oxford: Oxford University Press, 2005.

Jacoby, Susan. *Freethinkers: A History of American Secularism*. New York: Metropolitan Books, 2004.

Jakobsen, Janet R. "Ethics after Pluralism." In *After Pluralism: Reimagining Religious Engagement,* edited by Courtney Bender and Pamela E. Klassen. New York: Columbia University Press, 2010: 31–58.

Jenkins, Philip. *The New Anti-Catholicism: The Last Acceptable Prejudice*. Oxford: Oxford University Press, 2003.

Karim, Jamillah Ashira. "Between Immigrant Islam and Black Liberation: Young Muslims Inherit Global Muslim and African American Legacies." *Muslim World* 95, no. 4 (2005): 497–513.

Karim, Jamillah. "Through Sunni Women's Eyes: Black Feminism and the Nation of Islam." In *Black Routes to Islam*, edited by Manning Marable and Hishaam D. Aidi, 155–166. New York: Palgrave MacMillan, 2009. http://www.huffingtonpost.com/2012/03/29/progressive-muslims-launch-gay-friendly-women-led-mosques_n_1368460.html?page=1.

Karst, Kenneth L. "Paths to Belonging: The Constitution and Cultural Identity." *North Carolina Law Review* 64 (1986): 303.

King, Ryan D., and Melissa F. Weiner. "Group Position, Collective Threat, and American Anti-Semitism." *Social Problems* 54, no. 1 (2007): 47–77.

Korteweg, Anna C. "The Sharia Debate in Ontario: Gender, Islam, and Representations of Muslim Women's Agency." *Gender & Society* 22, no. 4 (2008): 434–454.

Kymlicka, Will. *Multicultural Odysseys: Navigating the New International Politics of Diversity*. Oxford: Oxford University Press, 2007.

Kymlicka, Will, and Wayne Norman. "Return of the Citizen: A Survey of Recent Work on Citizenship Theory." *Ethics* 104, no. 2 (1994): 352–381.

Lambert, Frank. *The Founding Fathers and the Place of Religion in America*. Princeton: Princeton University Press, 2003.

Lapechet, Jaye. "Virtual Communities: The 90s Mind Altering Drug or Facilitator of Human Interaction?" Berkeley: University of California [no date]. At http://besser.tsoa.nyu.edu/impact/s94/students/jaye/jaye_asis.html#fn5.

Late Corp. of Church of Jesus Christ v. United States, 136 U.S. 1 (U.S. 1890).

Lee, Simon. *The Cost of Free Speech*. London: Faber and Faber, 1990.

Leonard, Karen. "American Muslims and Authority: Competing Discourses in a Non-Muslim State." *Journal of American Ethnic History* 25, no. 1 (2005): 5–30.

Leonard, Karen Isaksen. *Muslims in the United States: The State of Research*. New York: Russell Sage Foundation, 2003.

Levin, Abigail. *The Cost of Free Speech: Pornography, Hate Speech, and Their Challenge to Liberalism*. Basingstoke: Palgrave Macmillan, 2010.

Lienesch, Michael. *In the Beginning: Fundamentalism, the Scopes Trial, and the Making of the Antievolution Movement*. Chapel Hill: University of North Carolina Press, 2007.

Limbaugh, Rush. "Why This Mosque on This Spot?" *The Rush Limbaugh Show*. August 17, 2010. Retrieved March 27, 2012. http://www.rushlimbaugh.com/daily/2010/08/17/why_this_mosque_on_this_spot.

Loller, Travis. "Murfreesboro Mosque Ruling Raises Questions." Associated Press. Last modified June 11, 2012. http://www.courier-journal.com/article/DN/20120611 / NEWS03/306110040/?nclick_check=1.

Macfarlane, Julie. *Islamic Divorce in North America: A Shari'a Path in a Secular Society*. New York: Oxford University Press, 2012.

Mansbach, Richard W., and Kirsten L. Taylor. "Identity Politics: Nationalism and Ethnicity." In *Introduction to Global Politics*, edited by Richard W. Mansbach and Kirsten L. Taylor. London and New York: Routledge, 2007: 418–453.

Marshall, Thomas Humphrey. *Citizenship and Social Class and Other Essays*. Cambridge: Cambridge University Press, 1950.

Mason, Patrick Q. *The Mormon Menace: Violence and Anti-Mormonism in the Postbellum South*. London: Oxford University Press, 2011.

Mauss, Armand L. "Sociological Perspectives on the Mormon Subculture." *Annual Review of Sociology* 10, no. 1 (1984): 437–460.

McCloud, Aminah Beverly. *African American Islam*. New York: Routledge, 1995.

McLoughlin, Emmett. *American Culture and Catholic Schools*. New York: Lyle Stuart, 1960.

Michaels, Ralf. "The Re-Statement of Non-State Law." *Wayne Law Review* 58 (2005): 1209–1259.

Miller, Timothy. "Controversial Christian Movements: History, Growth, and Outlook." In *New Religious Movements and Religious Liberty in America,* edited by Derek H. Davis and Barry Hankins, 9–24. Waco, TX: Baylor University Press, 2003.

Minkenberg, Michael. "The Policy Impact of Church-State Relations: Family Policy and Abortion in Britain, France and Germany." *West European Politics* 26, no. 1 (2003): 195–217.

Modood, Tariq, Anna Triandafyllidou, and Richard Zapata-Barrero, eds. *Multicultural-ism, Muslims and Citizenship: A European Approach*. London and New York: Rout-ledge, 2006.

Moes, Matthew. "Education Law and Muslim Students." *Capella University, School of Education*. Accessed July 10, 2012. http://www.theisla.org/filemgmt_data/admin_files/EducationLaw%26Muslims.pdf.

Momen, Moojan. *An Introduction to Shi'i Islam: The History and Doctrines of Twelver Shi'ism*. New Haven: Yale University Press, 1987.

Moore, Kathleen M. "Muslims in the United States: Pluralism under Exceptional Cir-cumstances." *The Annals of the American Academy of Political and Social Sciences* 612, no. 1 (2007): 116–132.

Moore, R. Laurence. *Religious Outsiders and the Making of Americans*. Oxford: Oxford University Press, 1986.

Morris, Charles. *American Catholic: The Saints and Sinners Who Built America's Most Powerful Church*. New York: Vintage Books, 1998.

Naturalization Act of 1790. 1 Stat. 103 (1790), repealed by Naturalization Act of 1795. 1 Stat. 414 (1795).

Naturalization Act of 1870. 16 Stat. 254 (1870).

New York Times. Editorial, August 19, 2012. "Ramadan in Murfreesboro." *New York Times*, viewed September 18, 2012, at http://www.nytimes.com/2012/08/20/opin-ion/ramadan-in-murfreesboro-tenn.html.

Newman, William M., and Peter L. Halvorson. "An American Diaspora? Patterns of Jewish Population Distribution and Change, 1971–1980." *Review of Religious Research* 31, no. 3 (1990): 259–267.

O'Connor, Kathleen Malone. "The Islamic Jesus Messiahhood and Human Divinity in African American Muslim Exegesis." *Journal of the American Academy of Religion* 66, no. 3 (1998): 493–532.

Oman, Nathan B. "How to Judge Shari'a Contracts: A Guide to Islamic Marriage Agree-ments in American Courts." *Utah Law Review*, Vol. 2011, no. 1, (2011): 287–334.

Orgad, Liav, and Theodore Ruthizer. "Race, Religion and Nationality in Immigration Selection: 120 Years after the Chinese Exclusion Case." *Constitutional Commentary* 26 (2010): 237–296.

Ozawa v. United States, 260 U.S. 178, 198 (U.S. 1922).

Peek, Lori. "Becoming Muslim: The Development of a Religious Identity." *Sociology of Religion* 66, no. 3 (2005): 215–242.

Pew Research Center. "Muslim Americans: Middle Class and Mostly Mainstream." May 22, 2007. Retrieved August 3, 2011. http://pewresearch.org/pubs/483/muslim-americans.

Pew Research Center. "Muslim Americans: No Signs of Growth in Alienation or Support for Extremism." August 30, 2011. Retrieved May 5, 2012. http://www.people-press.org/2011/08/30/muslim-americans-no-signs-of-growth-in-ali enation-or-support-for-extremism/.

Pew Research Center. "The Future of the Global Muslim Population: Projections from 2010 to 2030." January 27, 2011. http://www.pewforum.org/Global-Muslim-Population.aspx.

Philipson. David. "Jews and Industries," *Menorah* 4, no. 1 (1888): 100–107.

Pickus, Noah. *True Faith and Allegiance: Immigration and American Civic Nationalism.* Princeton, NJ: Princeton University Press, 2005.

Pocock, J. G. A. "The Ideal of Citizenship since Classical Times." *Queen's Quarterly* 99, no. 1 (1992): 35–55.

Portes, Alejandro, and Rubén G. Rumbaut. *Immigrant America: A Portrait.* Berkeley: University of California Press, 2006.

Prell, Riv-Ellen. "Triumph, Accommodation, and Resistance: American Jewish Life from the End of World War II to the Six-Day War." In *The Columbia History of Jews and Judaism in America*, edited by Marc Lee Raphael, 114–141. New York: Columbia University Press, 2008.

Preuss, Ulrich K. "The Ambiguous Meaning of Citizenship." Paper presented at the Center for Comparative Constitutionalism, University of Chicago Law School, December 1, 2003. Unpublished paper available at http://ccc.uchicago.edu/docs/preuss.pdf. Viewed September 6, 2011.

Project MAPS 2004: Muslims in the American Public Square and Zogby International. *Muslims in the American Public Square: Shifting Political Winds & Fallout from 9/11, Afghanistan, and Iraq.* Retrieved July 31, 2008. http://www.zogby.com/American-Muslims2004.pdf.

Pyle, Ralph E., and, James D. Davidson. "The Origins of Religious Stratification in Colonial America." *Journal for the Scientific Study of Religion* 42, no. 1 (2003): 57–75.

Pyne, Tricia T. "The Politics of Identity in Eighteenth-Century British America: Catholic Perceptions of Their Role in Colonial Society." *U.S. Catholic Historian* 15, no. 2 (1997): 1–14.

Rahman, Fazlur. *Islam.* Chicago: University of Chicago Press, 1979.

Reid, Alan, Judith Gill, and Alan Sears, eds. *Globalization, the Nation-State and the Citizen: Dilemmas and Directions for Civics and Citizenship Education.* London: Routledge, 2010.

Reynolds v. United States, 98 US 145, 166–167 (U.S. 1878).

Rezk, Rawya. "Muslim Women Seek More Equitable Role in Mosques." *The Columbia Journalist, Religion and Ethics News Weekly*, November 12, 2004. Episode no. 81. Viewed August 23, 2012, at http://www.pbs.org/wnet/religionandethics/week811/cover.html.

Richey, Russell E., and Donald G. Jones. "The Civil Religion Debate." In *American Religion*, edited by Russell E. Richey and Donald G. Jones, 3–18. New York: Harper & Row, 1974.

Ridings, Catherine M., and David Gefen. "Virtual Community Attraction: Why People Hang Out Online." http://jcmc.indiana.edu/vol10/issue1/ridings_gefen.html#s1.

Riesenberg, Peter. *Citizenship in the Western Tradition: Plato to Rousseau.* Chapel Hill: University of North Carolina Press, 1992.

Ritzer, George F., ed. *Encyclopedia of Social Theory.* London: Sage Publications, 2004.

Rouse, Carolyn. "Engaged Surrender: African American Women and Islam." Berkeley: University of California Press, 2004.

Saito, Natsu Taylor. "Alien and Non-Alien Alike: Citizenship, 'Foreignness,' and Racial Hierarchy in American Law." *Oregon Law Review* 76 (1997): 261.

Schuck, Peter H. "The Reevaluation of American Citizenship." *Yale Law School Faculty Scholarship Series.* Paper 1696 (1997). Paper available at http://digitalcommons.law.yale.edu/fss_papers/1696. Viewed May 21, 2012.

Scott v. Stanford, 60 U.S. 393 (U.S. 1857).

Senzai, Farid. "Engaging American Muslims: Political Trends and Attitudes." *Institute for Social Policy and Understanding.* April 2012. http://ispu.org/pdfs/ISPU%20Report_Political%20Participation_Senzai_WEB.pdf.

Serjeant, R. B. "Sunnah Jami'ah, Pacts with the Yathrib Jews, and the Tahrīm of Yathrib: Analysis and Translation of the Documents Comprised in the So-called 'Constitution of Medina.'" *Bulletin of the School of Oriental and African Studies* 41 (1978): 1–42.

Setrakian, Lara. "A New Muslim (Virtual) World." ABC News. http://abcnews.go.com/International/story?id=6433768&page=1. December 10, 2008.

Sizemore, Chelsea A. "Enforcing Islamic Mahr Agreements: The American Judge's Interpretational Dilemma." *George Mason Law Review* 18 (2011): 1085–1116.

Smith, Jane I. *Islam in America.* New York: Columbia University Press, 1999.

Smith, Steven D. "Constitutional Divide: The Transformative Significance of School Prayer Decisions." *Pepperdine Law Review* 38 (2011): 945–1020.

Solieman, Ishra. "Born Osama: Muslim-American Employment Discrimination." *Arizona Law Review* 51 (2009): 1069–1096.

Spickard, Paul. *Almost All Aliens: Immigration, Race, and Colonialism in American History and Identity.* New York: Routledge, 2007.

Spivak, Gayatri Chakravorty. *Can the Subaltern Speak? Reflections on the History of an Idea.* Edited by Rosalind C. Morris. New York: Columbia University Press, 2010.

Taha, Mahmoud Mohamed. *Risalat al-Salah (Treaties on Prayers),* in Arabic, 4th ed. Umm Durmān (Omdurman): Matb'aat al-Nasr al-Tijrārīyah, 1969.

Taha, Mahmoud Mohamed. *The Second Message of Islam.* Syracuse, NY: Syracuse University Press, 1987.

Takim, Liyakat. "The Indigenization and Politicization of American Islam." *Politics and Religion Journal* 5, no. 1 (2011): 115–127.

Tamanaha, Brian. "Understanding Legal Pluralism: Past to Present, Local to Global." *Sydney Law Review* 30 (2007): 375–411.

Tan, Sor-hoon, ed. *Challenging Citizenship: Group Membership and Cultural Identity in a Global Age.* Burlington, VT: Ashgate Publishing, 2005.

Thompson, Emily L., and F. Soniya Yunus. "Choice of Laws or Choice of Culture: How Western Nations Treat the Islamic Marriage Contract in Domestic Courts." *Wisconsin International Law Journal* 25 (2007): 361–395.

Time Magazine. "Religion: Recognition for the Holy See." December 26, 1983. http://www.time.com/time/magazine/article/0,9171,926427,00.html.

Tumbleson, Raymond D. *Catholicism in the English Protestant Imagination: Nationalism, Religion and Literature 1600–1745.* Cambridge: Cambridge University Press, 1998.

Turner, Richard Brent. *Islam in the African-American Experience.* Bloomington: Indiana University Press, 2003.

Turner, Richard Brent. "What Shall We Call Him? Islam and African American Identity." *The Journal of Religious Thought* 51, no. 1 (1994): 25–53.

Uniform Law Commission. Child Custody Jurisdiction and Enforcement Act. Accessed September 17, 2012. http://uniformlaws.org/Act.aspx?title=Child%20Custody%20Jurisdiction%20and%20Enforcement%20Act.

Uniform Law Commission. Premarital Agreement Act Summary. Accessed September 17, 2012. http://uniformlaws.org/ActSummary.aspx?title=Premarital%20Agreement%20Act.

United States Constitutional Amendment. [XIV], Section 1. Ratified July 9, 1868. http://www.loc.gov/law/help/citizenship/fourteenth_amendment_citizenship.php.

United States v. Bhagat Singh Thind, 261 U.S. 204, 206 (U.S. 1923).

United States v. Wong Kim Ark, 169 U.S. 649, 705 (U.S. 1898).

Vance v. Terrazas, 444 U.S. 252, 270 (U.S. 1980).

Vikør, Knut S. *Between God and the Sultan: A History of Islamic Law.* Oxford: Oxford University Press, 2005.

Wadud, Amina. "American Muslim Identity: Race and Ethnicity in Progressive Islam." In *Progressive Muslims: On Justice, Gender, and Pluralism*, edited by Omid Safi, 270–285. Oxford: One World, 2003.

Wald, Kenneth. *Religion and Politics in the United States.* New York: St. Martin's Press, 1987.

Weiss, Bernard G. *The Spirit of Islamic Law.* Athens: University of Georgia Press, 1998.

Wells, Charlotte Catherine. *Law and Citizenship in Early Modern France.* Baltimore: Johns Hopkins University Press, 1995.

Wenger, Beth S. "Rites of Citizenship: Jewish Celebrations of the Nation." In *The Columbia History of Jews and Judaism in America*, edited by Marc Lee Raphael, 366–384. New York: Columbia University Press, 2008

Whitted, Alex R. "Park51 as a Case Study: Testing the Religious Land Use and Institutionalized Persons Act." *Indiana Law Review* 45 (2011): 249–274.

Witte, John, Jr. *Religion and the American Constitutional Experiment: Essential Rights and Liberties.* Boulder: Westview Press, 2000.

Wood, James. "Abridging the Free Exercise Clause." *Journal of Church & State* 32, no. 4 (1990): 741–752.

Woodman, Gordon R. "Ideological Combat and Social Observation: Recent Debate about Legal Pluralism." *Journal of Legal Pluralism* 42 (1998): 21–59.

Wuthnow, Robert. "Divided We Fall: America's Two Civil Religions." *The Christian Century* 105 (1988): 395–399.

Yildirim, Yetkin. "Peace and Conflict Resolution in the Medina Charter." *Peace Review* 18, no. 1 (2006).

Index